The Stolen

For Rowena

Also by Patrick Rivers

The Restless Generation
Politics by Pressure
The Survivalists
Living Better on Less
Living on a Little Land
Diet for a Small Island (with Shirley Rivers)

The Stolen Future

How to rescue the Earth for our Children

Patrick Rivers

Green Print
Marshall Pickering
1a Beggarwood Lane, Basingstoke, Hants RG23 7LP, UK

First published in 1988 by Green Print
Part of the Marshall Pickering Holdings Group
A subsidiary of the Zondervan Corporation

ISBN 1 85425 005 1

Phototypeset by Input Typesetting Ltd, London
Printed in Great Britain by Anchor Brendon, Tiptree, Colchester

Contents

This book is dedicated to my granddaughter, Josephine

Acknowledgments

Out of the many who have encouraged and helped me I should like to thank Lou Barron, Alwyn Jones, Barrie and Sheila Naylor, Roger Palmer, Carol and Simon Spencer, and Clive and Sally Ponting. I am especially grateful to Dr Anthony Stevens for letting me quote so liberally from his highly relevant work, to Robert Waller for his unwavering conviction in all I have been striving to express, to Ronald Higgins for his fearlessly thorough critique of the outcome, to Jane Keay for her illustrations, and to Elizabeth Wallis for her kindness in indexing it.

Of all the others who helped me in various ways I should like to mention Dr Glin Bennet, Dr Brian Birch, Professor Alfred W. Crosby, Herbert Girardet, Dr Mayer Hillman, Professor Leopold Kohr, Dr Ian Spellerberg and Neil Wallis. Also the Librarian and staff of Monmouth Public Library.

I am indebted to the Joseph Rowntree Charitable Trust. And to my wife Shirley, who not only shared much of the work, but patiently suffered my flaws and limitations, and nourished me in so many ways.

Introduction

The Stolen Future is a book for ordinary intelligent men and women everywhere who share my deep concern about what we are doing to the world, and consequently not only to today's children but to those yet to be born. Hoping to alert people far beyond the Green movement itself, the book endeavours unashamedly to be a work of inspiration and lively observation rather than scholarship. It ranges widely over phenomena, more or less familiar, to reveal hidden but crucial connections between them. This is its chief claim to originality, for I have been more concerned with imaginative ideas than with incontrovertible facts. If at times I strain your credulity, its bibliography may yield reassuring sources. If too it seems odd that a book about the future should dwell on the past, this is because the past largely makes us the people we are, invested with the means to shape the future — for better or worse.

A few clarifying words on style. Aware that anything worth saying must first be readable, I have avoided academic jargon and fashionable 'buzzwords'. Statistics too are minimal except in Chapter 11 where they serve a special purpose. Throughout the text I use 'we', sometimes to mean 'all humankind, past and present', sometimes to mean 'we in the wealthy industrial states of the so-called Rich North', and occasionally to mean 'you and I who are together involved with this book'. In each case the context should make the meaning clear. Since English is a language shaped chiefly by men, its minefields of sexism can often be avoided only at the expense of style. Generally I refer to people as humankind. Where I use 'man' or 'woman' I mean exactly that. Everyday expressions like 'man-made' simply have to stand, and to avoid clumsy evasions I occasionally take the risk of using 'he' where I may mean both sexes.

For impact I have written about our early ancestors almost as if I had been around at the time, rather than hedge my bets with 'ifs' and 'buts' to appease conflicting authorities. All the dates are approximate and many of the assumptions here — and indeed elsewhere in the book — are based on intelligent guesses.

I believe it is long overdue: it confronts the most crucial issue of our time.

PART ONE

Natural excellence

1 · The C[illegible]

[illegible]

If we learn that someone was [illegible] [illegible]

We [illegible] [illegible]

[illegible]

point, we can reject the [illegible] [illegible]

1: The Challenge

We do not inherit the Earth from our fathers, we borrow it from our children

Anon

If we learnt that someone was stealing from our children we would do our best to find the offender and put a stop to it. But if the search led us to *ourselves* how would we react? With indignation, disbelief, inaction? Or would we want to learn more?

We could be doing so without knowing. Or perhaps disregarding conclusive evidence that we can't face — people do have problems in confronting the unthinkable. Either way, the charge is so serious that we would surely want to examine our behaviour, and if the accusation stood up, to make amends.

The evidence comes from distinguished authorities and countless concerned, thinking people all over the world. For years now they have been telling us in vain that by taking unnecessary risks with what we don't fully understand we are jeopardising the world that children expect to inherit. In short, stealing their future. The warning comes not only from scientists, economists, historians and futurologists, but from statesmen, philosophers and religious leaders, along with authors, poets and others.

The nub of what they are saying is simple. By the way humankind lives now, we are destroying the natural world on which our lives — *all life* — depends. This we do as a species, however innocent we may believe we are as ordinary individuals. The chief offenders moreover are high consumption industrial nations such as Britain and the USA. Humankind may be the world's dominant species, but we have become trapped in an evolutionary blind alley: endangered.

There are sound reasons why. Thanks to our extraordinary brain, we can exploit the natural world and all Earth's limited resources solely for our immediate use. Bright we may be, but apparently not bright enough to notice the disastrous effect of this on other species. Because life on Earth is interdependent, their loss is our loss; life cannot be sustained, the world becomes a less secure place and the future cannot be guaranteed. But this is not all. As the resources we are consuming dwindle, fewer are left for today's children, less still for those yet to be born: eventually none at all — no accessible oil, gas, coal or other vital minerals, no prime croplands or life-giving rainforests. In short, the way we currently use our unique brain is more likely to cause our extinction than our survival.

To understand this paradox we must turn back the pages of history.

Long ago in a primaeval age, our ancestors made a *quantum leap* in evolution. Over time they became aware not only of all that they experienced around them, but significantly also aware of their own existence as the experiencer. This unprecedented breakthrough was both a miracle and a mystery. In this new state of self-awareness, events that took place outside their heads simultaneously produced images inside them: that is to say the events became 'conscious'.

What distinguishes humankind from other species today is not the sheer size of our brain but this unique self-awareness, or 'consciousness' as it is more generally called. However, while this gift enables us knowingly to shape the world to suit our needs, it does not necessarily enable us to understand the consequences. The living world is not a simple place.

Fortunately, self-awareness also endows us with freedom of choice. We can, if we wish, change the way we think and behave. This means that, both as individuals and as a species, we have the means to make the next evolutionary quantum leap: from self-awareness to *Earth awareness*. We can elect to switch from unbridled exploitation to a total concern for all life. This is our ultimate choice. Unless we make such a move soon, our children have no guarantee of a future. If we fail to confront this prospect, we virtually seal their fate.

In the light of this, the warnings of well-informed authorities cannot be dismissed out of hand. They cannot all be wrong, neither are they all mad, misguided or mischievous. At the very least their message means that we owe it to our children to examine ourselves and discover why we carry on as if all were well.

If we claim that we have never heard of their warnings, then we are saying in effect that we read no serious books or responsible newspapers, and that we only switch on the radio or TV for the soap operas. If however we do know of the risks but ignore them, there seem to be only two possible explanations: either we find the warnings so marginal that we are able to dismiss them, or else they are so disturbing that we can't face them. If this seems to fit our behaviour, we need to ask ourselves how we can look our children in the eyes and assure them that we love them above all else.

The nature of the crisis

A few facts and prospects, plucked from the many now piling up, may remind us of risks we take and ignore.

Every minute sees the destruction of another 100 acres of the surviving rainforests, responsible for so much of the world's oxygen. At this rate of felling they could all be gone within forty years. Short term effects could include a billion human lives put at risk and the disappearance of half the Earth's species. Long term consequences could rival those of a nuclear war, now expected to kill more than half the world's people — most of us lingeringly.

The world has barely one acre of cropland to feed each person alive; every year there is less. In all the continents soil is eroding and deserts are advancing, yet within twelve years there will be another billion of us to feed. Well before then we could be facing worldwide famine with attendant pandemic disease.

By releasing pollutants into the atmosphere we are destroying the ozone layer that shields us and all life from the sun's lethal rays: over Antarctica the 'hole' is already as big as the USA and still growing. Moreover, industrialisation already shows signs of creating the 'greenhouse effect': a warming of the atmosphere and oceans, capable of drowning coastal cities and rendering arid vast areas of rich farmland. Affecting the entire planet, it is the most colossal and dangerous ecological experiment of all time.

Scenarios of mass lunacy such as these are not new. They have been published again and again, but with no appreciable effect. Moreover they are only the centre-stage drama. Behind the scenes a host of less spectacular plots are potentially just as menacing. Yet that is not all. They are merely symptoms of something infinitely more profound. Together they mean that humankind is blatantly disregarding crucial natural principles that sustain all life. These fundamental principles maintain not only vast but hidden cyclic flows throughout the whole web of life, but also the equally vital physical properties that set Earth apart from her lifeless sister planets. In consequence short term palliative measures are totally inadequate. As later pages will show, measures have to be radical — nothing less than a total rethink. If we fail to grasp the nettle, the consequences could range from an unacceptably bleak and risky future — ugly, oppressive, chilly, spartan, unhealthy, and radioactive — right through to the eventual collapse of the living world we know.

There is no escape from this dilemma of conscience. We may not personally wield the chainsaw, light the match or press 'the button', but all the same we are each happy to enjoy the benefits of remote actions taken by others, even if they have hidden costs attached. Yet, as the world's wider problems press ever closer, it becomes increasingly hard to claim individual innocence within our collective guilt. For ever since Chernobyl we have been forced to accept that the world is one village after all. In consequence, actions that people take in one place can profoundly affect people in other places, however far away.

We tend to ignore this uncomfortable connection because understandably most of us simply want to live our lives as we are used to doing. We either enjoy, or hope to enjoy, the life style constantly advocated in the media: well paid work rewarded by a well heated, comfortable and labour-saving home, TV, a garden and a car, nice clothes, eating out, holidays abroad, keeping up with trends . . .

All of this we envisage in a high consumption, industrial-based society set to run much as it does now, with material achievement and acquisitiveness sanctified, with national security allegedly protected by armed deterrence, and — in common with other affluent nations — sustained by material economic growth targeted to reach up to four per cent a year. Within this broad canvas, we hope to live even more enjoyably no doubt, more excitingly perhaps, but still reassuringly surrounded by the great body of our culture's acquired knowledge and beliefs, together with its ensuing values and rules.

Roughly speaking, these are our expectations and they seem on the face of it fair enough. We would be shocked to learn that, although they may be theoretically attainable, they cannot last. Simple arithmetic shows that if a nation's material-crunching economy grows at the apparently modest rate of four per cent a year, its output will double about every 17 years. As its economy grows, then so will its input of Earth's resources. This is dangerous economic nonsense. If every nation is aiming for the same target, even if not all of them hit it, clearly something has to give. Either the minority of rich industrial nations will use up Earth's dwindling resources even faster than they do already, or else the majority of poor nations will be even more deprived than they are now. In any event there will be precious little left for future generations.

The syndrome is not quite as straightforward as this of course: although doubling output inevitably sucks in more materials, the input may not rise as fast. Other factors also come in, such as technological substitution, thermal climatic change, pollution, land loss, population explosion, ecological breakdown — as we shall presently examine. However, because such exponential increases ignore natural principles, they can only be realised for a while, and even then only by condoning unconscionable injustices. The sobering truth is that our expectations are as unfair to most of our less fortunate brothers and sisters alive today as they are to all yet to be born. Most of us would feel uncomfortable to learn that the society we prize can only ever benefit a minority of people, and even then at the expense of the rest.

The essence of the challenge

If word got around that the economies of industrial nations such as our own might very well be suspect, insubstantial and fleeting, most of us would feel devastatingly threatened. Seemingly solid surroundings we take for granted would be as flimsy as a stage set. A prospect so awesome challenges all that holds the mind together. It implies that the rules and values by which we live are intimately connected with the ongoing world crisis of exploitation, injustice and risk that is stealing our children's future.

If the implication is true, we shall have to look for something else to believe in and work for: in short, a new culture based on a fresh body of knowledge and beliefs to replace the unsustainable rules and values of our present one. Not some idiotic attempt to go back to the Stone Age or even a lost paradise, but a new direction in our cultural evolution: one that aims to reconcile our own needs as a species with those of the living Earth.

To most of us the concept that the natural world has its own needs may be novel. Yet it is central to any attempt to rescue the future. Blessed by energy from the Sun, life on Earth is sustainable indefinitely only because all species are interdependent and everything is re-used. Renewal is Earth's fundamental need. The system is cyclic — or at least it was until humankind interfered. Yet in the way we live now we disregard that need; the economic systems that sustain our societies are based on throughput. Rescuing the future means seeing things from Earth's viewpoint rather than always from our own. This is the kind of quantum leap in imagination the operation demands. If we fail to embrace this challenging concept, we are in effect admitting that a way of life centred on material comfort means more to us than our children's future. There is a conflict between the two. We have to choose one or the other. In weighing the two options, we should anticipate our children's agony when they in turn may discover they cannot guarantee *their* children a future either. It is a fear destined to haunt each successive generation unless we confront it now.

If, after responsibly airing the problem, we opt to continue much as now, we have to ask ourselves whether we have any right to commit today's children to suffer and even die for what may be little more than our craving for comfort and distraction, without even consulting them on the issue.

The power of choice

The problem is far more deep-seated than we suspect, for it has to do with our original nature. Evolution has equipped each of us with a survival device that enables us to put out of our heads any thought too painful to bear. A psychological trick, it prompts us to seek escape from the inadmissible by means of distractions, or by delaying confrontation with some horrifying prospect, even though everything tells us we should not. It is the unthinkable factor, and later pages will elaborate on it. It helps to hide the fact that our species is distinctly flawed and limited, unready for its power and unable to connect its behaviour with the ensuing world crisis. Yet if we are to understand how we came to be where we are, faced with what we would prefer not to know, capable of destroying ourselves and the familiar world — and apparently hell-bent on doing so — we have to understand the past which has chiefly made us what we are. Unconventional though the approach may be, to alter the future we must first look to the past. We have to destroy prevailing misconceptions about our origins, our prehistory and the significant events that have created our present uneasy relationship with the rest of life on Earth.

Only in this way can we determine what our *real* needs are, rather than the ones we have been conditioned to accept. Only in this way can we expect to comprehend the mysterious workings of the living Earth. And only when our needs and those of Earth have been reconciled can we expect to reclaim the future.

When we examine the events that have dominated the whole million-year sequence of human life on Earth so far, we cannot fail to be struck by a mysterious predictability running through it. The turning point had to be now: it could not have happened sooner. The chance to exercise the ultimate choice may not be repeatable. For if we fail to meet the challenge, we may discover that we have reached, not just a turning point, but a point of no return. One day, when the crisis can no longer be ignored, world opinion will eventually change, but by then it may be too late.

Fortunately the options are not just the polarised ones of either 'saving the world' or doing nothing. These are the options: the more radical the changes we make, the more we postpone our extinction; in contrast the longer we continue as we are, the greater the risk to our common future. Having travelled so far along the wrong road, we cannot expect to retrace our steps in order to take the right one. Yet this does not mean that we are bound to continue on it, nor that all is lost: we can still look for by-roads to lead us away from the precipice ahead.

Clearly we cannot leave it to 'them'. Since 'they' led us to where we are we shall have to take the initiative ourselves — from the grassroots upwards. Happily we can each choose an agenda of action that feels right for us. At the same time we can begin work upon ourselves. With it we may acquire the responsibility and kind of behaviour that seem appropriate to the power we wield over the natural world. Instead of wringing our hands helplessly on the sidelines, we can all join in the adventure of changing direction and, each in our own way, move towards becoming part of the solution rather than remaining part of the problem.

The next chapter shows how life on Earth is confined to a thin, green membrane stretched over her surface that displays characteristics of a single living organism. Left alone, this living world functions superbly by principles that we ignore at our peril.

2: The Web of Life

Nature is often hidden; sometimes overcome; seldom extinguished.
Bacon

It is significant that at a time when we show every sign of rendering planet Earth uninhabitable we should be obsessed by Outer Space. People with undying faith in science and technology get excited at the idea of colonising a suitable planet beyond our own solar system: in the US, enthusiasts have already embarked on a serious research and training programme for doing so when launch day dawns. Sci-fi is one of the most popular subjects of television and popular fiction, with interplanetary travel the principal theme. The arms race, dominated by the Space race and SDI — the so-called 'Star Wars' initiative — soaks up more money and resources than all aid to relieve earthly poverty put together. Against such a background it is not surprising that space games and the like are every boy's idea of the perfect present.

The trend is a morbid symptom of our collective lunacy and ongoing stress. To the extent that it diverts us from the urgent need to care for our own planet Earth, it poses a threat to the future. Now that space fantasies rank so high in our priorities, a keen look at the realities is long overdue.

If we picture Earth as a speck of dust, on the same scale the nearest star turns out to be about 2 000 miles away, and darkness fills the unimaginable void between. Somewhere in the measureless universe, according to the laws of probability, a host of other planets are capable of supporting life, although we might have to travel way beyond the nearest star to find one of them. Marooned as we are on 'Spaceship Earth', the frightening loneliness encourages the fantasy of space colonisation that helps to justify the way we proceed to make Earth uninhabitable. Even our sister planets are hostile and remote, no more than lonely specks in the centre of immensities. Using the same scale as we did earlier, our own great sun appears as a fiery ball some six inches across. Mercury, closest to the sun is located seven yards from it, Earth is eighteen yards from it, and the outermost, planet, Pluto, is 710 yards away.

On Mercury it is so hot that metals are molten. Venus, the next planet out, is a lifeless hell beneath a shroud of perpetual dust, its day equal to 58 earthly days, its night the same length. Beyond us spins Mars, more like Earth, yet its colder, moon-like wasteland is demonstrably lifeless after all. Beyond Mars circle the two giants Jupiter and Saturn, five and nine times further out than Earth. Receiving tiny fractions of our intensity of solar heat and light, they are even less hospitable. Beyond them circle Uranus and Neptune; beyond them lies Pluto, smaller than Earth and nearly forty times further out, spending 248 years in each orbit; all three colder still, dark and empty.

In comparison with her sister planets, our own blue-green Earth is a unique haven for life that we take far too much for granted. The configuration of conditions on Earth, exactly right for life, are rare and miraculously ordered. Lying at the optimum distance from the sun, our planet is neither too hot nor too cold for life to arise and continue. The speed at which the Earth spins on her axis is equally critical, for by rotating once every twenty-four hours she retains most of each day's precious warmth.

Earth is positioned exactly where the sun's rays may carry the precise amount of energy to maintain life. Her atmosphere is unique within the solar system. Other planets are surrounded by poison brews such as methane, ammonia and carbon dioxide, heavy and suffocating. Earth in contrast is enveloped in a benign mixture of oxygen and inert nitrogen, together with low concentrations of carbon dioxide and water vapour: all the gases that life requires. She is indeed a blessed planet.

Into this scene, when the time seemed right, humankind entered and became the vessel for the unprecedented phenomenon of consciousness: the miraculous state of self-awareness. Yet evolution, not for the first time, had blundered. As a species we were not yet ready to be the vessel for so powerful a phenomenon, and so, instead of employing the gift to *enhance* Earthly life, we set about destroying it.

Earth: a single living organism?

So accustomed have we now become to treating Mother Earth as something between treasure trove, casino, and woman to be conquered that any view suggesting we approach her gently, or challenging our role of manager or steward, is naturally threatening. This being so, we are sure to feel uneasy with a concept that Earth and the thin green mantle laid upon her act as if they were a single, if complex, living organism. It would seem improbable that they might share the common aim of ensuring the necessary conditions for life to continue, and unlikely that Earth has needs just like any other living organism. Moreover it would run contrary to prevailing religious belief to suppose that Earth and her green mantle, the so-called biosphere, helped to create the exceptional conditions that made life possible in the beginning.

This revolutionary concept was formulated in 1970 by the British inventor and geochemist James Lovelock, while he was working with NASA's space programme. He named it the *Gaia hypothesis* after the mythologial Greek Earth goddess, and it has been the subject of serious if controversial study and speculation ever since. The hypothesis challenges the conventional view that life exists on Earth only because material conditions just happen to be right for it. Mystical though it may seem, hypothetical though it remains, its underlying premises seem to have a sound scientific base.

Intensive comparison of Mars to Earth suggested to James Lovelock that '. . . the entire range of living matter on Earth, from whales to viruses, and from oaks to algae, could in many ways be regarded as a single living entity, capable of manipulating Earth's atmosphere to suit its overall needs, and endowed with faculties and powers far beyond its constituent parts.'

It was already known that life itself has played a major role over three billion years ago in creating conditions on Earth suitable for it to flourish and blossom into all the myriad complex forms we know today. The very first simple cells of life were bacteria and algae, unable to breathe oxygen. Instead they actually produced oxygen as a waste product from the process of photosynthesis. Over a period of a billion years or so, this oxygen combined with minerals to form oxides. When the minerals could absorb no more oxygen, the rest escaped into the atmosphere, some of it to form a high-altitude layer of ozone.

This amounted to a curious turn of events. Until then the sun's ultra-violet light had helped to synthesise the amino acids of primitive life. To more complex and susceptible oxygen-breathing life forms, however, the ultra-violet light posed a lethal threat. The ozone layer neutralised this threat by acting as a shield. In consequence evolution had no need to stop at the level of anaerobic bacteria and algae, but was able to achieve the efflorescence of life we know today.

All this was known when James Lovelock made his hypothesis. To assume that all the elaborate and interrelated conditions for life to evolve and continue could be attributed to no more than sheer coincidence was too much for him to swallow. He took the intriguing implications a stage further. He posed the hypothesis that life itself continued the evolutionary process by co-operatively carrying out control functions necessary to maintain the right conditions for life. The process whereby control is achieved by immediate and automatic reactions is known as *cybernetics*; the steady state it accomplishes is called *homeostasis*. These two processes go on within our own bodies every moment of our lives. Gaia is no different.

The ozone layer described above is one such homeostatic mechanism: four others may be briefly described.

Of the four mechanisms, that which regulates the amount of oxygen in the air is perhaps the most important. Gaia, Lovelock's living Earth, keeps the oxygen level constant at exactly twenty-one per cent: any less and life as we know it would not survive; any more and spontaneous combustion would ensue. Forest fires would burn until every tree had been reduced to ash.

Living plants play a major role in regulating oxygen and carbon dioxide levels. By the amazing process of photosynthesis, trees and other plants are able to feed directly from sunlight: overall, taking in carbon dioxide and producing oxygen as a by-product. Their constant exchange of these gases contributes to the global cycling of gases through air, ocean, rocks and soil. Of all Earth's plants, the 25 000 different species of marine algae are perhaps the the most crucial. Dominated by microscopic plankton, they release from the oceans a vast proportion of the atmosphere's oxygen.

In the soil and seabeds, microbes produce the gas methane by fermentation at the scarcely credible rate of at least a billion tons a year, and this naturally occurring gas could well be a major oxygen regulator. Microbes, however, appear to be the star performers in the Gaian scenario. Since life began they have been interacting with the atmosphere to create the soil that absorbs carbon dioxide — the gas now threatening atmospheric balance in excesses that could well strain Gaia beyond her capacity to maintain homeostasis.

The second regulating mechanism involves the Earth's temperature. As in our own bodies, a stable temperature is also important if life on Earth is to continue. Despite dramatic cosmic changes, the Earth's surface temperature has stayed within tolerable limits for hundreds of millions of years. And just as several agents are responsible for keeping our own temperature constant, so many are involved in stabilising the Earth's.

Unlike any of her sisters, Earth is an ocean planet. Covering roughly four-fifths of her surface, the oceans help to stabilise her temperature. Within them are found most of her life forms and, but for the unique properties of her atmosphere, Earth would know no other life, for the sea would lie inert, the land arid. Yet because her atmosphere has the remarkable capacity to absorb evaporating water, the oceans have been able to share water with the land. Watered by rain and snow, the land teems with all the life forms we know.

Within the Earth's atmosphere a small proportion of carbon dioxide acts as an insulating blanket, trapping much of the heat energy radiated from Earth that would otherwise be lost in space — the 'greenhouse effect'. Plants too play a significant role, for water vapour helps to stabilise temperature. Transpiration from the leaves of plants adds to the humidity, which encourages rain to fall — an effect that can be witnessed dramatically in tropical forests where rain stops short at the very point that the lush greenery ends. Cloud and the greenery of plants and forests together affect Earth's *albedo*, a measure of her 'shininess'. This too affects her temperature by its capacity to reflect the sun's light and heat back into space.

A third mechanism mantains the rain's acidity. For soil to make available the mineral salts that plants need for nourishment, the rain falling on it must be sufficiently acid: too little and the nourishment remains locked up; too much and plant life succumbs. Normally the right acidity is maintained by the presence of ammonia in the air in small proportions kept constant by Gaian means.

Our last example involves the oceans. Life began in the oceans. Moreover they not only support at least half the total weight of life on Earth today, but they play a major role in maintaining life on land, in regulating climate and in moderating excesses such as those brought on by industrial man. Their health, so demonstrably essential for life, depends principally on the amount of salt they contain. Over time so much salt has been washed down by rivers that by now the oceans should have become as intolerant of life as the 'closed cycle' Dead Sea; nevertheless ocean salinity stays at the 3.4 per cent maximum that life can stand. Had it ever risen even to 4 per cent, life could not have evolved as it has; if it had soared to 6 per cent even briefly, ocean life would have promptly succumbed. Since so much of Earth's living matter is found in the sea, it may be conjectured that here lies the key to whatever regulates salt levels.

For the homeostatic balance so crucial for life, Earth's three elements of air, land and sea all depend upon each other. Plant life, mostly as trees, shrubs, flowers and grasses, is nourished not only by water and the gases present in air, but also through minerals dissolved by rain within the soil that is Earth's skin.

Since animals feed chiefly on plant-life, the two important forms of life have become mutually interdependent. Yet soil is no mere solution of mineral salts in rock pulverised by the insults of time. Soil is an organic living entity, a thriving community of bacteria and other tiny creatures, all essential to the 'higher' life forms above. Without these small creatures, the structure of soil collapses and eventually blows away in the wind or washes down to the sea. 'Lower' and 'higher' forms of life are similarly interdependent.

The oceans too have their complex systems of currents, tides and food chains, transporting the sun's energy to the depths and distributing fertility to all regions. The oceans interact with the air and land, renewing the air's spent oxygen and absorbing its excess carbon dioxide, as well as receiving the land's excess fertility. The whole functions as one giant system, perfected over aeons, sustainable for as long as the sun shines, in controlled balance and charged with incomprehensible order.

In exploiting Earth we have interfered with the critical physical and living cycles in all three elements: air, land and sea. In doing so we have placed at risk the balance which Gaia endeavours to maintain in order that life may continue. On land we have drastically reduced the green mantle of forests and other plant life, and the destruction is proceeding faster than ever before. This process has been accelerated by acid rain, caused chiefly by sulphur dioxide emissions from fossil fuel power stations and car exhausts.

Through years of burning fossil fuel and deliberate forest fires, we have raised the amount of carbon dioxide in the air by 12 per cent in less than a century. All these actions could raise Earth's temperature and seriously affect climates everywhere. It remains to be seen how Gaia attempts to restore equilibrium.

Since ocean life plays a major role in preserving stability, we should take heed of warnings from organisations like Greenpeace and Friends of the Earth. To exterminate the whales, dolphins and porpoises, to over-farm the rich continental shelves, to demean the ocean by dumping radioactive waste and other toxic man-made rubbish regardless of consequences . . . such acts could be pushing Gaia too far. For as later pages will show, once we show signs of becoming over-dominant, whether through sheer numbers or misbehaviour or both, we may expect appropriate retaliation.

In this we may glimpse both our prospect of early extinction and our hope for avoiding it. We can either continue as now and watch our numbers fall so drastically that the AIDS epidemic will take on the aspect of a curtain raiser; or we can pave the way for such a radical change in thinking, concern and action that it supplants the present body of knowledge and values that has contributed so generously to our destructive dominance. Gaia, if the hypothesis is valid, favours no one species more than any other. She remains impartial to the outcome just so long as the threat is removed.

The excellence of natural design

Contrary to general belief, the natural living world is not some anarchical, distant jungle. Despite its superficial chaos it is subject to strict laws which sustain it over time and keep it in balance. And it could hardly be closer. Our own guts are host to millions of benign bacteria that can live nowhere else. Without them we would all soon be dead. The soil beneath our feet is only fertile because of countless tiny creatures and fungi, and but for them we would all go hungry.

This living web of exquisite balance is the world that designed us, and for which we were designed. Like it or not, as a species we are part of it, temporarily dominant over the fraction that we can see, but otherwise no better or worse than any other species, and from Earth's viewpoint, highly detrimental! To ensure a world for our children we first have to clear our minds of the dangerous, lingering notion that the world was made for us alone. If we happen to be 'stewards' of it at present, this is more through an accident of evolution than through other-worldly intervention. No matter how we may have assumed this role, we hold the future of the living world in our hands: not only our children's destiny but that of all the other unique creatures — beautiful and ugly — that we depend on.

By the way we conduct our lives, every single one of us, we affect the health of the whole web of life. Moreover, as some four billion out of a five billion total are progressively overtaken by a Western way of life that ignores one natural law after another, we are in much deeper trouble than a weekend drive through the countryside might suggest.

Our mysterious self-awareness allows the luckier of us to experience the beauty and the wonder of this natural world that ecologists unfeelingly call the biosphere. It fills the oceans and lies delicately, as a thin, green film or mantle over the more favoured regions of Earth's surface. We may appreciate it because it surrounds us, but we do not stop there: we exploit it that it may serve us. Ever since we forsook it to build the first cities, we have entertained a desire to push it away from their perimeters. Parks, gardens and zoos, tended and tidied, we may create and enjoy; but Nature 'red in tooth and claw' must be tamed or put out of sight where we like to think she belongs. She deserves more consideration than she receives.

In common with all other creatures, we depend entirely upon Earth's living membrane for existence: for a life-giving climate, with its rainfall and snow, warmth and cold, humidity and aridity, its wind and calm, sunshine and shade; for fresh air, food and drink. It is crucial to our well-being yet we seldom look at things from *its* perspective, only from our own. Which is the nub of the problem.

The mysteries and the workings of the natural world cannot be adequately explained in words. Yet we can experience a sense of them if we walk deep into woodland, far from other people, touch the ferns and flowers, embrace the trees, absorb the sweet smell of earth and plants, the pungency of animals, and sit quietly with our eyes open. We should be there long enough for darkness to enfold us, to hear the myriad sounds of the night. If possible we should be there to see night give way to dawn and to listen for the first chorus of the day. Then if we are spared the noise of aircraft, chainsaw, tractor, traffic or other human interference, and we listen long enough, not only to the changing natural sounds around us, but to an inner voice that only speaks the truth, then the separation from Nature that we have come to believe is normal may be bridged for a while.

To understand the mysteries more fully we would need to spend time in places where today's people have not yet interfered. This is beyond the means of most of us. It would not be easy because few such places are left. If we could travel to one, we would have to spend days and nights alone in silence, observing and meditating, until we felt the flow of life engulf us. Then we might experience the inexpressible, remembered vaguely as a sense of timelessness, awe and wonder: as a journey back in time, to childhood and long, long before then. We would have to stay until we merged with our surroundings so that we might enter them; until they pervaded us and we became as one with them. Then as we forgot ourselves in this communion, so we might begin to rediscover ourselves and learn again what we have lost.

We would return to the present, humbled. We would have stood with artist and mystic in the elusive realm they strive to recreate. None of this would be easy, and the afterglow would fade if we attempted nothing more. Words are no substitute for intuition and experience, but they can be crucial to the continuing work upon ourselves. As an aid to understanding they can help, if only in clearing away the irrelevancies and frustrations that may stand between us and direct experience.

Words and concepts, like the knives and needles of a dissector, can nevertheless be dangerous. By trying to understand the workings of the natural world chiefly by observing and defining parts of the system, we may lose sight of the whole. The natural world does not lend itself readily to any process of analysis by reduction into parts, for the whole is immeasurably greater than their sum. The natural world keeps everything in sustainable balance by far more laws, rules and principles than we can possibly imagine. The few principles selected here are those most likely to cast light on our present crisis and uncertain future — some of them more than others.

There is no need to grasp every principle fully right now, for we shall return to them with examples of how, out of all the species now on Earth, ours alone ignores them. If ever there were other species that also ignored them, it seems they are no longer around.

For the time being it is only necesssary to hold in mind a sense of the miraculous order that the natural living world maintains by whatever is at work, either within it, or in the cosmos. The principles that maintain this order could be expressed in purely scientific terms, but then only the minority who are scientifically disposed would trouble to read them. This summary attempts to convey in simple language the excellence of natural design that surrounds us and how it comes about. Written with simplicity in mind, it may not always seem to follow strict Darwinian principles but may seem more as if Nature and species alike have 'intentions' and 'interests'. However, even if in strictly scientific terms they do not, this need not demolish the argument that things often seem to happen as if they did. Any 'pure' ecologists who might cringe at such colloquialisms can pass over the section.

Natural principles

The living world is divided into ecosystems, all connected to each other. An ecosystem comprises many different species, each with its own niche, and all living off a common environment which functions as a more or less self-sustaining unit. An ecosystem might comprise a substantial area of marshland with its unique, self-sustaining population of fish, birds, animals, insects, plants and bacteria; or a tropical rainforest, similarly teeming with life; or a 'meadow' of waving seaweed, rich in fish and crustaceans.

It has long been held that the greater the number of different species that there are in an ecosystem, the more it is able to withstand damage, for diversity from Nature's point of view is a kind of insurance policy against the loss of any one species through over-swift or excessive change. The principle that diversity means stability has recently been challenged by reference to specific examples, but until a satisfactory computer model of the global ecosystem has been devised, it would seem prudent to follow common sense and play safe.

If there should be such a sudden or violent change that an ecosystem collapses, the stability of other ecosystems everywhere is affected — just as they are affected by the expansion of any ecosystem. If an ecosystem — or indeed any individual within it — gains an undue advantage over others, it does so at some cost to the rest. Biologist and ecologist Barry Commoner has neatly summed this up as 'There is no such thing as a free lunch'. Payment cannot be avoided, merely delayed.

History abounds with examples of the consequences of ignoring connections. When the Romans made a desert of North Africa by punishing the land to grow ever more grain, they affected the climate from the Middle East to the Gulf of Mexico, and even to Britain, right through to the present day.

The splendour that is Venice was responsible for the eventual destruction of Mediterranean forests from Spain to Greece and as far north as the Baltic, felled for shipbuilding and for sunken piles to support her island palaces.

So much for the past. Today, agribusiness farmers boost crop growth with fertilizers and poisonous sprays that leach into streams and undergound reservoirs so that drinking water becomes contaminated with potentially carcinogenic nitrates and other toxins. For their unfair advantage both town and country dwellers pay dearly. Eventually the farmers' own families share in the misery: a case of 'Prosper now, pay later.'

The importance of recognising connections may be described as *the principle of division into ecosystems*.

Within the overall system, each species occupies its own unique niche. A niche in this context is not specifically a crevice in a rock or a cleft in a tree trunk. It is not so much a physical location as a vocation. Each species has a job to do, basically that of feeding itself and reproducing, and each does its work in a unique way. The 'higher' species have the extra task of rearing their young and once again each has its own way of doing so. The uniqueness of each species grants it a specific space in the complex society of life, not unlike a piece in a jigsaw puzzle.

A niche is multi-dimensional. Within its niche an animal, insect or fish seeks the specific diet it needs, and a plant the soil type it thrives on. The niche may also provide the most suitable micro-climate for a species, as well as space and an adequate amount of water and other resources for its needs. Here too it must be able to reproduce itself with a fair degree of safety from predators, while enjoying whatever shelter from the elements that it requires. (It is of course the ability to reproduce that chiefly distinguishes living matter from dead matter.) Each species over time becomes uniquely adapted to life within its niche and suffers if it is forced to deviate from its lifestyle. Sometimes a species can live outside its niche, but since such an existence can be harsh and subject to stress, the species seldom thrives for long.

The niche allows many different species, predator and prey, large and small, weak and strong, to partition resources and live side by side. Since each has its own job to do, its own way of breeding, its specific diet and way out of danger, each species is able to thrive. As the ecologist Paul Colinvaugh explains, by obeying the principle of *muted* competition, territorial animals respect the neighbourhood of others. It is the system of niches that enables foxes, rabbits, reptiles, birds and insects to inhabit the same patch of heathland in relative harmony. From time to time individual members may get eaten, but their numbers ensure that the species as a whole survives.

To 'trespass' on the niche of another is to come into direct as opposed to 'muted' competition and so run a greater risk of being eaten. Since every individual is food for the members of one or more other species, life is naturally hazardous. Nature is not cruel in the way humankind is however. All this killing is solely for survival; deliberate cruelty is confined to our own species. When a cat plays with a mouse it is only 'keeping its paw in' — practising for the next hunt.

The system of niches accounts for the amazing order that prevails despite the world's seeming chaos. It enables most plants and animals to live their lives without stress, largely free from the constant risk of being eaten. There is not the perpetual massacre that most of us imagine but peaceful co-existence: merely a muted struggle in which each species devises 'tricks' and strategies of opportunism to avoid wasting energy in futile, all-out competition.

As Charles Darwin insightfully discovered, the guiding principle governing the structure and function of all living organisms is simply the survival of the fittest species. To achieve this, each species in various ways has become sublimely adapted through the process of natural selection. All organisms produce many more young than would be required if all of them were to live, but only those best fitted for their niche survive and breed. Consequently these 'survival' characteristics spread throughout the species. All species are therefore different, but although they live in muted competition with each other, nevertheless they are all interdependent. For example, a North American beetle called *Oncideres* lays her eggs only on the limbs of mimosa trees. She then ring-barks these tree limbs so that they fall to the ground and rot, so providing the only food her larvae can eat. Pruned this natural way, the tree lives four times longer. Other seemingly inexplicable examples of interdependence abound.

It is not as facetious as it sounds to suggest that our own species has evolved in the way that it has primarily in order to propagate fruit trees! Our early predecessors were fruit eaters and their anatomy — our anatomy — developed splendidly for this purpose: it was nothing less than our ecological niche, our contribution to the web of life. From the trees' viewpoint, with our roaming habits, we did a magnificent job as distributors of their precious seeds, scattering them over a much wider area than directly below the trees where the fruit would otherwise fall. For once we had enjoyed the fruit and digested all but the seed, we would deposit it, well covered with grade one organic fertiliser, ready for its eventual germination. At that time in our prehistory we were helping to spread the growth of forests, essential for life. We no longer do. Instead we destroy them and cover the world with concrete, which from the viewpoint of the rest of life is, worse than useless. By comparison with all other species, from mosquito to elephant, we are bottom of the league. Without rivals.

Humankind is probably the only species to ignore the principle of interdependence and leave its niche of hunter-gatherer to poach systematically on the niches of others. As a species we are 'swarming'. We have relinquished muted competition in favour of unashamed aggression. It is a situation that the whole will not tolerate indefinitely. Paul Colinvaugh points out that we humans enjoy little peaceful coexistence, either with our own kind or with the rest of Nature. We are engaged in a deadly struggle and so, even though some may fare well, the majority must expect a harsh existence.

The foregoing principle is known as *the system of unique niches.*

Each living organism has evolved over time to be just about right for its niche, though never more than adequately so. The giraffe's neck is not really excessively long but just right for browsing parts of the tree that other animals cannot reach. If circumstances change, species evolve and change as much as is necessary to survive, but again no more than is adequate. Those that fail become extinct.

In the natural world, individuals normally kill others only from necessity, to defend themselves, their young or their territory or, if carnivores, when hungry, but never more than they need. In ordinary circumstances without pressures they rarely kill members of their own species, though they will if overcrowding occurs. We should not be too hard on the fox that kills *all* the henhouse poultry in one go: in Nature the hens would all be roosting high up beyond his reach. The first bird's startled cry would despatch any other foolish ones into the trees, and the fox would be lucky if he took more than one; any blame lies with the farmer for creating a situation for which the fox isn't programmed.

When members of any of the more intelligent species are in dispute, ritualised, non-mortal aggression is the common alternative to killing, intended as a warning or a gesture of supremacy, at most a wrestling match where the loser is allowed to escape. The spectacular clash of skulls of reindeer, rams and billy goats is a familiar example.

Within the whole there is never any lasting surplus. Waste, as we humans understand the word, is unknown. Anything left over by one individual — whether inedible husks, faeces, discarded skin or corpse — is delectable to another species. What one discards becomes another's nourishment. Vultures and dung beetles may not be cuddly but they do an invaluable job by cleaning up carion and cow pats, while the dreaded woodworms helpfully turn fallen trees and branches into good soil when nobody is around to gather firewood.

All of the foregoing summarises *the principle of adequacy*, or 'enough is enough'.

Change is constant. Any time that the environment or niche of any species materially changes, the species is subjected to stress. The new situation then represents a challenge that calls for an appropriate response. If the species is adaptable enough to make the necessary change, the stress disappears and all is well. However if it cannot, possibly because the change in its environment was too swift or violent for it, the species becomes so stressed that it either fails to breed or becomes easy prey to others until it is reduced to extinction. If this happens, other species then move into its niche and overall balance is usually restored. Sometimes however an ecosystem may be invaded by a species so aggressive that it takes over to the detriment of others. This is known as opportunism. As later pages will show, this happened when Europe colonised most of the world and introduced all manner of foreign species, from rats and mosquitoes to prickly pears. Original balance is then never restored.

Adaptability is a highly prized survival mechanism. As a

species well endowed with it, we have been able to spread throughout the globe. Yet it can be a gun that fires both ways: it can create a population explosion with subsequent unpleasant de-stabilising measures; and it can enable a species to survive in a degraded form, as is now evident in our willingness to accept a lower quality of life rather than make changes to improve it. In contrast, the popular giant Panda and the Koala bear are both endangered species because they have evolved to feed on only one species of plant — bamboo and one kind of eucalypt respectively. They are only endangered because we are encroaching on their habitats and they cannot switch to alternative diets. This is *the principle of response to change and stress.*

Constant change means that both living and dead matter is for ever being rearranged all over the face of the Earth. Nothing ever disappears, however, it is simply moved to somewhere else or converted into some other substance. A growing tree harbours a hundred species of bird, animal and insect whose droppings help it grow; a man fells the tree, burns it, the smoke settles miles away; the ash he digs into his garden to grow his vegetables which he eats; he dies, is buried; a tree is planted above his grave . . . and so the cycle is repeated.

In the web of life everything is connected to everything else. In a never ending cycle of birth, death, decay and re-birth there is continuous replenishment and renewal. For three billion years, life on Earth has survived natural disasters both from her molten interior and from outer space. Over time the whole has maintained its crucial stability and balance. Life on Earth — if we would only leave it alone to look after itself — could continue for as long as the sun shines. This principle is called *the cycle of life.*

The entire network acts like an amplifier. Because of a 'knock on' effect, a disturbance in one place can cause considerable, distant and possibly long-delayed effects elsewhere.

When Egypt's Aswan dam was built, the trapped waters denied the once-fertile lower plains their annual silt-laden floods. The deprivation not only cost Egypt an estimated 88 million square metres of cropland, but also cost the eastern Mediterranean its great beds of marine algae, and with them Egypt's huge dependent sardine catch. Here the 'knock on' effect contributed significantly to the near-extinction of this inland sea's whole fish population. It also forced Egypt to use much of the dam's hydro-electric power to manufacture fertilizers as partial substitutes for the lost silt, which is now displacing water in the dam! Clearly no one foresaw the connections.

The principle is not always based on erroneous technology.

Trendy gourmets throughout the West have developed such a penchant for frogs legs that Bangladesh, India and Indonesia alone export more than three million kg a year. Now the paddy fields need heavy spraying with toxic pesticides to cope with the plagues of insect predators that the inhumanely killed frogs once effectively kept in check. Rice gourmets beware!

If a large enough number of ecosystems were to collapse together, as would happen in a nuclear war, the entire living world would become stressed. Then its overall stability would be dangerously threatened for an indefinite period and surviving life on Earth could subsequently be dominated, not by us, but by bacteria and the anaerobic inhabitants of primal ooze.

The foregoing principle shows how *Everything is connected to everything else.*

There are constraints that operate to limit the growth of individuals and the species they belong to, for nothing — not even a cancerous growth — can keep on growing for ever: it is checked, either by the host's immune system or by his eventual death. Some constraints on growth are imposed from within individuals, while others work from outside. If, despite this, any one species becomes so dominant that it poses a threat to the rest, the whole eventually takes action to reduce the offending species' numbers so that balance may reign once more. This principle would operate if the world became so overpopulated by humans that they commandeered every possible acre of land for the sole purpose of feeding themselves. The most likely remedies would then be death-dealing famine and accompanying disease.

Because of constant change, both in the size and make-up of ecosystems and in the relationships between predators and their prey within them, occasional dissonance is inevitable before balance is restored. During this dissonant period certain species and individuals within an ecosystem might suffer stress, hardship and death. Over time however the whole would continue to function perfectly well. This contrasts with the man-made world in which specific parts of it may function extremely well, though often at the expense of the whole, which consequently works extremely badly. For example, modern cars have reached a state of efficiency and luxury that neither Mr Ford nor Mr Morris would have dreamed of, yet they poison the air, maim and kill millions, and the roads for them cover the world with concrete to the detriment of beauty, plant life and ultimately the whole. Similarly a multinational company may also reach peak efficiency through all its departments, but if it is making dangerous chemicals or weapons, and switching funds in a way that enriches the over-developed nations to the impoverishment of under-developed ones, it contributes to the malfunctioning of the whole. It is because such wider effects are ignored, even though they permeate the whole of industrial society, that the man-made world is in a mess and the natural world in retreat.

The thrust of self-interest

The rules and principles that sustain life on Earth, even over-simplified as here, do need to be stated *en bloc.* As it is with everything else on Earth, the rules are themselves interdependent and connected. To scatter them would break the thread.

We stand a better chance of understanding them if, for example, we know of the hidden affinities between self-interest, competition and co-operation. Every species is motivated by self-interest — the thrust to carry forward its genes from one generation to the next, even though stress may sometimes inhibit individuals from doing so.

In the ongoing competition of life, death is as inevitable as it is natural: essential for maintaining balance. Competition and co-operation join hands in their interdependence, and both of them are subservient to self-interest. For the interest of the Self cannot be adequately served without reference to that of others, and in this way self-interest can be identified as the rootstock of all morality. It is the force that dictates the constraints moderating all behaviour.

Our unique self-awareness grants us entry into the realms of intellect, aesthetics and spiritual insight. This gives each of us intrinsic value on our own account. It allows us to explore these realms as we wish, free of constraints. Only when we translate these into our behaviour do we run into constraints, and if we choose to ride roughshod over these constraints, we debase our individual value. In a world of limited resources there can be no alternative to the discipline of heeding constraints. Any species which gains such an advantage over others that eventually it impairs diversity and erodes resources, tends to become a threat to its own existence.

The guiding principles behind these interrelationships highlight the tenuous nature of our own hold on Earth. For perversely it is part of our present culture's body of knowledge, rules and values that we should feel free to amplify all our senses, expand our knowledge in every direction, exploit every opportunity and recognise no constraints. It has led to a free-for-all that is still in full swing. Only now that we have gained the post-Chernobyl concept of Earth as one 'village' is the absurdity of such a dream filtering through to some of us, implying as it does that the whole planet is up for grabs.

Even though most of us promptly consign such an impediment to our aspirations into the province of the unthinkable, a few now acknowledge that our plunder of the living Earth cannot go on forever, and thinking people are proposing instead that we should start to *manage* the planet. This could well signify a step forward, especially if it is accompanied by some moderation. So far, however, there is little sign of any. This is unfortunate, for without restraint on our needs and desires 'management' becomes little more than another name for exploitation, precisely because it disregards the critical link between self-interest and concern for others. Unbridled self-interest invariably leads to self-destruction.

For the top job of Earth Manager humankind's curriculum vitae is not impressive, as any objective look at our past performance reveals. If we search for evidence that we have added anything worthwhile to Earth's variety and diversity over the past 10 000 years or so, we draw an embarrassing blank. We have made no improvements to the whole. Any changes we may have made have been no more than local or temporary. We have indeed bred new strains of farm crops and livestock, but since they have widely supplanted original strains, their introduction has been made at the expense of overall diversity. The picture worldwide is one of alarming decline, gathering momentum with every year. Deserts are advancing, forests receding, soil eroding and fertility deteriorating as land, sea and air become ever more polluted. Moreover — for the first time in our history — the total number of species on Earth has decreased. Throughout the evolution of life on Earth, species have become extinct at the rate of one a year; now, under our management the rate is one a day, expected to accelerate to one every hour. It is estimated that by the turn of the century two million species of plants, animals, birds and reptiles will be gone forever.

From Earth's viewpoint the value of any species is not its intelligence, not its beauty, its size or its engineering accomplishments but only its contribution to the good of the whole — of *all* life. From this vantage point humankind takes on a different aspect. We get a glimpse of ourselves as others see us, and it is not at all flattering. It implies that we can claim no special status on Earth apart from our awareness.

From this unfamiliar standard no one can possibly own a piece of land, any more than as a species we can be said to own the Earth. Any one of us may own a piece of paper alleging temporary ownership, but in reality the most we can claim is occupation, and our rights are neither more nor less than those of others, alive and yet to be born, however hard we may fight to exclude them. We should leave Earth as others would wish to find her: as rich and pleasant as she was before us, or even more so.

Renewal is paramount. Replenishment and renewal are implicit in the cycle of birth–life–death–rebirth. Together they are the means by which life on Earth maintains itself, the key to continuity, the chief hope for our future. And they stand for the principle we most ignore.

The next chapter tells of humankind's arrival into the world of natural excellence. It explains how this world dictated the way that we are both physically and psychologically designed, and traces our transition from human-like ape through ape-like human until we became virtually the people we are today.

3: Our Inheritance

Contentment consists not in great wealth but in few wants
Epicurus

If we are to look into our future, we must first look into the past that helped to make us what we are, for knowledge of the past can invest the present with meaning. By understanding both of them we are better equipped to shape the future. When we do so however, once again we run into the mental block of the unthinkable. We are likely to take up a familiar posture of 'us and them'. Cocooned as we are by our concealing clothes, sophistication, arts, artifacts and our culture's rules and values, in no way can we identify with the pernicious image of hunched and hairy ape-men and their lives so 'nasty, brutish and short' that comes to mind when we try to picture our origins.

Sadly our ancestors are helpless victims of a disgraceful smear campaign. Some 40 000 years ago there were people around who were just as intelligent as we are, with a similar portmanteau of hopes and emotions. They enjoyed a well developed sense of responsibility, they were blessed with a good deal more intuition than has survived in us, and they were far more in touch with the surrounding world. Almost certainly they were unburdened by the deep sense of guilt that plagues this post-Hiroshima age of ours.

Our misconception arises largely because, as the historian Edward Hyams has written, our past has been uncovered not by poets, playwrights or artists, but by highly specialised scientists. Predictably, what they have interpreted has not been the whole truth, but yet another myth, coloured by their deeply felt need to defend the scientific attitudes of our own time. The scientists' knowledge is intellectual, not intuitive. Influenced by them as we are, we find it almost impossible to understand that the past is irrevocably embedded in our minds, spirits and bodies. The past is not remote, however much we would wish it to be. It is here and now. All that is deep within us will be there for as long as our species survives. If our past had been interpreted by poets, the accepted view of our forebears would not be the dry, subtly contemptuous one that we cheerfully accept now. We might then share the light by which our forebears saw, and be filled with wonder and admiration — even envy!

This is the goal of the present chapter. Many readers, however, will experience difficulty accepting the surmise and speculation liberally sprinkled throughout it. The chapter is intentionally written as if we had all been there at the time. To maintain the pace of its narrative, it is burdened with a minimum of tedious let-outs such as 'if', 'but', 'probably' and 'tend to'. The omission is made without apology. From more than ninety-nine per cent of near-human and truly human existence, involving millions of individuals over millions of years, nothing is left but here and there a few stone tools and hunting weapons and dry bones. The immeasurably more revealing cave paintings, dwellings and burial places, with their artifacts and seeds, apply only to the remaining one per cent or so of our earthly lifespan.

Almost all our assumptions about our past come from trying to interpret these scraps. Scientists have had little else to go on but some knowledge of Earth's climate and environment over the period, together with studies of recent and vestigial hunter–gatherers. Yet as the anthropologist Marshall Sahlins has pointed out, such studies are highly unreliable. Throughout Africa, America and Australia, European invaders either wiped out or drove out the original inhabitants of the best land. Those that are left have to make do on less favoured land, usually arid. Moreover, since most survivors have been contaminated by Western contact, their hunting prowess has gone to pot. They have discovered avarice, and — hooked now on tobacco — with their pride in tatters, they have also learned how to beg. Unsurprisingly, much of the speculation about our ancestors has been coloured the wrong hue. This chapter aims to put the record straight.

During our long evolutionary past we slowly acquired not merely our physique, but, as we shall later examine, the emotional and intellectual features that form our basic human nature today. The story of this evolution is necessary if we are to have more than a dangerously superficial understanding of ourselves. It is a story that helps to explain why we behave so perversely to each other, to other living things and to the world's limited and vanishing resources.

When we revisit our origins we may be haunted by a disturbing note of predictability, almost as if we are helpless players in a drama extending over millennia, written and directed by an unseen author. The plot centres round the premature arrival on Earth of our prodigious brain and its consequences: a cosmic experiment in evolution that got out of control. Few of us are aware of this, for we are too close to it and ignorant of our possibilities. Our problem is to escape from the limitations of our scripted role: to attain a higher level of awareness so that we may influence the author, either before we are written out or before the curtain falls on the final act. There is a feeling of time running out, a chilling sense that the drama has gathered inexorable momentum, already climaxing for the denouement. Yet urgent though the solution is, we must first of all know the truth about our past, till now largely denied us.

The innocent prologue

Life on Earth first appeared about three and a half billion years ago. However, as the anthropologist Richard Leakey and the science writer Roger Lewin have graphically explained, not until some time between 10 and 25 million years ago was the scene set for the sequence of events that would culminate in consciousness on Earth. The sequence began at a time when dramatic changes in Earth's crust caused some of her extensive mantle of trees to yield to open grassland. In the shrinking forests of the area that we now call tropical Africa, new waving grasslands beckoned to any species brave, curious — and perhaps foolhardy enough — to try its luck and start a new life. One species that made the break was a crouching ape, some three-and-a-half feet tall. With this diminutive, unlikely creature began the slow, yet seemingly unavoidable transition from person-like ape to ape-like person that continues to this day.

There is no need to go into the confusing details of the various species of hominid and humankind that rose and fell during this transition. It is enough to know that the first hominids were ramapithecines, not unlike brainy, giant chimpanzees, which came on the scene over twelve million years ago. They were followed by australopithecines between three and five million years ago. The first true human beings made their entry around the same time. These were the habilines, so called because they were the first toolmakers. Some two million years later came the large-brained *Homo erectus* people, the first of us to walk really upright. The much maligned Neanderthals, who were really not ugly at all, appeared some 100 000 years ago, around the same time as our true forebears, *Homo sapiens*. All these species lived for considerable periods, some of them simultaneously. All have disappeared down their respective blind alleys, except our direct ancestors, academically dubbed *Homo sapiens sapiens*, who arrived some 40 000 years ago.

Unlike the familiar forest, the new grasslands that our predecessors encountered abounded with unfamiliar predators. Fortunately our ancestors brought with them several unique advantages. Not least was stereoscopic colour vision, the better to identify their forest diet of ripe fruit. Lacking sharp teeth and claws, they had to be mentally sharp to survive, for most of their enemies had a superior sense of smell and it was crucial to spot them first. Forest vision not only helped to spare our predecessors from being eaten, it also replaced smell as a means of telling friend from stranger, for it registered instantly the distinguishing features of every face encountered. Paradoxically, this lack of a keen sense of smell was to operate to our predecessors' advantage and prove to be a key factor in their development.

The cradle-like bony structure that we call our pelvic girdle excites less interest than it deserves. If it were not for its curious shape we would still be walking on all fours, supporting ourselves on our knuckles in the way our closest relatives the chimpanzees and gorillas do. Our hands would never have been capable of their remarkable dexterity, and we could well have been similarly ossified on the evolutionary trail. The historian, Arnold Toynbee, explains: '. . . the development of hand and brain was contemporaneous and, at each stage, there was an interplay between them which assisted the further development of each of them'. This interplay typifies the sense of inevitability that runs through the human story.

Once our predecessors had left the forest, they soon learned the advantage of peering over the tall concealing grasses. If enemies could *smell* them first, then our predecessors had to make up for the deficiency by increasing their height. Each progressive development was assured by natural selection. The zoologist and anthropologist David Attenborough writes: 'The ape-men were small, defenceless and slow, compared with the predators of the plains, so advance warning of the approach of enemies must have been of the greatest importance and the ability to stand upright and look around might make the difference between life and death. It would also have been of great value in hunting.'

Almost in defiance of Nature, the necessary modifications to the shape of the pelvic girdle occurred. In consequence, hands no longer had to take the weight of the trunk; thumb and finger could oppose each other, grasping became possible and the hands were able to be ever more manipulative. In this way our predecessors gained the ability not only to make a wide variety of tools and weapons but also to *use* them effectively. In the long run up to this point, three influences had been at work: keen vision, poor sense of smell and — king pin of all — the humble pelvic girdle. It was the constant interaction between developing brain and hands that led our predecessors to cross the Rubicon from ape to human being, to gain self-awareness and irredeemably change the face of the Earth. A mysterious inevitability . . .

These interwoven advantages were not all. Our predecessors had the benefit of adequate size too: not so big as to be ungainly, but well above average among mammals. They were physically disadvantaged, yet they had one unparalleled weapon for attack and defence: their phenomenonally large brain. In the painful throes of evolution, this ever-increasing brain was to be a problem, and, as time was to show, a threat to survival later on. Even a million or more years ago, a baby's head was disproportionately large: so heavy that babies could no longer cling to their mothers' fur, which in any case was becoming ever scantier as they trod the evolutionary path. In order that mothers could move about with their babies, they learned to carry them in their arms — and no doubt other objects too. Possibly the very first inventor was the woman who made herself a carrier bag.

The first real people

Around three million years ago, when our hominid ancestors had been joined by the toolmaking, semi-upright habilines, they became so human that from now on the book will generally address them more politely as 'we'.

By then, to supplement our largely vegetarian diet we had turned to hunting, made ever more effective by the weapons we could now fashion. The benefit of stereoscopic vision also became apparent, for it gave us a precise sense of distance and a deadly aim. The tools we were making were essential for slitting the hides of the larger animals that our improved hunting skills yielded; later we would use even better tools for an ever wider range of purposes.

Around a million years ago, with the inevitable discovery of making and using fire, social evolution took another leap forward. Fire meant not only warmth and the ability to survive in colder regions — especially in the Ice Ages to come — but also protection from predators. It meant we could now cook our food as well. Previously inedible food such as tough roots became edible and we were also able to derive extra nourishment from other foods already on our menu. As our diet became more nutritious, two other developments began to show: height and weight increased, adding still more to hunting prowess; and our face changed shape. With a less fibrous diet, teeth and jaws became smaller, tongue shorter and face, as a result, more mobile. An upright stance had already shortened our neck and widened our throat; now our enhanced brainpower gained a vital new means of expression. Up till now communication had been largely through grunts and cries; the new, improved face and throat made language possible.

This led to a massive surge in development. Weapons and experience had already heightened hunting skill; now, with language, the men who commonly formed the hunting element of the group were able to make vast improvements to their organising abilities; with increasing success, they hunted animals larger than ever before. Fire also gave us a glimpse of the way we might one day dramatically change the environment to suit ourselves, for as a hunting strategy we learned to set stretches of forest and grassland ablaze and so flush out prey. To induce fire at an earlier date from inert grass and sticks had required nothing less than genius. With this subsequent act of arson however we took our first steps to move outside Nature: an ominous hint of genius in our nature had begun to stir.

Social life gained new dimensions. With a less bulky diet we took far less time to obtain and eat our food; the time saved could then be used in more enlightening ways. Thanks to language, complex thoughts and concepts could be shared; past, present and future discussed, myths related, stories told and plans made around the friendly fire.

Our archetypal nature takes shape

Powerful images and instinctive drives, imprinted deep within our psyche over a million years ago, remain with us to this day: they are the building blocks of our original nature. At times when we are able to enact them — from moment to moment and over longer periods — we are most likely to feel happy and fulfilled. It is when our twentieth century life style prevents us from expressing them that our troubles begin. Then we are apt to experience a sense of unease; we may feel restless, frustrated, depressed, threatened, and behave in predictably irrational, aggressive and other aberrant ways: all the usual symptoms shown by animals under stress. In short, we ignore our basic, *real* needs and fool ourselves by chasing ways of satisfying imaginary ones. All this is highly relevant to the present world crisis. Just how profoundly it affects our children's future will soon become apparent.

Our forebears perfected the hunting and gathering way of life some four million years before the first true, upstanding human beings came on the scene. These arrivals made few changes during the next million years or so. There was, after all, little point in changing something that had stood the test of time and worked so well. Despite a few innovations from time to time, day-to-day life and organisation were little affected.

Throughout this primaeval time our predecessors lived in small groups, chiefly extended families numbering some two dozen souls. Each group would roam over familiar country, using its knowledge of the seasons to gather food in the regions where, through their familiarity with the terrain, they could expect it to be plentiful. Each place where they settled for a time became home. Contact with neighbouring groups was always welcome, for most people were in some way related and everyone knew everyone else. These were occasions for exchanging notes on where the best food was, for grumbling about the weather, sorting out differences of opinion and exchanging gossip and stories; and they were times to throw parties, enjoy feasts and play games. Not least, they were also great opportunities for teenagers to get to know others they fancied. Since incest would have been a universal taboo, to avoid the debilitation of inbreeding, such opportunities were essential for the species' survival.

Because we tend to project our own contemporary problems and values onto our predecessors, it is tempting to picture them fighting and raiding each other's groups. Yet why should they have done so? Most people were in some way related and everyone generally knew everyone else. Certainly at times when animal predators were scarce they may have felt the need to invent external *human* enemies as substitutes. To do so helped to keep the group together, but it implied no compulsion whatsoever to injure or kill each other. The anthropologist Colin M. Turnbull substantiates this by pointing out that conflicts among contemporary hunter–gatherers are solved by non-violent submission, often accompanied by a simple agreement to part company rather than allow the argument to cross the threshold of violence.

Whenever squabblers felt tempted to misuse their primitive hunting weapons, others would generally be close at hand to restrain them. With the omnipresent threat of predators no sensible person ever ventured too far from the rest of the group. Those involved would doubtless have seized any opportunity to defuse a potentially dangerous situation. Today, after all, we often quarrel with our nearest neighbours, yet we rarely feel any urge to kill them.

For reasons we shall presently examine, possessions in those days would have been minimal, and so raiding in order to steal would have been most improbable. To create bad feeling merely to save a few hours chipping a stone spearhead or two would quickly have been revealed as counter-productive. In a survival situation such as theirs, co-operation paid dividends far too high to be lightly jeopardised. Raiding for food may conceivably have occurred several thousand years later beyond Africa, when rising numbers had brought on population pressures, and Ice Age extremes created lasting food shortages. However, in an Africa still blessed with ample trees, the droughts we associate with that unfortunate continent today would have been rare — raiding parties likewise.

In those days the group was all. The focus of their lives, it had become a survival unit to which every member could turn for support and protection. Without it a member was incomplete. To lose the group through mishap or rejection was a virtual death sentence. Sharing came naturally. Murder was almost inconceivable, war as yet unknown. Although doubtless there were squabbles over sexual partners and competition for leadership, in the interests of long term survival, aggressiveness was chiefly reserved for protecting the group from predators and for hunting. Steam could always be let off in ritual display of men and boys competing for girls and women, and in warning off would-be marauders. Any threatening strangers only served to bind the group more closely.

With no possessions save minimal tools, weapons and the crucial fire that women carried from place to place, they centred their lives round each other and the natural world on which they totally depended. The endurance of this way of life is testified by the way it survived floods, droughts, famines, diseases and predators, and eventually mass migration, at first from Africa to Asia and later from there to Europe, all within the period of a million years.

What sparked off the exodus from Africa is not clear. Possibly it was food shortage caused by population pressure, for the savannah cannot support many more than two people to the square mile. Probably this and many other factors coalesced: latent curiosity, perfected skills, better tools and weapons, better orchestrated co-operation and organisation — whatever the catalyst was, over ensuing millennia our ancestors established themselves in regions as similar as possible to those they had left behind in tropical Africa. From there they gradually fanned out to Europe, China and elsewhere in the temperate north.

The last Ice Age set in some 600 000 years ago and lasted intermittently until around 15 000 years ago. In the relentless, bitter cold, those who had ventured north experienced daunting challenges to survival, which called for appropriate responses. They met these challenges by donning skins and seeking shelter for warmth, and since vegetables were generally off the menu in winter, by eating more meat. It was a time of further migrations to escape the enveloping cold. When the polar regions accumulated ice and in consequence the ocean levels fell, some people crossed the temporary land bridge to America. In less affected southern Asia, opportunists braved the newly shortened sea crossing to start a new life in Australia.

Although as hunter–gatherers our ancestors were still securely within their grassland niche, new locations and hardships stimulated them to seek fresh solutions to unfamiliar problems. In the north for example, a greater reliance on meat had forced them to hunt ever larger animals, and the emphasis shifted from brute force to planning, cunning and organisation. Changes such as this marked the beginning of our uniquely human capacity to postpone the gratification of desires, and so paved the way for our quantum leap to conceptual thought. Here again can be sensed the sequence of inevitability, preparing us for the supreme transition to self-awareness.

Some time during the last Ice Age, perhaps only 100 000 years ago, genetic changes endowed us with the same brain size and roughly the same physique as that which we have today. Yet it was not until 40 000 years ago that our brain reached its complete physical development and we became virtually the people we are now. In Europe we had been forced by extremes of climate to make some of the most energetic responses in order to survive, and there the process of natural selection led to a strain of humankind almost akin to a sub-species. The rigours of the Ice Age had selected the fittest of us, the rest had perished of cold, hunger and the sheer inability to adapt. The climate and environment had proved to be a far cry from our African 'Garden of Eden' and in consequence the survivors were unusually adaptable, energetic, curious, tough, dextrous and socially organised.

By then we were building shelters from branches and fashioning greatly improved tools of bone, ivory, antlers and wood; we were burning wood and coal on our fires, and making pottery in kilns. We were decorating our artifacts and moulding clay figurines. And as hunters we had become so skilled and intrepid that in what is now Europe we were staging large scale elephant hunts.

This 'sub-species' was destined to become the latter-day Europeans: the singularly restless adventurers who would engulf the rest of humankind in their explorations and conquests, and lead the way in ruthless exploitation of the world's resources. In the unprecedented stimulus of the Ice Age this 'sub-species' shook off the last vestiges of our million-year African torpor. By then our biological evolution was complete. From then on our evolution was destined to be cultural. Freeing ourselves progressively from the confines and safety of our ancient niche, we were poised to shape our future as it suited us, rather than remain for ever constrained by our surroundings.

Life within survival groups

In many species males and females differ quite markedly in physique. In our own, men have always been generally bigger and more muscular than women, with longer legs and a narrower pelvis; consequently they have been the faster runners. This suited their protective role: keeping an alert watch while the whole group was out foraging. It also affected the way we organised the hunt. In its early stages, hunting was probably an equally shared activity, but as we sought larger and larger game and the dangers multiplied, the men increasingly made it their preserve. Over time the process of natural selection endowed men with more than their share of attributes needed for hunting and protection. As their appreciation of space and distance grew, their missiles and spears flew farther and with deadlier accuracy; their metabolism coped ever better with the hunt's sudden physical demands; and they became better able to plan and subsequently to work together as an efficient pack bonded by strict rules and codes. Persistence was a vital attribute. As Roger Lewin has put it, 'A carnivore that cannot keep its mind on the job soon goes hungry'. The strong sense of discipline that hunting demanded eventually spilled over to other group affairs. Men gradually assumed the major reponsibility for its smooth running and survival, taking the lead in setting and enforcing its rules. As boys grew up, men supervised their initiation into the demands of manhood, and in this way they passed on their attributes to subsequent generations. Within the group that had become the focus of everyone's existence, men's superior strength blended with their traits of scheming and cunning to give them dominant status — or at least the illusion of it.

Women however were still the more important by far. Although when couples fell in love and made love, they would almost certainly have formed a family within the group, there is no reason to suppose that we had yet directly associated copulation with subsequent births. Women therefore were revered for their paramount, mysterious and singular role of renewing life, and they were doubtless accorded the protection they needed and deserved.

Spending time near the home base while men were away hunting, women were well placed to give children the love they needed for their early development, and they helped girls through their transition to womanhood. They also took charge of the crucial fire and cared for older members and the sick.

Until the height of the last Ice Age, food that was gathered, such as plants, nuts, roots, seeds and fruit, probably contributed more nourishment to people's diet than the meat produced by hunting. Over time, hunting had developed into something of a sport to absorb the surplus energies of the men; it kept them out of mischief and the ceremony of distributing the rewards helped to placate their appetite for dominance.

The highly important responsibilities of locating and gathering food and healing herbs passed increasingly to women, whose superior powers of intuition gave them the edge over men in this skilled work. It is not generally appreciated that each plant had to be identified and in time named, not least to distinguish between what was nutritious and what was poisonous, what was food and what was a medicinal remedy. Women played the major role in this dangerous and vital selection.

For well over a million years, the Darwinian process of natural selection progressively refined humankind until our species became superlatively successful within its hunter-gatherer niche. Men evolved physically and psychologically to become elegantly efficient and deadly 'hunting machines'; women equally superlative intuitive gatherers, healers and carers. Together, men, women and children acquired the gentle and sophisticated social skills of 'give and take' that enabled them to live together harmoniously in small groups. This above all else was the key essential for survival.

Since untoward aggressiveness within and between groups would have been counter-productive to the overall aim of survival, the ruthless process of natural selection would have reduced it to a minimum. Nevertheless, groups would still have been required to restrain occasional power-hungry, uncooperative, quarrelsome non-conformists and the threat they posed. Ridicule, silent contempt or the ultimate counter-threat of rejection would generally have served as warning enough. Throughout Nature, so-called 'sports' crop up from time to time and are dealt with accordingly to ensure they do not breed. Remote though all this may seem, its importance to life today cannot be over-emphasised. Once we left our niche and took to city life the tables were swiftly turned. The new way of living called for different aims, new values. Under the process of cultural, as opposed to biological evolution, the residual non-conformists rose to the top and became the leaders.

As later pages will show, conditioned by our million-year past to be easily led, the rest of us obligingly conformed. The direction in which we were led took us to the brink where we now find ourselves. For this reason, the change of direction away from the brink can only be expected to come from the grassroots at the time when Earth awareness releases ordinary people from the constraints of their conditioning. This is the hope within the present crisis.

The original affluent society

Well before our exodus from Africa around a million years ago, and until we encountered the acute stress induced by the last Ice Age, we lived without inner conflict and for most of the time in harmony with other members of our group; each group moreover lived in concord with its neighbours and all were on equal terms with the rest of the natural world. Africa then — in sharp contrast to now — must have been the closest we have ever known to a Garden of Eden.

This is not to imply that our lives lacked struggle, then or since. Hunters would return empty handed, droughts meant empty bellies, savage beasts broke through our defences, fires went out, accidents befell us, mothers and babies died in childbirth, and disease would strike without discrimination. Yet we had evolved in competition with other species and we needed an element of struggle in our lives to be fulfilled, just as we do now. What made our lives secure and our culture so long-lasting was the adequacy of our species as a whole to meet most adversities. Natural selection ensured that only the tribes, groups and individuals best suited to the hunter–gatherer niche survived.

What natural selection fails to reveal is the height of social order and self-fulfilment we rose to, way above the monotonous plains of mere subsistence. In any attempt to reconstruct the past that still lives within us, we should avoid the mistake of equipping our ancestors with the bourgeois impulses and values with which we have progressively saddled ourselves ever since. It is an understandable and almost irresistible temptation, but if we fall for it we are likely to judge their situation as hopeless even before we begin.

More accurately, as Marshall Sahlins has explained at length, we lived then in the original affluent society — affluent because all our wants were easily satisfied. Wants can be satisfied in two ways: by producing much or by desiring little. Nowadays we have great difficulty in understanding those times because our wants have become excessive, even insatiable, while our means to satisfy them have remained limited. The resultant 'economic' problem — as we now call it — is a typically modern Western one. Its origins contrast sharply with ancient approaches such as oriental Zen. These alternative approaches propose that since our genuine material needs are few, they can be easily satisfied. If this is true, then any society able to satisfy these needs can enjoy perceived plenty, even on a low material standard of living. If so, as hunter–gatherers we were perhaps affluent after all.

In this light our own future may be better than we imagine. It means that there may be no need to plunder the planet as we do. Nor do we, as a species, necessarily have to sentence ourselves to a life of hard labour in a futile effort to close the unbridgeable gap between our limitless wants and inadequate means. For most of us it comes as something of a shock to find that we can learn anything from 'savages' long dead. The typical from-the-hip retort is usually that we are naively advocating some inane return to the Stone Age. What *can* sensibly be proposed, however, in our own very different age of five billion people will have to wait until later pages. Meanwhile it is encouraging to glimpse even a few rays of hope.

When we were hunter–gatherers we had no need to renounce acquisitiveness for we had never succumbed to it. The reasons were entirely practical, nothing to do with ascetism. Whenever we broke camp to move where food could be found, we had to travel light. Since anything superfluous was an encumbrance, we never institutionalised possessions in the way we do now. We were not 'economic man'. Our unencumbered life style of long ago spared us the present day curses of avarice and ambition which our consumer-powered economic systems depend on to keep going.

The need to travel light also encouraged another thoroughly convivial dimension of those times — the custom of sharing. There was no point in claiming sole rights to anything that could be used communally. By sharing the rewards of the hunt everyone in the group was kept happy.

As millennia passed by, the custom of sharing became deeply ingrained in our nature. It is forever there, however much the newer drives of avarice and ambition may have quashed it. Since these latter drives arise from mere conditioning, we can take heart and work for the change that can restore the balance.

In those far off, misunderstood days we were mercifully spared yet another modern compulsion: the work ethic. No one marshalled us into gangs and tyrannised us to spend our lives separated from our families toiling to build pyramids, amphi-theatres or temples we would never enter, nor in factories to make things we would never use. Our only routine activities would have been finding food and making shelter. As Marshall

Sahlins records, from observations of uncontaminated hunter–gatherers today, gathering plant food would generally have taken no more than four or five hours a day. For much of the time it would have been an unhurried, carefree and sociable sort of family activity, with plenty of time to chat and think. Hunting, in contrast, was no daily chore but a well-planned event. It was for men usually an exciting, unpredictable and sometimes dangerous challenge. Yet it would also have been rewarding, fulfilling, and at its best tremendous fun — the sort of holiday thing that top executives pay big money for nowadays.

Except in the winters of the temperate north, neither hunting nor gathering would normally have been arduous or unpleasant. Apart from making and repairing tools and weapons, chores as we know them barely existed. Although this allowed ample time for sleeping and pleasurable day-dreaming, the rest of the day was not so boring as we might suppose. As we know from contemporary well-fed tribes, it would have been comfortably filled by conversation and thinking, settling disputes, planning the next hunt, tending the fire, making love, grooming, finding medicinal herbs and caring for the sick, playing with the children, teaching them, visiting friends and relatives, entertaining, storytelling, dancing and ritual celebrations. Until our self-awareness began to dawn, we would have known most of the joy of *being* with little of the compulsion to be forever *doing*.

Not that life lacked the kind of problems touched on earlier. Once we had migrated north, we experienced extremes of heat and cold for which we had not been archetypally designed. Increasingly in the new harsh environment, sickness and death would strike suddenly, mysteriously and unexpectedly. If the crucial fire went out, fierce predators were ever-ready to pounce. In the rhythm of seasons unknown in the tropics, food shortages could force us to resort to infanticide. Moreover, if a journey for food was so long that old people could not make it, with deep reluctance they would be left behind to die.

Life within the survival group meant conforming to its rules and obeying those chosen to lead its various activities. Once again, applying contemporary judgement, it is tempting to imagine constant quarrelling and dissension. It must be borne in mind however that our survival as a species for a million years or more had depended totally on cohesion. A willing acceptance of hierarchy and expectation of loyalty would have been long embedded in our psyche. Doubtless the witch doctor or medicine man of the day often exploited superstitions with his own brands of tyranny, but as with group leaders, his powers would have been limited.

With a stretch of the imagination it can be seen that, for all its hardships and austerity, life in those times could have been more convivial, full and affluent than we have been led to believe, despite what modern ideas interpret as crippling material deficiencies. Our ancestors could hardly have missed what they had never known: neither the material plenty of our present age with its high-rise blocks, hair pieces, credit cards, compact discs, hypermarkets, designer jeans and microwave ovens; nor its limitless distractions, from Disneyworld, discos and Space Invaders through hard porn to heroin; and not even its odd blemishes of overcrowded prisons, motorway pile-ups, blocked drains, pneumatic drills, radiation and multi-megaton nuclear warheads.

The next chapter describes our ancestors' attainment of self-awareness and its destructive impact on the natural world. In the light of this, the chapter discusses whether humankind is evil, misguided or both.

PART TWO

The experiment that went wrong

4: The Dawn of Consciousness

Awake. Be the witness of your thoughts
The Dhammapada (Sayings of the Buddha)

There was no particular dawn, say half a million years ago, when one of our forebears woke up, stretched and then, unusually wide-eyed for that hour, exclaimed 'I think, therefore I am!' — after which the world was never the same again. Disappointingly, for the scene would have made splendid television, self-awareness could hardly have happened that way. It would have dawned slowly, possibly over hundreds of thousands of years.

Throughout our prehistory, one key factor after another led us inexorably and mysteriously to self-awareness: a more than adequate brain, apt anatomy, tool-making and the uses to which we put the tools, the breakthrough of language, the cerebral stimulus of hunting, the aftermath of migration from Africa, the challenge and response of the last Ice Age, and our intricate social network. Without language, which distinguishes us so much from the rest of life, we could never have made the evolutionary quantum leap to self-awareness. Tools and technology may be favoured by scientists as the one big factor but language dwarfs and pre-dates them. Language above all else enables us, *and us alone*, to transmit and receive the abstract thoughts and concepts that are crucial to self-awareness.

As a species we are exceptionally adaptable. More than once our forebears left one niche to explore another, firstly to quit primaeval forest for grassland, and again several million years later on leaving Africa. At first they sought and found climate and terrain resembling what they left, but further north fresh challenges strained their adaptability to the utmost. In a sense, each major trial of strength and ingenuity constituted a change of niche — and vice versa.

Over all this time, self-awareness dawned gradually. In their African niche our predecessors' way of life had been so harmonious with the rest of Nature that there had been no incentive to change: like today's disappearing gorillas they had 'never had it so good'. Content to accept Nature as she was, their lives held few fresh challenges to stretch them, few demands for responses that would stimulate their brains. Had they remained in Africa these brains might have languished even longer. Not until their venture plunged them into the rigours of the Ice Ages were they subjected to enough stress to enlist the billions of superfluous brain cells and synapses, lying for so long 'bone idle' within their over-size skulls. Stress fanned the flickering flame of consciousness into full awareness and eventually a dazzling new light illuminated aspects of their being that they never knew existed. The awakeners began to experience the surrounding world as if they were outside it.

From then on, the old life style with its intimate social fabric was doomed. Much as when they left the original forest, they set out to face whatever might lie in store for them. Yet this occasion held one significant difference: no fresh grassland niche awaited them. Faced with unprecedented challenges, they depended primarily on the attributes of adaptability, cunning, arrogance, knowledge and skills, passed orally through each generation. Their only other aid was a legacy of subconscious images and drives from a doomed past. The web of life that had once sustained them now seemed more like a trap. Discarding the irrelevancies of the past, they stepped outside it, and from then on faced the heady prospect of becoming masters of their destinies. They were free at last to create whatever substitute for a niche they might desire, along with whatever new social structures might suit it.

By then, aware that they enjoyed an existence separate from the surrounding world, our ancestors became sensitive to the transience of life and the inevitability of death — and no doubt were just as affected by the knowledge as we are in our own times. Consciousness had awakened them to create, to learn and organise. Yet it had also burdened them with greater fears and wilder imaginings. The great cold of the Ice Ages had inflicted terrible sufferings. The past haunted them and the future held fearful dangers. They no longer slept so well. In response they invented gods to reassure them. These early gods would not have had human form, nor did they live in the sky. They were the gods of the natural world, on which our ancestors still totally depended. To celebrate, to invoke and appease them, on cave walls they painted in stunningly beautiful and expressive forms the animals they hunted and — since life depended on them — also revered. And they laid flowers on their loved ones when they died.

The demise of natural excellence

Looking back from our own twentieth century, it is tempting to see the advent of consciousness purely as a phenomenon affording untold visions of revelation and achievement. And so it seemed until recently. Only now can we see that almost from the outset, innocent of fateful connections, we have been treading the waters of illusion.

From Earth's viewpoint the beginning of our self-awareness heralded the end of natural excellence. In an ill-conceived attempt at a kind of 'second creation', we set about subordinating every potentially useful thing on Earth, dead or alive, to our needs and desires. As Earth's self-appointed stewards, we began progressively phasing out the natural living world which, by unwritten but superbly co-ordinating laws and principles, had regulated itself magnificently for some 800 million years. Displaying prophetic arrogance, we substituted a lawless man-made alternative characterised by exploitation and expediency. Under our energetic hands, the green mantle of life that had cloaked Earth through all that time suffered damage that rivalled an Ice Age, yet without the prospect of eventual recovery.

The first of our major impacts was the vast forest fires that we deliberately started in order to flush out animals to hunt. We were too few in numbers to harm the green mantle when we use stone axes to clear land for farming, but as increased food supplies sent our numbers soaring, so the forests retreated.

Yet farming also imposed heavy costs, borne not only by the suffering Earth but also by ourselves. One of the earliest consequences was the first ever appearance on Earth of surplus. Its advent enabled us to forsake our traditional close-knit groups and congregate, first in villages and towns, then in cities, where unprecedented wealth and power progressively passed into the hands of a few. Surplus made possible armies, war and oppression, and led in turn to money and the enslaving concept of lifetime toil. From then on the affluent minority sentenced themselves to spend their lives vainly trying to satisfy what they erroneously perceived as their needs and desires, while the majority of their subjects lost forever the bona fide affluence they had once enjoyed.

By then, geographically separated from the natural world by city walls and psychologically alienated by city values, we blinded ourselves to our abuse of Nature in an obsession with amassing ever more surplus, regardless of consequences. Surplus manifested itself as one of the costs imposed by farming: not so much a boon as a self-inflicted punishment for ignoring natural principles. The problems that surplus created arose less from possessing knowledge than abusing it: part of the price we had to pay for losing our innocence.

The enigma of consciousness

The age-old Indian language of Sanskrit has some twenty different words for consciousness; in English there is not a single word that adequately describes our state of self-awareness which was to transform the world of 10 000 years ago.

Consciousness may not be our exclusive property. Animals too may be conscious, and some — especially those we have domesticated — show signs of higher levels than others. Yet their internal models of the world are simple, no more than adequate for their survival needs, and as such are very incomplete. Ours are far from complete too, but because our nervous systems are so complex and our needs correspondingly intricate, our internal models are correspondingly complex. The author Peter Russell has explained that our models contain the extra dimension of ourself: the 'modeller', seen as separate from the rest of life. Self-awareness may be considered as 'self-reflective consciousness', for we are aware not only of all we experience around us, but also of *our own existence as the experiencer*.

This awareness is both a miracle and a mystery. It has been rightly said that one must be profoundly impressed by the extreme wonder of the fact that an event that takes place outside in the cosmos simultaneously produces an internal image; that it takes place, so to speak, inside as well, which is to say becomes conscious. Consciousness has been variously expressed as 'the world's reflection of itself', and '. . . our ability to draw conclusions from what we see to what we do not see, to move our minds through space and time, and recognise ourselves in the past on the steps to the present'. By releasing us from total domination by our instincts, self-awareness allows us a degree of free will not enjoyed by other animals. It is essentially a property of the human mind with its conscious and unconscious realms. The whole, according to Jung, constitutes the psyche.

Consciousness did not just happen. As Arnold Toynbee wrote, 'This achievement was so immense and the effort demanded by it must have been so, that it is not surprising that the dawn of consciousness should have been followed by a million or half a million years of torpor, before Man began to exercise actively the spiritual and material power with which his wakening consciousness had endowed him'.

Nevertheless, if the long wait still seems strange, it should be remembered that we are limited, not only by the inadequacies of our world view, but by the near impossibility of acquiring a cosmic viewpoint. Who among us has not lain awake at some time, trying to imagine what lies beyond the farthest star, and reeled at the immensities of the thought? On a cosmic timescale a million years shrinks to the span of a moment. If we can bring ourselves to adjust our minds to this concept, then, on a cosmic timescale, significant and successive Earthly events such the discovery of agriculture, the birth of science and Hiroshima's agony appear as simultaneous. In short, 'the first spade in the ground exploded the atom bomb'.

Arnold Toynbee suggested that the increasing speed, vehemence and variety of change between the time of the prehistoric 'industrial revolution' and the harnessing of atomic energy had the look of 'a grand finale that is heading towards a climax'. If he is right in this analysis, it should serve as a reminder that in our efforts to avert demise, time is emphatically not on our side.

The mythical records.

The fall from innocence that came with our self-awareness is recognised in the myths of many cultures. When the Bible recorded our change from hunting and gathering to farming, it was also recording the time when we left our original niche. In the allegory, Adam and Eve personified transitional humankind. When they were tempted to sample the forbidden fruit of knowledge, we can imagine them restrained by the instincts that bound them to the familiar niche, urging them to stay with what they already knew. Tempted enough, however, any of us will fall; personifying ordinary people with all our limitations, accordingly they fell. The mythical fruit symbolised self-centred awareness together with the knowledge that a great slumbering brain could be woken and put to work on mastering Nature, standing in the way as she seemed to be.

If Adam and Eve had been able to foresee the consequences, they might have held back, for the implications were explosive, frightening and irrevocable. As they prepared to leave their long-nurturing niche, they could not be expected to understand that, by succumbing to temptation, they would come to see the niche as a prison. At the time they believed that once freed they would be able to satisfy all their latent and boundless needs and desires. They could not have known that The Fall would mean a profound change in the way they spent their lives: a shift from simply *being* to compulsively *doing and having*. Limited as they were, they could not have anticipated the inability of Nature to satisfy their needs and desires for ever; nor that, however completely they mastered her, their luck would eventually run out.

They succumbed nevertheless, and subsequently Cain put the knowledge to work by taming Nature in order to grow his corn. When Cain murdered his brother, Abel the gentle pastoralist, he 'was condemned by God, yet favoured by man'. Marked as an assassin he might be, but as the possessor of the knowledge to amass money and power he was able to tempt in turn those who threatened to punish him. And as might be expected, they succumbed to his promises. From then on they were condemned to share his plight. There was no escape, for in the myth, farming is 'a punishment laid on man' for his arrogance in believing that by mastering Nature he could usurp God.

Caveman or genius?

To determine what has been our true nature impelling us through our million-year past, we can view humankind in two ways. One way could be called 'psychopathic genius', the other 'bewildered caveman', though in practice we are probably a blend of both, with one or the other alternately in control. To explore this concept we need to take a look at our origins. When we do so, we find that throughout pre-history, even before there were people around with brains our size, our predecessors enjoyed tremendous, untapped capacities for technology, organisation, creativity and emotion.

The 'psychopathic genius' viewpoint implies that our nature is such that whenever we find ourselves in a position where we can exploit and demolish Nature we use all our capacities to do so, and therefore we are somehow inherently evil. The 'bewildered caveman' view in contrast implies that as hunter–gatherers we lived in some kind of Arcadian idyll in tune with Nature, and that the invention of agriculture which followed self-awareness was in some way a culmination of The Fall which ruined our true nature. In short, that we acquired imperfections more than we inherited evil.

In the 'genius' view, the breakthrough of agriculture allowed our ancestors to escape from the restrictions of their primitive, unchanging ways, so that true human nature was able to come out of the closet and find expression. Or, put another way, the genius was at last able to discard his outlived 'psychic carcase' much as a butterfly forsakes its chrysalis to get on with the job for which Nature designed it.

This view offers an explanation for our subsequent abuse of technology, by suggesting that our ancestors failed to exploit Nature for most of their time as hunter–gatherers only because they lacked the technology to do so. Humankind then comes across as a colossal evolutionary blunder, disguised for a million years until some catalyst such as the rigours of an Ice Age released our full destructive capacity. It suggests that today we are, by our very nature, not only apart from Nature but *anti-nature*, as evidenced by the way we are destroying the natural world. As geniuses we can scarcely plead stupidity as an excuse for doing so!

If this is so, it implies that Nature can be saved only by one of two corrective events: either by using our extraordinary intelligence we must somehow impose effective constraints on our destructive behaviour and so become 'stewards' of the world; or else we must save Nature by destroying ourselves.

In the 'caveman' view, the 'genius' proposition is stood on its head. This view suggests that, since we have spent up to 99 per cent of our time on Earth in small hunting and gathering groups, the kind of person that we were then is, in some profound psychological sense, basically the kind of person we still are today. In this view The Fall is significant because it led to the technology that enabled our ancestors to build the man-made world we have developed today. This view notes that on an evolutionary timescale, 10 000 years or more in an increasingly man-made world is as nothing compared with the million or more that we spent as an integral part of the natural world. Indisputably, during most of that time we became supremely designed for it, for had the design not been excellent, the period when we were part of Nature would not have lasted so long. If instead we were right for our man-made world, and vice-versa, it would show every sign of lasting. Which it manifestly does not!

A third view, favoured in these pages, suggests that we are part 'bewildered caveman', part 'psychopathic genius', with one or other alternately in control and a good deal of bickering behind the scenes as to who should be boss and when. In this view we are not so much evil as *weak*. By some evolutionary blunder we have been endowed with consciousness long before we had acquired the degree of responsibility necessary to moderate its potential harm. This harm consists principally of the way we exploit planet Earth to suit ourselves, regardless of the effect of so doing not only on the rest of life but on the physical capacity of the planet to support life at all. Our weakness takes the form of inherent flaws and limitations highly conspicuous today. As subsequent pages will explore, in our hunter–gatherer days many of these qualities were vital assets for survival, but in the unnatural milieu of modern cities they severely impede us.

Our discreditable track record confirms that although we may perform brilliantly at specific tasks, we are so inept at connecting our actions with their remote effects that we fail to understand wider and more important long-term issues. The consequences are chillingly apparent. Before humankind appeared on Earth, the natural world had supported life for over 800 million years. If it were not for our meddling, life could thrive for as long as the sun shines. We are now supplanting it with a man-made world which inevitably bears all the hallmarks of our inadequacies. So imperfect are the workings of the man-made world that it is leading the natural world headlong towards the chaos that precedes breakdown. Confused as we are by the well-meaning savage inside us who cohabits so uneasily with an irresponsible prodigy, we have promoted ourselves far beyond our abilities. This, the third view of our basic nature, is the one examined throughout this book.

Cavemen we may be at heart, but we shall still need every ounce of genius we can muster if we are to meet the challenge that faces us. And we shall have to apply it in wiser and gentler ways than in the past. For it will take more than mere technology to solve the problems created by technology: nothing short of a change of heart and mind in fact, as well as some hard work upon ourselves.

The next chapter reveals how powerful, inherited images and drives from our past still influence us for better or for worse today.

5: The Living Past within Us

We carry the whole living past in the lower storeys of the skyscraper of rational consciousness. Without the lower storeys our mind is suspended in mid air. No wonder it gets nervous. C. G. Jung

We enter this world with our tiny naked bodies packed with billions of cells, each one miraculously carrying the complete genetic code of the unique human being we could become. This microscopic bundle holds far more than our physical characteristics such as hair and eye colour, height, sex organs and individual body smell; even more than the greater part of our character, personality, aptitudes, type of intelligence, temperament and dexterity. Most of us know this. What we may fail to recognise is the notion that the bundle also carries the means by which we have survived as a species during the million or more years that earlier chapters in this book have tried to bring to life.

Many people find it hard to believe that behaviour can be inherited, even though it is apparent in all our primate cousins and every other living creature. This scepticism is understandable. Not only do we like to think we are above the rest of Nature, but — unlike other species — most of the time we behave as we have been taught. It is part of society's blanket conditioning. As part of it, society also teaches us what to forget and, as later chapters will show, this creates serious problems not only for ourselves but for the natural world as well. The impact of these problems will be less if we can distinguish between behaviour that is inherited (nature) and that which is acquired as part of our cultural evolution (nurture).

The genetic survival kit that tells us how to behave goes by more than one name: instinct or inherited memory are the common ones. For Jung however these were inadequate and misleading terms. He saw them as universal images from the past of fundamental emotions and behaviour that we hold within our unconscious, common to all of us. He described them as 'inherited, instinctive impulses and forms that can be observed in all living creatures'. Over the years he identified several of them and aptly called them 'archetypes'.

Archetypes are not just 'academic' abstractions. Together they help to explain how we came to be in our present predicament. Even more to the point, they could also lead us out of it. An understanding of them could extricate us from the stress largely responsible for the collective madness now culminating in the world crisis. As individuals we would stand a better chance of coping with life if we allowed archetypes to reveal more knowledge of ourselves. With enough people in the world willing to work on themselves in this way, future prospects would be altogether brighter.

Since prehistory, these images and their associated drives have transmitted our basic human nature to each new generation. The images are forever trying to tell us how life should be. Fashioned during our long affinity with the natural world, they hold the knowledge of our primal, physical needs of food, shelter and warmth. They hold the form and expression of how we should relate to others — friend and foe. They also hold the knowledge of the kind of surroundings that we need in order to experience a sense of well-being. In societies of today, these surroundings would be the closest approximation to our original ecological niche that, under the circumstances, we can devise.

The images together comprise a system within which the complete scenario for individual life has been programmed. The psychiatrist Anthony Stevens, who has made an exhaustive study of the subject, writes: 'As the story unfolds, new archetypal motifs emerge, expressing the point which the inner action has reached. Much of the time we pay little attention to this inner theatre, which will never close until the very end of the last act, but occasionally . . . one suddenly finds oneself on stage, committed to a part of the performance. At such moments an archetype has taken hold and one is transfigured by its numinous intensity.'

The following pages explain how, in today's industrial societies, we ignore many of these inherent images, and how they become distorted by our efforts to conform to the unnatural man-made world. Although part of our nature, they have become anachronisms: survival models of a million years ago, trapped in a time-warp and, as such, irrelevant to the way our industrial society obliges us to live.

Associated with these images are powerful instinctive drives. Some of the drives prompt us to take immediate action in unexpected situations that might threaten our survival: to fight or take evasive action for example. Others operate over the longer term, helping us to transform the images into reality. A simple way of grasping the second concept is to look at how a bird builds its nest. The bird has an inherited idea or image of what the nest should be like; its instinctive drive is what prompts it to set about building the nest. A more complex example taken from our own lives would be the idea that we have of a family of our own; the specific drives would then be those we need to enact in order to bring the family into being — from courting, to sexual intercourse, home-building and child-rearing, right through to feeding and protecting them. When a bride out shopping says 'I'm getting my nest together', she is enacting an inherited image.

In the early days of our unfolding self-awareness we would have responded unconsciously to our images and drives. As our self-awareness grew and the images became increasingly complex, they would manifest themselves from time to time: in dreams and also in wakefulness, whenever some appropriate outside stimulus unlocked them. On such occasions they would serve as systems of readiness to determine how we should act in response to any new situation. At other times we would know of them only as dimly perceived concepts and emotions — glimpses of our inner spirit, elusive and inexpressible. They influence us powerfully every day of our lives.

Together these images amount to much more than the sum of their parts. Latent in our unconscious, they hold the knowledge of the *whole* human being we are capable of becoming. This potential is our universal basic human nature. Yet even this is not the whole picture, for within the pattern that they create is woven the uniqueness of each one of us.

The betrayal

As babies, all that we need is our mother or a mother figure, but as we grow up we need the extra reassurance of a small, unchanging group of caring people centred round her. Later still, from about the time we begin to crawl and take an interest in our surroundings, we expect to experience the challenges of the natural world for which we were designed: we are eager to experience one by one its myriad sights, smells and sounds, its alarms and reassurances.

Sadly life doesn't necessarily unfold this way. In the artificial world of towns and cities, we oscillate from over-protection to premature shock. We are cut off from the natural world for which our inherent images and drives have prepared us: in its place we progressively encounter a profoundly alien milieu of electronic noises, angular shapes and synthetic chemicals eaten, inhaled and touched. We are designed for none of these. They are as alien to our psyche as they are to our immune system. In straining to cope we stretch our innate adaptability to the limit, even beyond. From the outset, denied mother's ever-present voice and smell, and the constantly reassuring movement of her warm body, put to sleep in the terrifying loneliness of a cot, and probably bottle-fed, we become confused and disturbed. Later, isolated from virtually everything for which our long past has designed us, alone amongst the lonely, we spend the rest of our lives vainly trying to adjust to the mismatch.

It is to this that we owe much of our lifelong stress and self-delusion. We are not what we think we are, for we grow up in a culture which, however energetically it conditions us to fit its mould, never entirely succeeds. Although we may never consciously recognise it, deep within many of us there festers a sense of betrayal that will influence every thought, feeling and action throughout our lives. Like a re-enactment of The Fall, we shed our innocence only to don the mantle of disillusionment. The sense of betrayal is deeply felt by young people no longer able to visualise any future. Through no fault of their own, overshadowed by the Bomb, they are forced to compromise with a feverishly snatched present. In trying to offer a worthwhile future for them, we would do well to look beyond facile solutions based wholly on political and economic expedience.

There is much to explore and understand: the limitations of our inherited original nature; the thrust of our subsequent cultural evolution; the escalating 'needs' now despatching us down an evolutionary blind alley; and the needs of the natural world on which we ultimately depend for survival — as we always have done.

To relate the betrayal to everyday life we can be helped by comparing ancient and modern. 'Stone age' children would accompany their mothers as they foraged, aware of how food grew, learning one plant from another, distinguishing food plants from poisons and generally growing accustomed to their surroundings. In contrast, 'nuclear age' children are bundled off to supermarkets and dumped on trolleys while packets of this and tins of that are loaded round them. They are incomplete, ignorant of connections and usually remains so.

'Stone age' children, like their modern counterparts in a Third World village of the Poor South, would learn how to live from all the members of the group, always secure with siblings and friends. 'Nuclear age' children are whisked off to schools, away from family and into the hands of strangers, numbering hundreds, even thousands, only to be confronted with a syllabus apparently unconnected with life. In place of the warmth of love and reassurance radiating from the extended family that they are designed to expect, they encounter blank indifference and the growing risk of cruelty and sexual abuse. They become unbalanced, confused, disillusioned and withdrawn. Having lost their innocence they lose their integrity; they learn the rewards of being defensive, manipulative and calculating. For the rest of life, in varying degrees, they will be shunted from group to group: from school to workplace, from home to new neighbourhoods, even to a new country. They must accustom themselves to successive workplaces and friends, clubs, teams, relationships, marriages, in-laws. . . nothing remains constant for them except the certainty of change.

From early life, the part of our being that is the past, expects to encounter the green and reassuring excellence of natural design, once our true heritage. Instead it finds itself in a harsh, unfamiliar and ever-shifting substitute that is the man-made world. A vital part of us withers and dies. And at the very end we go, still puzzling what it was all about. . .

The past still lives

The truth that the past is still alive in us is yet another aspect of the unthinkable that we have to confront. This has been confirmed by Edward Hyams. We need our sense of the past, he stresses. Our deeper nature is composed of fragments of it, pre-selected for their importance to our survival and retained in our genetic inheritance as our necessary images and instinctive drives. When we deny our past, we repudiate our origins. In doing so, we render ourselves no more whole or healthy than someone who has lost his memory. It is not enough to act as if the past were done with and to concentrate only on the present, because although the present has position in time it has no magnitude. As he puts it: 'To think, feel or act as though the past is done with, is equvalent to believing that a railway station through which our train has just passed, only existed for as long as the train was in it. A community which ignores or repudiates its origins in its present acts, is no more whole and healthy than a man who has lost his memory.'

In our examination of how we came to be where we are, a recognition of our past is paramount. The society we live in is no different from any other in its need for a body of knowledge and beliefs that embraces — and is embraced by — the rules and values by which its members are able to live. This great body becomes the prevailing culture. To rescue the future, we shall need a new culture to replace the existing one. It must enable us to rediscover our sense of oneness with the natural world.

The beginning of the search has to be inward in an endeavour to distinguish between illusions about ourselves and the reality. To understand the collective behaviour that has got us into our present mess, it is necessary to identify what is universal to humankind about the way we think, feel and behave: the traits we all share, even though cultures in different parts of the world have been historically isolated from each other. These traits represent the past alive within us. They are archetypal and they are highly relevant to the present, as well as to the future.

As earlier pages have shown, during our million-year past all the crucial thoughts, feelings and behaviour that helped us to survive were absorbed into our genes and passed on to the present time, coalesced into what we call 'human nature'. They showed us how to respond to challenges and threats from our competitors, and how to behave towards each other so that the survival group could function efficiently and harmoniously. Human nature became the key to survival in the niche in which we lived for so long.

When self-awareness spurred us to leave our ancient niche, we radically changed our way of life. First we became farmers, later on city dwellers — as most of us are now. Despite this unparalleled change in our milieu, life-style and social organisation, our original nature remained unchanged. Even today, after millennia of cultural evolution, the same nature is still alive and well. From deep within our unconscious, however outmoded and irrelevant, it exerts a powerfully disturbing influence over all our thoughts, feelings and behaviour.

By virtue of the images and instinctive drives within our original nature, the elusive quality of wholeness is enshrined within each one of us. We need to enact them in the course of our lives if we are to realise wholeness and become complete, rather than partial human beings. For this to happen we need wish for little more than to be spared too much of life's inevitable buffetting, for then wholeness is able to evolve naturally. The more fortunate of us may achieve wholeness without effort, but most of us are so damaged by the man-made world that it is denied us: we never evolve to become the complete human being so tantalizingly encoded in our genes. In consequence, most of us find a measure of wholeness only if we have been lucky enough to find out from some source — such as a meeting or a book — that it really is possible; that it matters; and that to enjoy it, as later pages explain, we have to do some hard work on ourselves.

The images and drives, together with their accompanying emotions, express themselves in the gentler, higher human qualities such as love, friendship, sharing and curiosity; just as they do in the less socially acceptable ones of overt aggressiveness, competitiveness and status-seeking. They also express themselves in social rules and values, and in language, creativity and religion.

If we now examine some of the more powerful images and drives, we shall see how much they influence not only our lives but the shape, tone and rules of the society in which we find ourselves. We shall also see what happens to our lives and to this society if the images merely lie dormant and are never activated by the kind of stimuli for which they were originally designed; what happens when they are activated by inappropriate stimuli; and also the consequences of their being activated at a time in our lives when we are not yet ready for them. In each case we are frustrated from achieving our rightful sense of well-being, as well as our necessary wholeness. As Jung has repeatedly emphasised in his writings, the archetypes he identified are worthy of study and respect.

Drives and images in everyday life

Our concern for children's future requires us to examine the kind of society that brought about the world crisis now putting it at risk. If our attitudes and behaviour are reliable indicators it displays grievous shortcomings: materialism, people treated as objects, 'me first' and 'me too' attitudes, distrust, insecurity, aggressiveness, over-competitiveness, crime, violence, child abuse, marriage breakdown . . . By studying our principal inherited images and drives we can understand how they have helped to shape contemporary culture. From there we can see that when we enact them inappropriately or are unable to actuate them at all, we become stressed and behave irrationally and anti-socially.

Anthony Stevens singles out the mother image for its significance. He explains that if a child grows up close to his mother, all the tender feelings, behaviour and perceptions that are involved in mothering are released: love, trust, family ties, sharing, etc. Not only is mother herself fulfilled, but her child is more likely to grow up to become whole: for the way in which he experiences her foretells how he will experience life and the world.

The psychologist, E. H. Erikson, on 'basic trust', stressed that a mother's ready presence whenever a child needs her builds in him the assurance that life is good, so that later on when he encounters strangers he will feel that they are worthy of his trust and co-operation. On the other hand, as Anthony Stevens confirms, if the unnaturalness of the man-made world deprives him of either a good enough mother or a loving substitute, he is likely to grow up to be self-centred and insecure, innately distrustful of others.

It is self-evident that when such a child grows up he will tend to seek substitutes for people and develop attachments to material things — safe and understandable in a way that people are not. Incapable of trust, he treats people as objects, or to put it the other way round, his failure to relate to people breeds an obsession with things. Moreover, he will be denied the security of strong family ties, at first with his parents and siblings, and again later if he marries and has children of his own.

If it is absolutely necessary for both parents to go out to work when their children most need their love, their role should only be taken over by people who show the same love. Since this is rare, family ties are usually weakened. Many fathers would much prefer to stay home and help with children if only they were not so heavily conditioned to be 'men'. In the nuclear family, the demands that healthily inquisitive children innocently make are often beyond the capacity of both parents, let alone just one. Such traits as an obsession with material things, treating people as objects, excessive aggressiveness and ambition, an insatiable appetite for the security that comes with recognition . . . all these can stem from inadequate mothering. Ironically they have become valuable items of baggage for many of us in our climb to the top. This shows markedly in politics and industry, where the behaviour of top people profoundly influences society's rules and values.

The archetypal bond between mother and child, or its absence, can have unexpected and far-reaching political and ecological implications.

The father image is less powerful than the mother image, but it does substantially shape our society. A boy needs an adequate father if he is to develop a secure masculine identity. A girl also needs one if she is to develop a mature feminine identity able to deal with the masculine aspects of the psyche and, of course, men themselves.

If mother is perceived as the centre of the family, then father is seen as an important source of knowledge about the world beyond it. Although both parents help the child adapt to adult life and to understand society's rules and values, father traditionally assumes the major role. Because of this, if children grow up with an inadequate father, or without any positive male role models, they are less likely to conform to social rules. As long as the father image remains unlocked they will tend to see order, hierarchical authority and discipline as automatically running counter to individual freedom. Self-control and responsibility will then sit uneasily on their shoulders and they may not reach their full potential of courage.

If a child's father is too easy-going, or although strict is seldom around, he may grow up to be anarchic, without much appreciation of the need for rules and values. On the other hand, with too strict a father who is generally around he could grow up dogmatically defending the status quo. When there is no positive father image, children may manifest the ensuing damage in many ways. They may find it hard to accept life's responsibilities and disappointments. Unknowingly mourning the lack of an adequate father, they are likely to relate closely to groups of other young people long past adolescence, and to cling to the ideal of youth throughout life.

If we scrutinise contemporary society we soon come across examples of aberrant behaviour due to inadequate fathering. As we shall later see, much of it stems from the emphasis our masculine-dominated society places on the work ethic and *macho* attitudes. Any father is bound to be a distant figure if he relates more closely to a group at his workplace than to his family. If he leaves home early and returns late and tired he will see little of his children except at weekends. Even then they have to fit in with all the competing distractions he seeks in order to recover from the trials of the week. His absence or inadequacy contributes generously to society's ills.

Marriage, or any other name for parental bonding, is a universal institution with all the characteristics of an inherited image. In the ancient survival group, even though all members might share in the care of growing children, the natural family of parents and siblings generally persisted. It needed the support, reassurance, companionship and protection of the main group, just as the main group depended upon it for regeneration and stability. The natural family was never isolated in the way a modern nuclear family is.

If our upbringing and family life are at fault, all else in subsequent life is almost certain to go wrong. The conventional nuclear family that we build as a refuge from the stress of the modern world is emphatically not archetypal. Sadly, the smiling quintet of mum, dad, two kids and a dog on the packet of cornflakes is about as unnatural as the contents. Its unnaturalness offers a clue to the fragility of marriage. In Nature the whole is invariably dependent on the part, the part upon the whole. In the man-made world, when the extended family becomes as geographically fragmented as it is now, its tenuous links all but break. It virtually ceases to exist as a supportive group, and in our stressful state we tend to turn against those who could help us most — as most Christmas reunions amply demonstrate!

When lives are shattered, the State instead is required to pick up the pieces. Today's 'cornflakes' family resembles a limb without a body and its failure to function is understandable.

Since no young child in the ancient group was ever alone, as soon as he was ready to widen his interests beyond mother to include others, not only were adults available but plenty of children as well. If he were to persist in aggressive, selfish or generally anti-social behaviour, he would soon be left out of their games. Rather than risk rejection, he would learn by bitter experience to forego such bad habits long before they became part of his character. Today this valuable lesson is generally learned too late in life if at all, and society bears the tell-tale scars.

The three interdependent images of mothering, fathering and family, together with their enacting drives, deeply affect the nature and stability of our society. If they are never triggered into action, if they respond to the wrong stimuli or they are enacted at inappropriate times, the individual can never become whole. Instead he grows up as yet another damaged person, forever endeavouring to satisfy false needs instead of true ones and prone to anti-social behaviour. A vicious syndrome begins in which damaged people produce a sick society which in turn produces damaged people. There is convincing evidence that this syndrome is rife and that it contributes to the prevailing world crisis in ways not yet appreciated.

Getting together

Since our million-year survival depended on our living together in small groups, an urge to club together still persists. With the least excuse most of us will join or form a group of some sort. This imperative binds together the whole complex tapestry of modern society: from families to streets or villages, to towns and cities, right up to the mother country. Within the whole is a pattern of clubs, societies, committees, teams, unions and various working relationships — in shops, offices, factories, hospitals, regiments, ships . . . Few of us can tolerate being alone for long.

Unlike the virtually everlasting group of prehistory, our contemporary imitations constantly come and go. It is not hard to see why. Since the majority of them are far too large for either comfort or efficiency, they are always prone to erupt into disagreement and disintegration. Yet size is not the only problem, for the aims we declare are not always our true ones. Whatever may be their ostensible motives, members usually come together for a variety of other reasons: self-interest, fear, loneliness, guilt, revenge, boredom, class-consciousness — the list is long.

Members of the ancient group, in contrast, were there instinctively for mutual protection. They could conceive of no alternative life style. Over time, membership would change: through births and deaths, as youths chose brides from other groups, from sub-division into new groups and through amalgamations. Yet every group was held together by the synergy of each member's portmanteau of inherited, universal drives and images — virtually all designed to achieve just this aim. Through this, every group enjoyed a continuum extending back far beyond memory. Above all, every group shared a universal aim, fully understood and respected by each member: sheer survival, nothing less. To achieve it, self-interest and group-interest were fused into one. Over the rocks and rapids of time, as in the sharpness of every moment, the stream of common humanity swirled unceasingly around and through the group. And no one was ever an island.

Although hierarchy is no longer the height of fashion, even so it is yet another universal image: survival groups could function only with authoritative leaders. To plan and execute the hunt someone clearly had to be in charge. This person was not necessarily the one who led the group in other situations. Whenever lives were at stake, for example, someone already appointed would be required to make a swift decision and to accept responsibility later if things went wrong. Anthony Stevens made the point succinctly when he wrote that hierarchy evolved to prevent 'the evils of anarchy, disorder and the ultimate disintegration of the group'. If our species were to continue down the evolutionary trail, two powerful imperatives had to be passed on to each generation: not only a formal hierarchical structure in society, but exceptional willingness on the part of each member to accept it. Later pages will show how these imperatives have been used and abused in contemporary society to bring about our predicament.

Two other important drives, still very much alive within us, stem from our ancient life-style in groups, and both arose from our hunting origins.

The first concerns the simple act of sharing beyond immediate family — a distinctly human quality, found among few other primates, and fundamental to the development of civilization. While it may perhaps have existed before humankind took to hunting, it was certainly cemented by the sheer need to make the most of the ever larger carcases hunters brought home. As has been noted, by sharing the bounty they not only ensured that everyone was fed, but in times of abundance they had the ideal excuse for throwing the parties that lessened any tribal friction.

The second of the two drives is equally relevant to life today, even though more complex and controversial. In certain situations we tend to bond more closely, even exclusively, with members of our own sex. As our ancestors turned to hunting ever bigger and more dangerous game they had to be even more sure of their aim and their ability to run fast. Put differently, it could be said that natural selection favoured the swift, the intrepid and the cunning. Either way, hunting came to be more and more the domain of men, and the psychological as well as the physical attributes for it were implanted, passed on and enriched by learning through countless generations. To this day, the attributes reveal themselves in diverse, sometimes disturbing ways: as a craving for excitement and danger, a tendency to be more at ease away from the rest of the group in the company of other men; a yen for a sense of achievement, especially as a means of impressing women with their prowess; a highly developed capacity to scheme, plan and co-operate with other men to achieve their aims — by low cunning if need be; and an entrenched belief in their superiority over women in what they reckon to be the important things of life, childbirth mercifully apart. All traceable to the ancient hunt!

All this does not imply that women lack a comparable urge to bond closely with other women. As men absented themselves ever longer over their (at times unnecessary) diversion of hunting, women assumed increasing responsibility for the safety of the rest of the group and for the care of the sick and elderly. This enabled them to build an intimate rapport with their children and exert their own influence over them without men interfering. It also meant that when there was no undue risk from predators they could get on with the essential job of exercising their superior knowledge, intuition and skill in locating the whereabouts of staple plant foods and remedies — and peacefully gathering them. In this way the more passive qualities of selfless love, compassion, tenderness and caring generally became more generously implanted in their psyches than in those of men: or, put more technically, 'sex-linked, genetically inherited archetypes, reinforced by cultural evolution'.

Despite incontrovertible evidence that this tendency is universally evident in all human societies, it has become highly controversial. In the distorted values of our achievement-orientated societies, it has been misinterpreted as allocating women an inferior role. This is simply not so. The tendency is supremely significant, for these passive qualities are the ones that define civilization. They may contribute to our separation from the rest of Nature but they do not set us *above* the rest. The difference is not detrimental to either ourselves or to Nature. It is an honourable distinction. For these are the fundamental qualities that determine whether any civilization is worthy of the name: not the male-inspired brilliance of its technology; not its organizational complexity or its mass of acquired information; not its wealth nor the size of its bridges, tunnels, dams and other monuments, and certainly not its military strength and destructive capability.

It is the archetypal qualities of women that will chiefly determine whether or not our children may expect a future. If men do not interfere.

The first male chauvinists

Once our Stone Age predecessors had improved their weapons and organization enough to hunt larger game, they felt obliged to do so, whether it was strictly necessary or not: probably the first ever manifestation of the so called 'technological imperative'. The taste for meat fuelled the desire to hunt, and diet underwent significant changes. Once we had migrated north, this shift in custom was destined to play a key role in our survival. When the Ice Ages descended on the migrants the climate subjected our predecessors to unprecedented hardships. The lush subtropical vegetation that had covered much of Europe and northern Asia gave way to tundra. This supported grazing animals, but for most of the long and bitter winters it was inhospitable to humans. Thanks to our greater hunting prowess these animals were able to sustain us, and as our skill and courage grew, we hunted game even as formidable as the small elephants that had migrated to Europe.

From an ensuing addiction to meat and through sheer necessity, we depended increasingly on the hunt, and its success depended ever more on men. Physically the more powerful sex, men had already installed themselves as the group's protectors. From then on, as its principal providers, they were well placed to enhance their power by setting its rules as well.

When the ice eventually receded and edible vegetation returned to northern Europe, our ancestors again enjoyed the more varied diet that gathering was able to provide. By then however, men were reluctant to relinquish their superior status. Moreover, men in neighbouring groups to the south, unaffected by the Ice Age, would no doubt have spotted the enviable power that those to the north had acquired during their rigours, and they would have eagerly followed suit. In such ways as this the new social order could have spread.

In places where subsequently they practised the arts of farming, the tables were turned. At first, since women had been the chief providers of plant food, to them fell the work of tilling the fields. According to the historian William H. McNeill, in many such places women gained added independence and authority, and history suggests that matrilinear lines prevailed. For a time the spread of agriculture saw the rise of priestesses and female deities along with worship of the Great Mother of fruitful Earth. Among predominantly hunting people however, patrilinear families still remained the rule. In general the switch was no more than temporary, however. When farming methods eventually improved and draught animals were introduced for ploughing, the men took over the work of tilling, and wherever they could, they re-asserted their authority. Once we took to living in cities, lasting male dominance was assured.

The profound effect on men of their million-year hunting heritage cannot be underestimated. It shows even today in ways that offer opportunities for rewarding speculation. It may lie at the root of their inherent restlessness, never perhaps more prevalent than in today's Western societies. Offer many a man all that he may be expected to desire — loving family, home, comfort, gadgets and career — and yet, contrary to all logic, he still falls victim to the 'thornbird factor'. He hunts elsewhere for other means to satisfy what he can rarely define, regardless of the agony he may suffer himself and inflict on others. Men deprived of hunting for game may hunt in other ways.

Similarly, in an age lacking suitable predators, the inherited image that men hold of themselves as protectors of the group may also be thwarted. Unable to protect their group or family as they would wish, men may turn to unduly protecting possessions and property instead. And this is not all. Deprived as they are of any single, overwhelming image as powerful as giving birth, men may seek all manner of alternatives to live with their inadequacies. Yet men are not alone in seeking substitutes. All of us show the effects of inherited drives that we are unable to enact in the way for which they were designed.

Men today patently set the rules and values of societies just as forcibly and universally as ever. Even so, as with so many archetypal traits, masculine dominance has outlived its value. Paradoxically the phenomenon that came about originally to enhance our survival now threatens it, for the values that men have imposed are precisely those that have led to the exploitation of Nature and the crisis in which we find ourselves.

Why rules and values

Within any civilised culture a body of knowledge and values can arise, grow and survive only if it is founded on values accepted by most of its people. That which is moral to one person may seem the opposite to another. So it is with different cultures. Throughout the world, despite the 'creeping Coca-Colonisation' of US economic influence, there still exists a wide range of religions, arts, customs, manners, laws, rewards and punishments. Underlying them is an archaic common denominator: despots build upon this, anarchists eschew it, and either extreme spells trouble.

This universal morality resides in the collective unconscious propounded by Jung. It is an image, inherited from our long past that no culture, no individual can ignore without courting eventual demise. Its presence in our psyche offers hope for our future. It encompasses the principle that we are designed by evolution both to embrace life-affirming values and to eschew the opposite, to trust and show trust and to shun anti-social behaviour. When constraints are missing we are all capable of taking advantage of their absence. Then nothing but the strength of our culture's positive values or the restraining influence of other people will stop us. Whole societies at times may similarly go off the rails. All history abounds with instances, while in this century two World Wars have been followed by the collective Western lunacy of the present world crisis. Subsequent pages will explore what constraints may be re-enacted to rescue the future.

When we were still part of Nature we would have known intuitively what was life-affirming and what was not. The swiftness of cause and effect would have brought home the consequences to us whenever we had contravened natural principles or undermined the group. Life now is no longer so simple. Having set ourselves apart from Nature we are afforded no such ready protection from ourselves. In place of intuition all we have is our code of knowledge, beliefs, rules and values, coupled with an occasional sense of guilt. Together the code and the guilt encourage us to behave tolerably well for most of the time and to prefer the pleasure of approbation to the pain of guilt and the possibility of rejection. Actor and writer Peter Ustinov displayed rare insight when he observed that: 'A twinge of conscience is a gift of God'.

Universal morality underlies much that is common to different religions, many of which sanctify prevailing social rules and values. There is nothing new in this: it was originally a key role of religion. Anthony Stevens writes that religion provided the justification, the means and the motive to induce each member of the survival group to sacrifice narrow self-interest to the wider interests of the community as a whole. Religion ensured cohesion in the group by strengthening the resolve of its members to serve it. It enhanced survival prospects — not only for the group but for each member of it. The ideas of the moral order have been buried within us so deeply and for so long that they cannot be expunged.

As we did in prehistory, so do we still seek a cause greater than ourselves, to commit ourselves to and even to die for. Our ready submission reveals both the glory and the pathology of the human condition: for the cause may not always be a religious faith; it may be the pursuit of knowledge, as in science; it may be music or art; it may be the preservation of knowledge and values — perceived as 'my country' and the readiness to go to war for her; it may be space exploration. . . even the pursuit of crime. Sadly it has yet to be manifested in the more crucial cause of saving the natural world from our ravages, although Earth awareness is now stirring.

Language is a universal form or image that we take too much for granted. We forget — if indeed we ever knew — that in our prehistory, lacking an armoury of teeth and claws, unable to run as fast as either our predators or our prey, we had to make up for our deficiencies in other ways. Sheer cunning came to our rescue, but only after men had formed well trained hunting groups. Had it not been for language, such organisation would have been impossible. Without language, our brain would not have developed as it has: consciousness could never have arisen in us, neither could we ever have made our subsequent attempts at civilization. Distinguishing us so fundamentally from all other species, language is perhaps our supreme gift.

Humankind has a perverse knack however of debasing just about everything it creates — and most of what was created for us. Procreation turns into pornography, delight in play to football hooliganism, knowledge of natural principles to exploitation of natural resources. If we can possibly demean any benefit we do. Language is no exception. We have grossly distorted its original purpose, and as Chapter 8 will elaborate, in the electronic age of the communications explosion we are still only at the beginning.

Of all the other universal human traits few attract more violent argument than aggressiveness and how much it is nature or nurture. That it is universal cannot be disputed. That some cultures display more than others is equally obvious. More to the point: how much of it is justified?

As Chapter 3 explained, we project onto our forebears our

own shortcomings. By blaming them we hope to absolve our guilt. They do not deserve to carry such a burden. Richard Leakey and Roger Lewin have made the point: ' . . . the archeological evidence of cannibalism, notions of territorial and aggressive instincts, and of an evolutionary career as killer apes . . . have been woven together to form one of the most dangerously persuasive myths of our time: that mankind is incorrigibly belligerent; that war and violence are in our genes'. Objective analysis yields a different answer. We survived a million years not through aggressiveness but by co-operation, passed on by natural selection until it became an inherited image. A species programmed to destroy itself could never have survived so long.

None of this implies a total absence of inherited aggressiveness. Anthony Stevens explains its positive role succinctly: 'As social animals we are programmed from a very early age to shrink from people whom we do not know and stick to people whom we do. This fundamental distinction between attachment and xenophobia is crucial not only for the preservation of the individual, but also for the survival of the group. Societies are closely integrated systems, each glued together by adherence to the familiar, all separated by hostility to that which is strange. The sinister truth is that for communities to thrive, enemies are as necessary as friends. External danger binds the group together, reduces personal animosity, enhances mutual trust, promotes altruism and self-sacrifice. A society surrounded by enemies is unified and strong, a society without enemies is lax. Men in groups are the same the whole world over: when there are no outsiders to fight, they turn on their compatriots. For a rush of adrenalin and a cure for boredom, for camaraderie and thrills, there is nothing like a good scrap.'

Although both sexes have always reacted appropriately when threatened, and especially when protecting their young, unwarranted aggressiveness has principally been a male trait, erupting as a kind of foreplay when competing for female attention. In prehistory, men would have reserved their aggressiveness for this ritual and for exceptionally demanding occasions such as hunting, defending the home base and pre-empting an attack on the group.

It seems that our aggressiveness, as between human beings, only began to develop into a serious problem when our ancestors settled down to farm, for only then did they acquire territory and possessions. The more they had to protect, the more belligerent they became: the more effective their weapons, the more frequently that skirmishes degenerated into war.

Insatiable curiosity is another universal human trait. Present in every healthy child, it is magnified in adolescence and crystallised into our psyche by maturity. Curiosity it may have been that tempted us to leave our original niche. It still leads us into every conceivable temptation, filling us with a restlessness that often makes a mockery of our professed desire for a peaceful life. It implies that if ever we did attain such peace we would eventually become bored with it.

This restlessness is associated with an inherent need for challenge. Like other primates we evolved with challenge; for in our prehistory, although we competed little with each other we were in constant, if muted, competition with other species — interdependent yet opposed, in everlasting balance. Today, struggle is synonymous with problems, and if we have none, we soon invent some, for we are problem-solving animals. Once we had become 'civilized' and we had largely escaped from the pressing problems of everyday survival, the spur of immediacy no longer pricked us. Yet we were impelled to continue as if it did.

In our own time, exploring and curiosity no longer lead us, instead they push us. By now however we have no clear destination, only excess baggage. Our restlessness may be considered yet another part of the punishment of The Fall. Having left the safety of our primal niche we are committed to a quest for we know not what. It is more a restlessness of the spirit than the feet. We are torn between pressing on and harking back. Yet having promoted ourselves far beyond our abilities, the thought of failure haunts us more than the emptiness of the unknown ahead. The limbo of uncertainty is part of the price we pay for consciousness.

Although in order to gather and hunt for food, our predecessors doubtless covered considerable distances in the course of each year, nevertheless they would have returned to places they knew throughout the seasons, for there they would find ripening fruit and seeds and bountiful hunting. At each place where they tarried they would live in the familiar shelter of previous years. In such a way they would have gained a sense of place: not 'property' as we experience it, but, as today's vestigial tribes still do, a degree of permanence, welcome to a nomadic life style. There is a weight of evidence to suggest that a sense of place is universal today, manifested as home, garden, village town, city and country. And yet, as with all else human, it is open to abuse, experienced as the territorial imperative that can drive us to fight legal, and sometimes bloody battles.

A sense of oneness with all the natural world was once universal too. The lust to dominate Nature came later. Nowadays the image of accord with Nature survives tenuously only where the man-made world has not yet intruded. Even so, arising from deep within us, where they have long been buried beneath the debris of conditioning, unsettling images of the natural world we have left behind arise to haunt us. However vestigial, the urge to *connect* shows itself in many ways.

We see it in the flames of a log fire and feel drawn to gather round for more than mere warmth. The burning sun reminds us of the savannah for which we forsook the dark forest, and under its bright rays nakedness can feel good. In our homes, domestic animals, fish, sad caged songbirds, flowers and indoor plants, all help to relieve our alienation. As do natural materials of wood and stone — even pathetic plastic simulations. In gardening and when walking through the country we like to be reminded of Nature, however tamed. We crave the soft, uneven outlines of the natural world as relief from the angular hardness of town and city. Once beyond the city's limits our innate aesthetic senses revive and renew us, however uneasily they may prompt us. Yet we seldom risk too much: for we have journeyed too far for comfort in our craving for comfort, too far for safety in our search for safety. We hover between two worlds, never belonging wholly to either.

A re-awakening of our primal image of dependence on the natural world would not only be a life-saving anchor in the gathering storm, it would unify all people. Other than the storm's worsening, perhaps no other way will serve.

The next chapter describes our true, original nature, and shows how, by suppressing it in modern societies, we we help to aggravate the crisis.

6: The People We Really Are

You cannot shake hands with a clenched fist

Anon

We are not the people we think we are. Deep within us lies our original nature, fashioned by our million-year past, and founded on the powerful primal images and instinctive drives still active within us. It differs sharply from our conventional image of ourselves.

Although it is possible to sketch this nature in outline, the description that follows is manifestly incomplete. Human nature is patently far too mysterious and complex to be revealed by such a rudimentary exercise as this one has to be. We are not frogs to be brought into a classroom for dissection, nor mere objects for analysis by reduction. Our whole is infinitely greater than the sum of our parts. Nevertheless it is possible to distinguish our true, original nature from the false and distorted imitation that we have adopted throughout our cultural evolution in order to survive in the human-made world. For the industrial society, that stamps the world and is now our habitat, came into being, not as if people mattered in themselves, but through a haphazard mixture of accident, expediency, greed and oligarchy.

There are sound reasons why our true nature differs from its modern distortion. Whenever mammals such as ourselves find themselves in a threatening environment, their behaviour changes dramatically and turns nasty. Showing all the customary signs of stress they become unnecessarily aggressive, quarrelsome, excessively competitive and neurotic. They display all the signs of depression and eventually fall sick. They also behave oddly if consistently over-rewarded: feed them an excessive, over-rich diet and they become greedy, disorientated, dependent and — again — unhealthy. We are no different except that in our stress we also lapse into fantasies.

The consequences of being both threatened and over-rewarded are nowhere more evident than in the capital cities of the Rich North — the industrialised top twenty per cent of the world's population, located chiefly in the northern hemisphere.

Our present society comes across as threatening for a host of reasons: its cities are visually polluted, noisy, dangerous and overcrowded, its bureaucracy and other dominant institutions have grown increasingly powerful, faceless and computer-dominated; it is ruthlessly competitive; and it over-rewards a minority at the same time as it impoverishes the majority. In the population density of any big city, its unthinkable vulnerability to the Bomb adds an extra dimension of fear and anxiety.

Yet this is not all. What society demands of us and what we are naturally able to give are in a state of chronic dissonance. While society may profitably pander to our greed and our desire for comfort and distraction, it lacks believable aims and offers little spiritual sustenance. What is more, since it demands from us more aggressiveness, competitiveness, selfishness, ruthlessness and hypocrisy than we can comfortably muster, our abundant human qualities, such as kindness, love, trust, compassion, co-operation, tolerance and good humour, suffer and wane.

In the light of this, it should come as no surprise that in contemporary industrial society we dramatically change our nature and behave disturbingly like other higher mammals under similarly severe stress. No great stretch of imagination is required to see our connection with the big cats that ceaselessly pace their zoo cages or lie morosely in a corner; or with overcrowded laboratory rats that fiercely turn on each other without apparent reason; or with tightly penned pigs that habitually devour both their tethers and their young. The endemic depression, suicide rate, drug addiction, rape, child abuse, wife-battering, 'granny bashing', football hooliganism, gang warfare, mugging and racial violence so characteristic of our time do not reflect our original nature. They are manifestations of its anti-social aspects grotesquely magnified and distorted out of all proportion. Like the Nazi 'Wotan', they are manifestations of the psychopathic genius, ever ready to take advantage of our weaker moments and assert himself. At heart we are kinder and gentler than our city-centred, industrial society permits us to be. And a good deal weaker, more fragile, fallible and limited, less mature, perceptive and sagacious than our arrogance permits us to acknowledge.

Take any human being, strip him of the influences of misguided cultural evolution, put him into an environment where he no longer feels threatened, offer him love and reassurance and, as he heals his soul, so will you discover his original nature. The evidence that this nature is basically good still survives. Anyone who has travelled to places remote from the influence of towns and cities — especially in country districts of the Poor South — will speak of the spontaneous warmth, trust and sheer joy in living evinced by most of the people there. Not by and large the merchants and other entrepreneurs, the bus drivers, waiters and officials contaminated by cities, but the settled craftsmen, farmers and their families. They show it despite the lurking stress of knowing they are poor alongside those who are so plainly better off and may be the chief cause of their own poverty. The contrast is most noticeable in China, India, Africa, the Caribbean, South America and many of the islands of the Pacific.

Our original nature is alive and well among the few hunter–gatherers still living without contact with the rest of humankind. Though easily corrupted, they can be found in Africa, South America, within the Amazon Basin, and Borneo. Until a mere 200 years ago North American Indians exhibited much of this nature, not least in their reverence for the natural world and their incredulity and horror when European ploughs 'tore open' the soil they likened to their mother's breast.

In our own societies we can detect this original nature in children before they have been conditioned and corrupted. In dreams and on rare occasions when we are alone or at ease in small groups free from fear and underlying stress, we may discover it in ourselves. The way in which it survives, against all odds, bears out one of the fundamental principles of this book. To encounter it is enough to fill the heart with hope.

In this context we can begin to understand how much of our original nature is at odds, not only with our own thoughts, feelings and behaviour, but also with our existing society's body of knowledge, beliefs, values and rules. The vision of reconciliation is elusive and the task of realising it daunting. Yet we should beware of dismissing it out of hand, for it is intimately concerned with our ancient drives and images. And when we neglect these, we do so at our peril.

Our original nature

As earlier pages have shown, in prehistory, as part of the web of life and before we left our niche to crowd into cities, we would have been naturally loving and trusting of those we knew, reassured by family and friends in the supportive survival group. Rejection from it we feared above all else. For certain events we would have formed groups with others exclusively of our own sex.

Consciously or not, we *needed* enemies to bind us more strongly to members of our most essential groups. Apart from this we treated others as equals. Within this framework we had a compulsion to co-operate and share, and so break down the barriers that could have alienated us from each other.

Although unsettled by sudden change, nevertheless we could be extremely adaptable. We were spurred on by the supreme pleasure we gained from exercising our skills.

While we could be easily tempted, nevertheless our intense curiosity was tempered by living for so long without changes to our way of life. Because of this we lacked incentive to pursue things to the limit, preferring small steps to bold leaps. We enjoyed occasional excesses, but because of our nomadic way of life we would never have known acquisitiveness: we could not have craved what we had never known.

Although at times quarrelsome, as people can be, we would not normally have been aggressive unless threatened. We eschewed violence except when confronted by the need to defend ourselves, and even then with no more than minimum force, for we derived no pleasure in killing nor in cruelty for its own sake. Since neither murder nor warfare was in our nature, we preferred to settle disputes by reasonableness, although always prepared to display ritual aggressiveness before prudently admitting defeat.

Although nomadic within a familiar area, we would settle for a time in previous sheltered places. With a strong sense of place we were nevertheless not overtly territorial unless unnaturally overcrowded or deprived, or otherwise felt that our well-being was being threatened.

In spite of our susceptibility to temptation, as gregarious, sociable creatures we recognised the need for a strict code of rules and values, not only that we might live together harmoniously but also that we might thereby survive. Born into the neo-womb of the surrounding group, we would have accepted that freedom had to be balanced by order, hierarchy and discipline, both from within and without.

Taught from childhood the way of life necessary for survival, we developed a pronounced tendency to be easily swayed by the charismatic influence of others. Whilst this might lead to a passive acceptance of tyranny, we knew that any harm arising from a leader's abuse of power was limited to the group itself. We knew that with consensus the leader could be changed.

We were aware of an aim in life beyond sheer survival, and greater than ourselves; even above the survival of our group, although we might never come to understand its nature nor know how to fulfil it. Living in muted competition with other species, only with a sense of struggle and accomplishment could we feel fulfilled.

We would have felt the need of a strong sexual identity and

an urge to express it lovingly and physically with others of the opposite sex. With a deep sense of family and a desire for children, we readily formed a bond with our chosen partner for at least as long as our children demanded our combined love, care and instruction. Surrounded by an extended family, all willing and able to share in this responsibility, we would have recognised that the duration of our bonding need not outrun its time.

We would have had a keen appreciation of service to others, expressed in different ways according to our sex. For women much of this was in such qualities as love, tenderness, compassion and caring, especially though not exlusively towards family. This endowed women with a special aptitude for fulfilling the tasks and roles most crucial to ongoing survival, enabling them to understand better than men what was important in this vital respect and what was not.

For men the expression of service may have been orientated more to the cerebral problem-solving and physical prowess developed by the hunt, particularly if associated with a challenge to meet danger and overcome obstacles. Persistent and restless, they often preferred to pursue such activities away from home within a group of other men. They showed a singular fascination with organisation and things, especially tools. Both sexes had a well developed sense of *protectiveness*, albeit in different ways.

All would have a sense of affinity with the rest of life. We did not feel set apart, but as one with the familiar natural world upon which we totally depended. This knowledge required us to treat all life with awe and respect and to take from Nature no more than our well-being and survival required, instinctively returning to the rest of life at least as much as we had taken.

These were our basic needs and our responses to them. Yet we were no more than human. When bored, frustrated, cold, wet, or hungry, we could be stubborn, bad tempered and rebellious. We could be spiteful, jealous, vain, dishonest or lazy at any time. We could also gossip, plot and lust as much as anyone today. But not for long. None of us could push our luck too far while the risk of rejection remained real. Moreover, since such peccadilloes were confined to any group obliged for a while to suffer them, they posed no serious threat — one good reason why we came to live with the full expression of our original nature for a million years or more. Only later, when we had congregated into city states, might thousands be sent to their death at the whim of some despot similarly indulging himself.

Contrary to contemporary values, we were not born free.

Total, unfettered freedom was unnatural to us then, just as it is now. Archetypally designed for an intimate group, if today we no longer belong to one, we concoct substitutes. If life now lacks the restraints and responsibilities that would have been imposed by a group, we behave anti-socially until the balance is redressed — as later pages dramatically reveal.

So deeply buried under a mountain of accumulated conditioning and stress does our original nature now lie that much of it has been stifled or lost almost beyond retrieval. Yet if we are to enter a constructive new era in our cultural evolution, it must be resuscitated. This is at once the hope we can offer our children and the work that we can begin upon ourselves. It is possibly the noblest way to fulfil our gift of self-awareness.

Our dark side

In the days of the survival group, the supreme punishment for any misdemeanour was exile. It had the ring of a death sentence, for the group was a body, of which we were but a limb. Even now we are still haunted by fear of rejection and we adjust our behaviour constantly to reduce the risk of it happening to us.

The psychiatrist Robin Skynner explains that our immediate family is the first and most crucial of many groups to which we shall attach ourselves through life, and we soon learn that while the family readily accepts some kinds of behaviour, feelings and opinions, it recoils at others. We dare not risk being rejected by the family — by mother especially — and so we pretend that these offending feelings don't exist. If this trick develops into a habit, we grow up with a sort of screen inside us, unaware of what is on the other side, even though the unacceptable feelings are still there and affecting our behaviour. To ease the ensuing stress we project them onto others.

Anger he quotes as a good example. If we feel that anger is inconsistent with our image of ourselves, we deny ourselves the luxury of feeling and showing it. We then project it onto others by believing that they are angry, and most probably with us, when all the time they are nothing of the sort. If we feel there is something intrinsically wrong with anger, we are likely to disapprove of anyone who shows it. Similarly if we have grown up with guilty feelings about sex, we may see sex in every conceivable situation and person however improbable, and so feel 'purer' than others and superior to them.

It has been aptly said that denying a feeling is like trying to drive a car from the back seat so that you won't be told it's your fault if you hit something. You may kid yourself that you're safer in the back, but of course the risk is greater. At the wheel you're obviously less likely to have an accident, but if you do you will have to accept responsibility for it; and that, as Robin Skynner stresses, is an inconvenience you are trying to avoid at all costs.

This dark side of our nature on the other side of the screen corresponds to what Jung has termed the *shadow*. It harbours our impotent rage, all our inadmissable ideas, the source of all the unpleasant things that we could do — and sometimes secretly might like to do — but usually do not. By keeping these on the other side of the screen we are able to hold onto our idealised image of ourselves. We may even relish it when we see or learn of someone committing any of the sins hidden there, wallow in the self-satisfaction of feeling holier-than-thou, condemn too vehemently to be convincing, or simply indulge in silent envy.

The horror that we may be rejected because we inadvertently reveal some part of our 'shadow', by deed or slip of the tongue, accounts for all our lurking feelings of guilt and our desire for self-punishment and atonement. It also helps to explain our reluctance to step out of line and express outrage at injustice or empathy with life's losers. We shy away from renouncing the pleasure of others' approval. Worst of all, unable to accept the idea that there could be evil in ourselves, we project it onto others — who generally don't deserve it.

Fortunately we have been provided with a vigilant inner censor whose job it is to see that most of the time we behave tolerably well. But for this censor we would not survive long as a species. As individuals, we would we not be allowed out and about, for we would all be raging psychopaths, unable to trust anyone. The censor — sometimes called by Freud the super-ego — helps to ensure that we conform to whatever social rules we have internalised, and most of the time we accept the loss of freedom that is the consequence.

Since the 'shadow' holds the unthinkable fear that there may be no hope of a future, one of our first steps in showing concern about the world our children expect to inherit is a willingness to confront it. We shall not make much headway unless we give up rationalising, finding scapegoats or burying our heads in the sand, rather than accepting our fair share of blame for the present mess. It is part of the necessary work upon ourselves. We have to shed any cherished illusions about our virtue or innocence and learn to analyse our dubious motives and unacceptable feelings whenever they surface. We have to examine the validity of forever protesting that it's none of our business. For as Jung has put it: 'Recognition of *the shadow* . . . leads to the modesty we need in order to acknowledge imperfection'. Just as much a part of our being as our heart or our eyes, the 'shadow' demands to be recognised. If we refuse to accept what it holds, whether through apathy, puritanism, ignorance or fear, we encourage it to manifest its 'appetites' in ways beyond our control.

Humankind has a *collective shadow* too, part nature, part nurture. It reflects the dark side of technological progress: as noise, pollution, slums, ugliness, factory farming, loss of wildlife, vanishing natural resources and the ever-present Bomb. It helps to explain the moral vacuum which allows chronic worldwide poverty and hunger to co-exist with unprecedented expenditure on armaments, space exploration, trivia and the pursuit of comfort. It reflects the seamier side of our misguided culture's past, with its torture, massacres, genocide, religious persecution, tyranny, slavery, witch-burning and Hiroshima. A candid study of it reveals depths of cruelty unknown in the occasional, seemingly violent behaviour of other species: not even among those which we have either caged or domesticated so that they undergo severe stress or deprivation.

All that we have done to Earth, all the rampant destruction, is no more than a manifestation of what goes on inside each of us, on either side of the screen. For the trouble in the natural world is the trouble in ourselves. Our collective 'shadow' embodies our thirst for power and exploitation, and from there our ability to annihilate the familiar world we know. It is little more than an act of naive projection to blame the mavericks who climb to the top in the rat race, for since we relish the rewards and protest so feebly, they may be forgiven for assuming that they are acting on our behalf as well as their own.

All thoughts, feelings and behaviour, that are possible yet unthinkable, are relegated to the other side of the screen, to be part of the shadow within each one of us. It is a mechanism that we have learned to use in order to preserve a superficial sanity in a world of collective lunacy. This ability to hide what we cannot confront behind a screen is an outmoded survival device which now paradoxically threatens to destroy us. Yet our mere awareness of it could prove a source of inestimable hope. And a collective willingness to confront it would transform hope into realisation.

The next chapter returns us to the story of humankind and the aftermath of our discovery of agriculture. It explains how ruling elites in the earliest city states exploited the inherent images and drives in our original nature and so set the pattern for all our subsequent history.

PART THREE

Ensuing havoc

7: The Price of Civilization

Progress should not speed man faster than his soul

Chinese proverb

The first farmer was probably a woman. Ever since men became obsessed with hunting, women had been the principal gatherers of grain, fruit and vegetables. It is easy to conjecture how the breakthrough might have come about. There was this woman, musing by her pestle and mortar after recent rains, when she had this idea that the seeds of grain, which sometimes grew where she had spilled them, might be saved. Later she could scatter them where they could ripen without being trodden on, and later still gather the heads with certainty from one small, handy site, rather than roam far afield and find little. After that stroke of deductive genius it would have been a logical next step to clear the weeds from a patch of promising ground and scratch the seeds into it. She and her sisters would have begun to farm.

True to character, men were not to be outdone. When they had customarily driven hunted animals into traps, some man would have figured that instead of killing the youngest with the rest, he might carry one or two home and tether them to browse and fatten until ready to eat. After that the next logical step would have been to keep some animals long enough to breed from them, rather than rely so much on the vagaries of the hunt. In this way men would have become the first pastoralists.

Clearly we cannot be sure who came first, farmer or pastoralist. We do know however that over 10 000 years ago our ancestors had domesticated sheep in what is now Iraq, goats in Iran a thousand years later, then pigs in Turkey, and after that cattle in Greece.

Such accomplishments demanded profound changes in life style. Once we undertook the responsibilities of farmer and pastoralist, we were obliged to forsake our nomadic ways and, for a few years at a time, settle down in villages. Around our villages we cleared the land by fire and axe, and then moved on to repeat the sequence as soon as dwindling crop yields were no longer worth harvesting. It was the 'slash and burn', shifting farming, still practised by multinational companies in South America's rainforest and by impoverished or ignorant farmers the world over; not unlike the pattern of farming in North America that climaxed in the horrendous dust bowls of the Thirties.

In the Middle East, between the Mediterranean and the Persian Gulf, people on the move had found a vast region of easy terrain and fertile virgin soil where a primitive form of wheat grew luxuriantly. The region was blessed with the right amount of reliable rainfall for cultivation, a climate ideal for farming, and navigable river access to the sea. This 'Fertile Crescent' — as we came to call the arc-shaped region — offered advantages unknown anywhere else at that time. A focus for migrant tribes, it held the promise of a place where they could settle down to husband their stock and grow crops forever. Tribes that settled there coalesced into villages and, over time, some of the most successful villages grew to become the first cities.

This period, some 9 000 years ago, was another milestone in our history. To organise and feed one-time nomads in the cheek-by-jowl life style of cities destined to harbour thousands represented a major challenge. If life were not to disintegrate into bitter squabbling and bloody chaos, social structures would have to be rigid, complex and hierarchical. New means to settle disputes would have to be devised. Planners too would be required to lay out the cities, along with architects to devise more substantial buildings, weavers and spinners to make clothes, and craftsmen to fashion pottery, axeheads, blades, scrapers, grindstones, pestles and mortars, as well as necklaces and bracelets.

Our biological evolution had been completed some 90 000 years previously. Spurred on by the challenge of running cities, we were now taking another quantum leap in our *cultural* evolution. Until then, as primitive subsistence farmers, we had been chiefly absorbed in merely scratching a livelihood. The early cities and their associated settled farming held the promise of unprecedented surpluses — of time, food and artifacts.

The appropriate response to such an immense challenge was soon forthcoming, for a vast reservoir of talent lay untapped, waiting to find expression. Over the past million years, all the planning and organisation that the hunt entailed, with its strong element of delayed gratification, had equipped the male brain with singular attributes that could now be pressed into service. After a relatively brief period of enforced quiescence, men were able to assert themselves once again, and the new city-based societies of The Fertile Crescent emerged as rigidly patriarchal.

In this way a pattern of organisation, power and surpluses became firmly established, destined to spread not only throughout the rapidly growing settlements of that unique time and place, but throughout subsequent history, to cities yet to be born, even to the present day.

The new shape of human culture

One of the earliest cities was Jericho, first settled more than 10 000 years ago at a time even before we had learned how to make pottery. Jericho's origins pre-dated agriculture because people were drawn to an extensive oasis formed by an ample, ever-flowing spring which continually added to the fertility of its soil. There, with sickles of bone embedded with flints, they harvested a crude, wild wheat grass long before they knew how to plant it.

Jericho was the precursor of the age of cities in which we now live. It sealed the end of our biological evolution and marked the dramatic beginning of our cultural evolution which is still in progress. The degree of self-consciousness that made Jericho possible could never have been achieved by mobile hunter–gatherers, nor by 'slash and burn' farmers forever forced to keep on the move. Civilization could only arise in settled communities. These communities grew from villages that resembled the archetypal group to become cities that did not. The consequences of the change to farming communities, both for us and the natural world, have been predictably momentous. Because of the manner in which we responded to the challenge of city life, it may be said that the birth of consciousness anticipated the death of Nature. For in the process of selecting the species of plant and livestock which suited us and in eliminating those that did not, we upset the vital balance on which the whole of life ultimately depends.

Neither was the manner of our response to the challenge wholly beneficial to humankind. Under the combined impact of agriculture and city living, human populations grew as never before. As a consequence the forests, which had covered the post Ice Age world, progressively shrank, and hunter–gatherers who still lived outside the new way of life retreated into the dwindling wilderness. As early farmers and city dwellers, we prized our impressive accomplishments at the same time as we learned to belittle, revile and eventually destroy those tribes that had been left behind in the race. Yet, as we freed ourselves from the constraints of the ancient niche which still held some, we had not yet awakened to the knowledge that we were destined to become trapped in our own burgeoning fears and attachments.

The Sumer syndrome

At the south-eastern end of the Fertile Crescent lay the jungle swamps of the plains between the rivers Euphrates and Tigris in what is now Mesopotamia. Floods from these rivers regularly enriched the swampy soils with the alluvial silt they deposited from far off mountain slopes. This was the place where, some 6 000 years ago, tribes settled to drain the swamps, to sow, irrigate and reap their crops, and to organise the crop rotations. As the network of irrigation and drainage channels grew, it became apparent that only central organisation could mobilise the labour force, control the waters, extend the area and keep the whole scheme running smoothly. In this way the city-states of Sumer came into being.

The citizens spoke a language sufficiently advanced to convey and understand complex instructions. Their leaders possessed the imagination, foresight and self-control to work for rewards that would take months — even years — to be realised. Humankind, the newly emerged social animal, was everywhere imposing its will on the previously intractible realm of Nature. This uniquely ambitious venture however demanded far more than inspired organisation and audacity. It was essential that the rest of the citizens should share their leaders' faith. To unite everyone in this exhilarating triumph and to show their own faith and power, the leaders established a priesthood to conscript the ancient nature-gods that they might serve as divine patrons — or servitors — of human sovereign states.

As William McNeill explains, 'Sumerian theology held that men had been created expressly to free the gods from the necessity of working for a living. Man was thus considered to be a slave of the gods, obliged to serve ceaselessly and assiduously under pain of direct punishment: as flood or drought and consequent starvation. As the wealth of the temples grew, the splendour and elaboration of the sacred routines increased, until the appeasement of the gods bcame a major economic enterprise, involving the professional attention not only of the priests, but many types of crafstmen as well. Such behaviour was based on the assumption that a god had to be cajoled and propitiated lest he send flood or disease, or raise up some murderous enemy against his people.'

As a means of sanctifying the work ethic the concept was brilliant, for the more frequent the disasters, the harder people had to work. Moreover, the very insecurity of life guaranteed priestly power and influence. Since priests were the only people through whom the gods deigned to communicate with men, a generous share of the harvest was always stored in the temples.

Conveniently distanced from lesser citizens, the leaders in the various city-states consolidated their advantages by establishing the principle that the surplus created by all should not be equally shared but reserved for the privileged elite. Leisure too was to be unequally distributed. They established themselves as a ruling class which held that private luxuries were a just reward for the incalculable public services they performed.

The better to carry out these services, they surrounded themselves, not only with the priesthood, but with bureaucrats: administrators to interpret their wishes, clerks to keep accounts, servants to minister to their needs, and — significantly — an army to protect the state from plundering hill tribesman and envious neighbours and, when necessary, to protect themselves from their own citizens. They also encouraged a merchant class to exchange surplus food for materials they lacked, notably metals.

The irrigation scheme was far too complex to memorise from day to day, season to season. Too much water and soil, too many people had to be kept on the move according to a strict timetable. Mere spoken words were not enough; they had to be written down. In response to this need, around 5 000 years ago, humankind's newest essential tool came into being: the Sumerian script.

Breakthrough though it was, the script incised on its clay tablets was clumsy and complex. Since only the leaders could understand it the script affirmed their power over their dependent, illiterate followers. 'Follow my leader' was easy to enforce because it was already an inherited trait from the days of the survival group. That the citizens were now mobilised to perform tasks they could not understand within unnaturally swollen groups was immaterial. Submitting willingly, they displayed total faith in their leaders and in the gods with whom the leaders communed. By mastering human nature the leaders were able to master Nature. All this we know from the written records of Sumer. With local variations it would have held good for any city of the time and for earlier cities. It set the pattern for cities yet to come: religious ceremonial centres surrounded by separate areas in which the ruling elite lived in luxury, adjacent to the priesthood, administrators and the army, while ordinary people lived at a distance beyond them all. As cities grew, so did the ruling classes and the power they wielded.

Predictably the rulers of Sumer over-promoted themselves. Their wisdom failed to keep pace with changing circumstances. Effective operation of the irrigation scheme called for unified control, but rivalry between the city-states of the region meant that this control was not achieved until too late — and then it was imposed by a conquering neighbour. The same inter-state rivalry, fuelled by insatiable greed and ambition, kept them in an almost constant state of war.

The dream of peaceful co-existence and everlasting farming was fading fast. In the space of a few thousand years the constraints on behaviour that had worked so effectively in the archetypal survival groups were largely eroded. Leaders of each state that now constituted the 'survival group' openly misappropriated surpluses in order to build ever bigger armies. With close settlement there were no longer effective buffer zones between neighbouring groups to lessen tensions. Once long ago in the intimacy of the survival group, leaders and those they led had enjoyed mutual trust. Now that the two classes were distanced from each other physically and socially, the leaders were able to get away with murder — and no doubt often did. Meanwhile in the pervading climate of mutual distrust, war between rival states became unremitting and the armies of the rulers were obliged to face both inwards and outwards.

In time the region encountered other problems too. Populations had grown both in Sumer and in regions to the north. To build more and bigger cities and to keep their ruling elites in militarily defended luxury, the demand for timber grew. The mountain slopes, which gave birth to the life-giving rivers, became progressively denuded of forest. With the slopes stripped of their protective sponge-like cover, flood waters swelled out of control and wrought havoc on the irrigation systems hundreds of miles below. Heavy and untimely floods carried silt from the slopes to clog irrigation channels and bury growing crops. As the silt deposits inexorably worsened, whole cities had to be rebuilt on top of mud-filled predecessors. The early settlers had foreseen the primal alluvium as the source of all the region's wealth and greatness. That which had promised to be a resource to exploit forever, now threatened to engulf and destroy their successors — all within the span of a few thousand years.

The land became salt-laden too. Salt-saturated water, washed down from deposits, laid bare on the slopes, evaporated in the fields and reduced crop yields even further. In earlier days farmers had controlled this problem by resting land between crops, but as population growth put extra pressure on them they had to abandon the practice. The excess salt that crippled the fields of Sumer constituted Earth's first known instance of chemical pollution.

Around 3 500 years ago, barbarians from the north finally conquered the disintegrating civilization. However, they lacked the necesssary knowledge or will to maintain the irrigation systems. With the soil polluted, canals silt-laden and flood barriers in disarray, the world's first 'hydraulic civilization' came to a close. In succeeding centuries hardy nomads struggled on, but when the dying soil could no longer support them, they folded their tents and left. Today most of the plains and hillsides that once abounded in luxuriant sub-tropical greenery would scarcely support a mouse.

Before mismanagement of the region had taken its toll, the resourceful Sumerians, lacking mineral deposits, had learned how to bake the clay sub-soil to fashion farm implements of near-metallic hardness. Today the same clay lies naked, devoid of topsoil long eroded, baked hard by a fierce sun masked only by frequent sand storms. Here and there sparse flocks of sheep over-graze the vestiges of meagre herbage that tenaciously cling to life. Elsewhere virtually all life has departed.

This land, empty and irredeemably barren, now mocks the foolishness of the clever but short-sighted men who stripped it of wealth and life. As pioneers in a world they believed to be infinite in its resources, they had no word for ecology in their language. Neither had they predecessors from whose mistakes they might have learned the lessons that could have saved them and the land on which they totally depended. Limited and fallible as they were, they may be excused for failing to foresee the connections between their behaviour and its consequences. Lasting as it did, ten times longer than our own industrial counterpart to date, their hydraulic civilization has numinous lessons for us who imitate it today.

The role of surplus

As Arnold Toynbee has recorded, what happened to Sumer merely highlights the inevitable sequence of birth, death and decay that beset nearly all the early cities and city-states. Since then the same fatal sequence has led one civilization after another to collapse, not only in Asia, Africa and Europe but also in South America. There have been significant local variations, as in Egypt, sustained by the waters of the Nile until construction of the Aswam dam, but nevertheless an unmistakable common thread has run through them all, so relevant to our present world crisis that it justifies repetition.

In each state, alongside the spread of learning and the arts, there arose a powerful ruling class dominated not by 'ordinary' individuals but by mavericks, fanatics and gamblers. Distanced from both the land and the people, and consequently freed from constraint, its members acquired the means to abuse surplus. Instead of returning surplus, either to the land for renewal or to the people as reward, they used it to institute a bureaucracy, priesthood and army: an unholy trinity designed to further their own ambitions for power, prestige and comfort. In time this became established as a male-dominated power structure. Enjoying a life of its own, quite independent of the state, it was then well-placed to draw up the state's rules and impose values which suited its members.

The consequences were eventually catastrophic. In dominating and exploiting Nature to benefit the state, and *per se* themselves, they neglected to renew the land. As the agricultural hinterland of each state lost its fertility, so its rulers were obliged to acquire fresh land wherever it could be found. Forced to look ever farther afield they found themselves saddled with the responsibilities of empire. Feeding on the wealth sucked in from the empire, art, architecture, philosophy and law might flourish for a while — even for centuries. However, the state would become more and more dependent for survival on commerce, transport and technology, maintained by costly military or naval supremacy.

When inevitably the soils of the empire became farmed out, the state would find itself with a disappearing economic base and consequently no longer capable of sustaining its burden of top-heavy wealth. As the fabric of each society subsequently crumbled, so its power structure eventually fell apart. The state was then in its death throes. With the authority of its rulers gone, it became easy prey to incursive neighbours. Its people would either be absorbed into the society of its conquerors or else would disperse and leave the buildings of the old state to crumble into ruins.

In Sumer, until the closing stages, the people who toiled to transform the city-state's single resource of alluvium into wealth did at least *eat* the fruits of their labours. Elsewhere benefits to the toilers were sparse, their labours more bizarre. In ancient Greece successive rulers conscripted armies of slaves to build cities, sports stadiums and mighty temples that the slaves could seldom if ever enjoy. In Egypt, under the direction of the priesthood, the people were obliged to spend the greater part of their lives constructing colossal pyramids and excavating cavernous tombs. Here were housed bizarrely the corpses, not only of their rulers with their wealth and entourage, but also those of countless sacred bulls; some sites held millions of clay pots, each one a vessel for the mummified body of a revered bird. In Rome, slaves from all over its empire were forced to construct vast amphitheatres. There its citizens could revel in the ritual slaughter of untold numbers of wild animals, brought expressly for the purpose from Africa — as well as the prolonged deaths of unfortunate slaves and wrong-doers.

From the dawn of city living, the abuse of surplus, together with its attendant injustices, has been the order of the day.

With the advent of agriculture our numbers over the face of the Earth rocketed. That they were able to do so was largely because we defied natural laws. By failing to renew the land from which we extracted so much, we cut short the critical cycle of birth, death, decay and re-birth: in this way we purloined what belonged to other life forms, trespassed on their niches, and broke the benign cycle of interdependence with them. In all of this we showed no regard for the connections that maintain the balance of the whole. By commandeering an ever-growing surplus we acted without constraint and so ignored the eminently sensible principle of 'enough is enough'.

Our inherent flaws and limitations can now be seen in sharp relief. The Sumer syndrome amply demonstrated not only our need to submit to a cause greater than ourselves, but also our willingness to do so even when it manifestly conflicted with our best interests. The overwhelming majority of ordinary people asked nothing more than to be left alone to get on with their work of craft or farming, to live their lives anonymously and rear their children. This was not to be. Except in rare intervals of protracted peace, women would find themselves deserted, their menfolk rendered reluctant soldiers through the whim of successive ambitious rulers. Throughout history, our leaders — *nearly all of them men* — promoted themselves to the level of their incompetence. Yet in our apathy and confusion we have made heroes out of our tyrants and gods out of our heroes. We have remained indifferent to our latent power, unaware that, short of wholesale massacre, no ruler's army can suppress a whole population indefinitely.

Our compliance is understandable however. Conscripted into cities, we perceived ourselves as working for the gods who kept Nature at bay. We submitted because work was accorded religious significance. We worshipped our own collective power over the previously intractable realm of Nature. Sustained by this exhilarating faith, we spent our lives toiling in oversize groups, under the domination of tyrants, conditioned to pursue aims that we barely comprehended.

For this the psyche paid a crippling price. The life style was so alien to what we had known in our long and recent archetypal past that we became severely stressed. As earlier pages have recounted, our true nature was eventually overwhelmed by a warped substitute which we progressively acquired, simply to survive within the constricting framework of rules and values imposed by the state. Unlike the values we had left behind in our ancient groups however, these new values paid little heed either to our true needs or to those of the planet Earth on which we ultimately depended. Accordingly, humankind and planet suffered alike.

Throughout the ensuing millennia since Sumer, nothing of consequence has changed. The 'Sumer syndrome' serves as a disquietingly accurate model for the vast majority of subsequent cities and civilizations — Hellenic, Roman, Syrian, Islamic, Aztec, Inca, Maya, Mongol — even to this day, when the end of the story can be predicted but has yet to be told.

The story of these and other civilizations has been a chronicle of the abuse of surplus. Hunter-gatherers possessed neither the means nor the incentive to create it. The 'dawn' people soon acquired both. Through ever-improving organisation and technology, they wrung from Earth both her living and mineral reserves, and used the surplus so created to extract still more. This taming of Nature for our own ends is the fruit of knowledge for which the mythical records ascribe punishment.

The abuse of surplus is part of our collective 'shadow'. It overshadows our achievements in art, wisdom and religion, and our appreciation of aesthetics. Under the euphemism of 'wealth', surplus has given us limitless power for which we have not yet acquired a matching sense of responsibility. More than anything else, it accounts for the question mark that hangs over our future.

The making of history has been dominated by the making of war. Although each rising and falling civilization enjoyed respites from warfare, little time passed before, somewhere on the map, men fought each other for one cause or another, be it in perceived self-defence, to liberate or be liberated, or to assuage a thirst for avarice, revenge or conquest. While sometimes they may have shared their leaders' aggressiveness, more often they would have been dispassionate, reluctant participants. Over the years, for one reason or another and in the names of various gods, masters or passions, men have left their homes and families to fight, torture, rape and pillage. And all the while that these disturbed minorities were wrestling vainly with the dark side of their natures, the great majority of men and all women, whether constrained by poverty and obligations or sustained by conscience, carried on with the more important, if humdrum, business of living. Throughout it all, women, more attuned to the half-forgotten natural world, nurtured their men and the children that were born to them, all the while that they bore the brunt of each day's essential work.

Repeatedly the exploits of misguided and adventurous men

have reduced to ashes the fires that have illumined the teachings of philosophers, poets and seers, striving through the ages to re-awaken our consciences. Time and again, when it had seemed that we might attain the moral stature that could moderate our fearsome power to destroy ourselves and Nature, we have regressed into the darker side of our collective being.

Whenever constraints are weakened, the barbaric genius lurking and smirking deep in every one of us is all too ready to assert himself and have the devil of a time at the expense of morality and any awareness of vital connections.

The next chapter depicts what happens when flawed and limited 'cavemen' such as ourselves try to run today's complex artificial world.

8: A Species under Stress

'Nature has let us down, God seems to have left the receiver off the hook, and time is running out'

Arthur Koestler

We share with all the other millions of species alive today the distinction of surviving evolution's discrimination. Throughout Earth's three-billion year history, one species after another has evolved only to become extinct and make way for newcomers. The evolutionary trail is littered with failed experiments. The dinosaur's body grew so ridiculously out of proportion to its brain that when eventually the climate changed it had no hope of adapting. The man-like apes that were our ancestors mysteriously petered out. Our one-time contemporary, Neanderthal man, succumbed to the rigours of the last Ice Age, along with the mammoth and a host of smaller animals. The now extinct Irish elk was encumbered by its huge antlers. Nearly all of the flightless birds of New Zealand succumbed to the rats, cats and dogs brought by successive immigrants. More species have become extinct than are now alive. Throughout the world today humble turtles and beetles are endangered, not just through us but because once they are on their backs they simply cannot right themelves.

Ironically self-dubbed *homo sapiens*, we have joined the club of endangered species chiefly because, in contrast to the dinosaur, we have a disproportionately large brain. The duality of our nature is manifest: one part of our brain fails to connect properly with another, while the whole is in a state of precarious imbalance. Since the man–made world is entirely a product of this defective brain, we should not be surprised that it too malfunctions. As it relentlessly supersedes the natural world that is our life support system, so we head for the same fate as other blunders on the evolutionary trail.

Even reckoned at a three-million year maximum, our sojourn on Earth will have been one of the briefest: on a cosmic time scale, a stable million years as hunter–gatherers, followed by an apparently instantaneous efflorescence of technology and organisation leading to imminent extinction. It will have been a pathetic testimony to the evolutionary blunder of selecting humankind as the vessel to receive Earth's first known experiment in acquiring consciousness.

Yet this need not be. Once we are able to identify our more serious defects, so we gain the ability to overcome them and alter the direction of our cultural evolution. It is a question of using our self-consciousness differently. This dubious attribute, which has brought us to the brink of extinction, is all that we possess to secure our survival. Nothing can salvage the whole bizarre experiment from abject failure but ourselves.

The drives and images that were right for our ancient niche can be wildly inappropriate for life within the super-industrial state. Few of us now hunt, even fewer gather. In place of survival groups of around thirty there are nation states of millions. We cope with the vagaries of Nature by either 'Disney-fying' or destroying her. No longer capable of distinguishing friend from foe by familarity of face, we see enemies everywhere, even if we have to concoct them. No fierce predators any longer prowl around Battersea or The Bronx apart from our own species. With survival of a kind assured, when life loses its meaning we invent one in such guises as God, money or work.

We face challenges today that have no archetypal counterpart ready to spring instinctively to our aid; we have inherent drives pining away inside us for stimuli that never come. A horse knows from birth how to be a horse; a cuckoo from the egg precisely how to be a cuckoo. In contrast, devoid of our protective niche, footloose and free from constraints, we have little of relevance to guide us apart from our culture's great body of knowledge, beliefs, rules and values: and even *that* can be shown to be outworn.

In industrial societies, what most of us display as human nature is not a reflection of our true selves. We are not what we think we are. Yet while it may be fairly easy to paint a picture of our original nature, now engulfed by all our acquired cultural evolution, it is less easy to portray the warped nature that has nudged the old one out of the way. Dependent on laws and customs, this usurper varies from nation to nation. Arising as it does according to the degree of stress in society, it also varies not only between city and country, but also according to class. Since our upbringing damages each of us is in various ways and to different degrees, our acquired natures have far less about them that is truly universal.

But this is not all. Our collective behaviour bears little resemblance to the way we act as individuals. We are much nicer people than the daily headlines imply. Our better side flourishes in the sort of face-to-face situations that typify our ancient past. Most of us show less inclination to shoot our next-door neighbours than our real or concocted enemies, be they Russians, Argentinians or Libyans. We behave less barbarically as we approach the checkout counter than when we hurtle towards the contra-flow bottleneck. In small groups we tend to behave less like savages.

Citizens in nation states with populations numbered in millions tend to display many of the symptoms of stress. We do things in the name of causes that we would find abhorrent in the humdrum of familiar daily life. There is no need to point an accusing finger at a phenomenon so extreme as terrorism in order to find loathsome behaviour: it happens all the time in industry, business and commerce. Law-abiding family men in the boardrooms of tobacco giants can cheerfully divert their marketing efforts to the impoverished Third World once they see home sales drying up. Respectable purveyors of chemicals in the aerosol propellants depleting the ozone layer have run intensive lobbying campaigns to protect their interests, despite the evidence that we shall all be at even greater risk of cancer if they succeed. But it is not just 'Them' that suffer from the duality of living in two non-communicating realities. Most of us, faced with the task of selling a secondhand lawnmower, forget to mention that it has a habit of stopping because the carburettor is clapped out.

A species under pandemic stress

We have already seen how we came to be where we are. If we are to understand just what we are, we have to face the uncomfortable knowledge that we are not after all masters of the world with a glorious past and an illimitable future. From Earth's viewpoint we are a grossly imperfect creature with crippling limitations. Inherent flaws such as an inability to stop or see connections could prove fatal. In accumulating surplus we violated the principle of adequacy. Admittedly we never asked for our more-than-adequate brain: evolution simply endowed us with it well before our simple life style had need of such an extravagant instrument. Our mistake has been to use it, not simply to acquire the technology that could raise us above the worries of day-to-day survival, but to let it lead us to the present crisis.

So far we have used no more than a part of our brain: the rest is wrapped in mystery. The prospect of bringing into use its latent powers offers hope for the future. As the philosopher Arthur Koestler has perceptively observed of such a challenge:

'The new frontiers most worthy of being conquered lie, not in space, not in Antarctica or the oceans' depths, but in the convolutions of our own cerebral cortex.' Here could be the means of reconciling the pathological genius with the bewildered savage, for only then will our sense of responsibility catch up with our runaway technology and restrain it. Meanwhile most of us in industrial societies must remain lulled by our defects into believing that the half life they permit is our full potential. Spiritually we crawl when we could walk upright. We muddle on in our alien environment, suffering the kind of anguish and aberrations that afflict any of the wild animals we have caged in our zoos. Ours is the bewilderment and paralysis of a bat or hedgehog confronted by untimely daylight.

Evidence of widespread stress abounds. Up to a third of marriages in Britain are likely to end in divorce, most of them among the poor where stress-inducing conditions are predictably greatest. One survey has found that three out of five women are afraid to go out alone after dark, another that one in twelve women interviewed had been raped and one in seven sexually assaulted.

In the rich 'Top Twenty' per cent of the world, spending on tranquillizers matches the total public health expenditure of the world's poorest nations. In Britain alone, doctors write some twenty-six million prescriptions a year for the various benzodiazepine tranquillizers, and an estimated three million adults use these potentially harmful drugs daily. One person in four will suffer identifiable psychiatric illness at some time in their lives. One hospital bed in three is occupied by patients with mental illness or handicap. More than a million Europeans are confined to mental homes or hospitals.

Although hard drugs make the headlines, our socially acceptable addiction to ethyl alcohol in various strengths, flavours and different-shaped bottles is responsible, in excess, for more deaths, illness, serious accidents and misery than all other drugs added together. In 1987 well over two million anguished people in Britain contacted The Samaritans; almost a quarter of a million attempted suicide and 4 000 succeeded. Every day in Britain someone under the age of twenty-five commits suicide, almost a twenty-five per cent increase in a decade. In the United States, where teenage suicide is a grave and growing problem, a new phenomenon of 'cluster suicides' has been identified — one death triggers others in the same locale.

Some of us are more affected by stress than others. Although poverty, especially in the midst of affluence, is a prime cause, it is rife among the affluent. It is common among people who conduct their 'image-sensitive' public lives according to very different standards from their private lives, for in doing so they are obliged to ignore at their peril the warnings of 'the shadow'. Around 40 per cent of executives hospitalised through mental breakdown end by committing suicide.

The aggressive, competitive and other anti-social traits, *de rigeur* for those who to climb to the top, eventually filter down to become the accepted values for the rest of society — who then set about poisoning the cultural environment, which in turn poisons everyone. According to the psychology professor Cary Cooper stress costs Britain up to ten per cent of its GNP in lost productivity through heart disease, alcoholism and mental illness. Research shows that working couples with children are particularly prone to work-related stress, through conflicts of interest and responsibilities. In consequence their children suffer too.

We exhibit stressful behaviour not only when there is too much going on but also when there is too little. For we have survived as a species only because of our ability to cope with struggle. But for this we would have succumbed to the Ice Age. Much of the restlessness men exhibit may be attibutable to their being deprived of an outlet comparable to the hunt. All of us may display stressful behaviour through lack of the intimacy offered by a small group. And since the clutter of too many possessions is contrary to our original nature, here may lie a clue to the chronic discontent they fail to mollify.

Throughout our time on Earth we have abused almost every thought, emotion and sense, along with almost everything we have ever invented or created. Tools soon became weapons, farming turned into exploitation; machines, initially our servants, became our masters; printing became propaganda, and television a means of selling soap flakes; the miraculous microchip quickly found its place in missile guidance systems, in the same way that Einstein's genius, to his utter despair, led inexorably to the Bomb.

The unique and supreme human quality of selfless love, we have similarly abused, as 'smother love' and narcissism. Curiosity has turned from discovery to disillusionment, persistence to the pursuit of money and power, appetite to gluttony. Not content with language as a means to gain understanding, we demean it to a means of persuasion. Not content with sex as the source of procreation, the affirmation of love, ineffable pleasure and joyful lust, we frustrate its purpose, bend and pervert it, commercialise and trivialise it, and even pretend that it does not exist. Attitudes have changed only with the advent of AIDS and the supreme irony that sex can now carry the seeds of death as well as birth.

Unable to cope with the enormity of consciousness, we play dangerous games with it by swallowing, sniffing, smoking or injecting any substance that might alter it. Rather than change the state of our environment we cope with its defects with pills that change our state of mind. When the gift of consciousness becomes a burden, so too does the gift of life.

Under the rules and values of today's 'free enterprise', society we sell our brains to the highest bidder. There would be little wrong in this if all were well with the man-made world. Since all is demonstrably not well, technological innovation is channelled, not to where it could help solve desperate human problems of inequality, poverty, hunger and illiteracy, but to where wealth has already accumulated. This is not surprising. One of the principal defects of our species is ingenuity without appropriate responsibility. It confirms that while we can be brilliant at specifics, we are inept at making connections, unappreciative of wider issues. Far more than merely inadequate, collectively we can be demonstrably dangerous; as a species we are seriously unbalanced with a built-in paranoid streak. To understand why, we need to look at the design of the brain behind this mismatch.

Our brain is in effect two brains joined together. The lower of the two is our archaic old brain, governed by instinct and primitive reflexive emotion, which we share with reptiles and lower mammals. Superimposed on this relatively crude organ is a 'new' brain, the convoluted neocortex, which has endowed us with language, logic and the reasoning powers of conceptual thought. In the last half-a-million years the neocortex has expanded at a speed unparallelled in evolution. Some anthropologists have compared it to a 'tumorous overgrowth', a rare, benign mutation contrary to natural selection.

As earlier pages have shown, for at least a million years our predecessors scarcely used the neocortex. For the last 40 000 years or more the brain that was to take man to the moon was idling inside his skull. Clearly in creating the human brain, evolution widely overshot the mark. The consequences are apparent: given surplus brains we predictably abuse them — much as we abuse virtually every other natural gift.

It appears that because of the neocortex's rapid rise it failed to achieve adequate co-ordination with the archaic brain on which it was superimposed. Evolution had added a new, superior structure with functions that overlapped those of the old one, yet without giving it unambigious control: the genius forever bickering with the caveman.

If indeed the new brain has never become completely integrated, it would help to explain why emotion and intuition have always been at loggerheads with intellect; why faith and reason have been incompatible; why history has been punctuated by repeated holocausts, and why morality today lags so far behind innovation.

Yin and Yang

Our remarkable brain is not only divided laterally into the neocortex and the 'old brain' but, for most of it, also vertically divided into left and right hemispheres. These quite separate organs are joined together deep inside our skull by a bridge of nerve fibres called the corpus callosum. The two hemispheres have different physical and psychic functions. Put simply, the left side is the more active side, responsible for 'doing', for science and technology and manipulating the environment. It is essentially rational. The right side is more passive, receptive, for monitoring events and for perceiving and understanding the world as it is rather than changing it. The right side is intuitive and instinctive.

The two sides are often in conflict with each other. Suppose some crisis is brewing and we have to make a speedy decision in a situation where facts are sparse. Shall our judgement and subsequent action be based on facts or intuition? In a different dilemma we might have to choose between 'rocking the boat', which could be unpredictably destabilising, and *laissez faire*, which might merely make matters worse.

In each of us, one hemisphere or other tends to be dominant and therefore the more assertive in any situation. Life is seldom black and white however, and for the sheer survival of the brain's owner, each side must know what the other side is up to. This is where the bridge of nerve fibres joining the two hemispheres comes in. As well as communicator it also acts as mediator during the conflicts of duality that we encounter for so much of the time.

The divided brain helps to explain certain differences in thought, feeling and behaviour between the sexes. Men tend to be left hemisphere dominated — rational and active; women right hemisphere dominated — receptive and passive. In short, the hemispheres tend to stand for head and heart. It must be stressed that the accent is on 'tend', for in each sex there are many individuals who are exceptions to the rule. Nevertheless, unlike the preceding 'new and old brain' theory, which must obviously remain a hypothesis, it has been possible to establish this explanation by experiment and observation.

From prolonged studies, other qualities dominant in either one hemisphere or the other have emerged. Left side attitudes are extrovert, right hand ones introvert; the left way of functioning is conceptual, that of the right perceptual; the left side is more materialistic, the right more aesthetic; the left is more analytic, the right more deductive; the left deals in words, the right in images; the left approaches life with orderliness, the right with spontaneity; the left contributes mathematics, science, technology and theology to society; the right contributes painting, sculpture, music and mysticism. And so on . . .

Men generally manifest traits such as obsessional or compulsive behaviour, persuasive use of language, rationality, and the tendency to break down information into details, the logical deductiveness of science, technology, and exploration and manipulation of the environment. Women in contrast show more holistic perception, intuition, tolerance of paradoxes, and a propensity to perceive the world as it is rather than subject it to some purpose or design.

The Chinese have long known about such complementary tendencies. For them the left-sided ones — predominantly masculine — manifest qualities that they call the yang principle, the right-sided, more feminine qualities, the yin principle. The Chinese have never ascribed moral values to yin and yang. 'Immorality' springs largely from imbalance between the two extremes, a flaw that can occur in either sex. At all times and in all individuals there is dynamic interplay between the two. In societies and culture, as in people, there are cycles in which first one is dominant and then the other.

In Western terminology activity can be of two kinds: in harmony with Nature (yin) or against her natural flow (yang). In these terms, whatever we may do becomes either 'eco action' or 'ego action'.

Ever since the Renaissance, the driving forces of Western society have been egoistically motivated by the left side, in other words, masculine dominated. Throughout education the accent has been predominantly on the 'three Rs' rather than on the arts, on drama, music and dance, which are accorded a correspondingly inferior priority in later life. Not surprisingly, in today's rational, competitive and exploitative social climate, the 'irrational' qualities of intuition, aesthetic appreciation and personal passivity are allowed to languish.

There is far more to the concept of yin and yang than this outline can convey, and later pages will return to it, but it is enough to show how it governs the way we live each day. Because of some five centuries of masculine-dominated conditioning we have been rendered victims of a psychic and intellectual lopsidedness that constitutes a serious flaw in our nature. Since men are influenced chiefly by the yang principle, and since we live in a society where men write the rules and ensure that they are obeyed, technology (yang) rampages out of control, while morality (yin) limps pathetically behind.

To awaken human consciousness and conscience that we may rescue the natural world in time, this fatal imbalance has to be corrected by a swing to yin values in which the role of women will be crucial. There is risk attached to this, for too strong a swing to yin could lead to over-emphasis on intuition at the expense of reason, to total passivity and an acceptance of what should be put right. In the constant muted competition between Earth's species, such an imbalance would prejudice our survival.

Follow my leader

When we are very young, we absorb and imprint all that we hear, see and feel. Our developing brain and emerging psyche are pathetically at the mercy of the people and events that influence us. Although as children we are given to flashes of extraordinary insight, for the most part we lack critical faculties. As preparation for a life within small survival groups, we are archetypally designed to be highly suggestible. Not until much later on — if ever — are we able to discriminate between what is important and what is not, between good and bad, safe and dangerous, and so on.

Life was simpler in our original group. We would have been able to assimilate at a leisurely pace all the information and experience necessary for our survival, free from undue clutter or distortion. Nowadays we take in an unfiltered mish-mash of beliefs, attitudes, rules and values, out of which we need to make what sense we can about how we should think, feel and behave. With luck, a package of beliefs will emerge to equip us for life's journey. Yet it will not be of our own choosing, but chiefly composed of whatever our parents and other close associates have passed on to us. This has serious implications. Because what we are taught conflicts with what we inherently believe and desire, we run the risk of becoming stressed and neurotic. Our inherited credulity makes us all victims to early conditioning, some more than others. It numbs us into passive acceptance of the status quo. Under its influence each new generation cements into the edifice of knowledge and values the prejudices and misconceptions of its predecessors, locking us into the spiritually impoverished imitation of life that we assume to be the way to live. Many of us, however unknowingly, still hanker for a different kind of society where we would feel more at ease.

To see what happens in Nature when a species is thwarted in this way we might learn a lesson from the termites. Normally these small but important creatures build their communal homes as vast, elaborate pillars of chewed mud, superbly designed and with wall-to-wall air-conditioning. But they can only do so in groups of adequate size. When there are too few of them, they behave nervously and aimlessly and remain homeless, but once their numbers reach 'critical mass' they start merrily building. In other words they behave like termites. Such examples are common in Nature, and within them lies a clue to our own disturbed mass behaviour. Outside of reassuring small groups we feel profoundly vulnerable and display our own kind of defensively nervous and aimless behaviour.

By acting like petty dictators in the privacy of our homes we reinforce our children's conditioning. However unwittingly, mothers especially transgress through the way that they bring up their sons to be little men who don't cry or ever give in — just like Daddy. Flattered, Daddy naturally goes along with this. By over-stimulating the yang principle in infant boys we trap them in a 'macho' role that not only cripples them through life but, collectively, helps to ensure that our exploitative culture is passed on to the next generation. If we were possessed of some fiendish urge to generate antipathy to Nature in our young, we could hardly achieve our aim better than by imposing on boy children their accepted intellectual diet of sci-fi, toy missiles, TV violence, fantasy strip cartoons and electronic gadgets. The degree of damage they suffer is almost matched by the pathetic 'domestic' stereotype thrust on girl children, destined to play what are thought of as their socially inferior roles.

Nevertheless in guiding our children, we should be careful not to swing too far the other way. The yin–yang complementarity is the compass of life: like any compass it is pivoted in such a way that it points North no matter how far we may veer off course. Our true course lies at a mid-point between yin and yang.

As Chapter 5 observed, language plays a vital role in our lives. At all ages we are mercilessly susceptible to the hypnotic effect of words: cliches and slogans especially. For while language no doubt would have begun functionally as a means of exchanging information, it eventually progressed to communicating feelings and ideas. Over time it developed still further until it became an instrument of persuasion, wide open to abuse.

After our ancestors had begun to use language to convey simple instructions and make their needs known, they moved on to employ it in order to think in concepts and communicate them. From there it was but a short step from persuasion to perversion. The impact of this on our subsequent cultural evolution cannot be over-estimated. Within the small survival group the effects of persuasion on our highly suggestible nature had been minimal. However, once we forsook the old way of life for the hierarchical organisation of early cities, language which had been a vital survival device soon degenerated into an instrument of oppression. Sandwiched between our archaic suggestibility and the persuasive oratory of charismatic and self-seeking leaders, ordinary people hardly stood a chance. The priests of Sumer used it to enslave their subjects to the work ethic; Hitler was aware of its potency when he appointed Goebbels as his propagandist; it is the publicity industry's most trenchant weapon. The power structure of democratic society makes subtle and continuous use of it to maintain the status quo.

The persuasive power of language has been the means of creating a complex society and the body of knowledge, beliefs, rules and values that must accompany it. Society's leaders employ persuasion to obtain acceptance of the package. At the level of a whole culture this package embraces spectacularly diverse and controversial areas: specific customs, art, religious expression, family life, the nature of work: nothing less than the culture's entire politico-economic system.

When, in the earliest cities, we were marshalled in the cause of progress into ever-larger groups under ever more powerful leaders, we became increasingly submissive to them and to the rules and aims they dictated. We were bound to be part of some group or other: it was implanted in our psyche. And in doing so were not only enacting the ancient drive to 'follow my leader', but also the urge to transcend the Self in the interest of a greater cause. Whether the rules we observed meant forsaking family, donning a uniform or clerical habit, wearing long hair, short hair or no hair; whether the rules required us to seek conspicuous wealth or to observe a purifying frugality, we obligingly conformed. We learned, however reluctantly, that to obey the rules paid off. Initially they accorded us our very survival; later they granted us either immunity from pain or offered the prospect of pleasure — and sometimes both. If *in extremis* our allegiance demanded heroism, we were willing to provide it, even to the point of total self-sacrifice.

Little is changed today. Whether the aim of a group and its leaders entails joining a religious order, overthrowing a real or concocted enemy, raising money for a charitable fête or beating up the fans of a rival soccer club, we are able to embrace it wholeheartedly. It is not hard to see why. No matter what the aims may be they also serve to satisfy our inherent altruism, for paradoxically the self-assertiveness of any group depends eventually on the self-transcending behaviour of its members.

This is not the whole story. The larger the group and the further its leaders are distanced from its members, the more skilful the leaders become in manipulation. Similarly, the less say that members have in deciding aims and rules, the more opportunity leaders have to be ruthless and destructive before any member recovers enough of his lost identity to challenge them. There comes a time when a group can acquire a kind of 'critical mass': a point at which the insanity of its aims is matched by the submissive hysteria of its members; hence Hitler, war, the Bomb and *per se* the patriotic readiness to use it.

Our ready acceptance of any culture's great body of knowledge, beliefs, values and rules is made possible by our remarkable credulity. We are easy prey to the peddlers of the prevailing cultural code. It surrounds us like a neo-womb. We either remain conditioned to it or we rebel. The rebels are few in number however, for he who questions tradition is a dangerous hero. The power of the media amply demonstrates that most of us only too readily accept the explanations that others offer us. We are reassured from all directions by 'the patter of tiny minds'.

Fighting talk

Experiments with mice have shown that if they have plenty of space they behave sociably, elect amiable leaders, and behave like normal mice. When stressed by overcrowding however, they choose aggressive leaders instead to set new values, and they all begin behaving with mutual distrust — just like people. For us, overcrowding is not the only trigger. Any kind of stress will do: food shortage, the over-rapid change of 'future shock', the presence of unwanted strangers, deteriorating surroundings, fear and uncertainty. Society has become excessively male dominated, and since the male sex hormone testosterone is associated with aggression, it is only to be expected that the threshold of violence should have risen accordingly. In a 'macho' society, the once respectable response of flight borders on the unthinkable.

The aggressive violence that we witness in society today is yet another essential survival archetype turned sour through the unnatural conditions in which most of us live. In prehistory, constraints confined aggression to harmless ritual display. Now that the constraints have evaporated, the violence which had existed chiefly as a mere potential has now become a reflex action. Violence — both overt and covert — is so deeply etched into our Western way of life that we have learned to regard as normal the non-stop spectacle of so-called civilized nations confronting each other with arsenals capable of annihilating all humankind several times over. Originally designed for our survival, aggressiveness has become a fatal flaw, with the ironic prospect of destroying us.

Like all other social animals, we need to distinguish between friend and foe. We act accordingly. The more aggression towards enemies that we can muster, the more love, loyalty and unselfishness we are able to lavish on our kith and kin. The two kinds of feeling are opposite sides of the same coin. Both have important survival value, for we need enemies almost as much as we need friends. We are imaginative creatures however, and when under stress are capable of all kinds of paranoia. Archetypally we need an enemy and if there is none handy, it is no problem to invent one — as beleaguered politicians know only too well. Patriotism is little more than group loyalty allied to the culturally acquired territorial imperative and its archetypal twin, which insists on inventing enemies.

As later chapters will elaborate, the latent energy that fuels our aggressiveness may well be put to life-enhancing use. For there is no need to invent enemies: today's world has no shortage of them, whether injustice, poverty or the destruction of Nature.

There's no stopping us

We have a naive habit of insisting that if something is good, more of the same will be better. A flagrant breach of the law of adequacy, this habit goes a long way towards explaining such disparate phenomena as the arms race, nuclear 'overkill', food 'mountains', burgeoning bureaucracy, runaway consumerism, merger madness, monstrous multinationals and 'workaholics'. As a solution to anything at all, this doctrine of 'enough is never enough' has been exploded by the quote: 'Anyone who believes that exponential growth can go on in a finite world is either a madman or an economist.'

We succumb to the same flaw in the way we extend every sense and attribute to the limit, and sometimes beyond. It shows in our insatiable appetite for food, sex, possessions, power, comfort and excitement. To describe it the author Herbert Girardet aptly coined the description 'amplified man'. Statistics of amplification are plentiful: each American uses on average a thousand times as much oil as an indigenous African, and fifty times as much metal. He eats eight times as much grain as an African and a hundred times more meat than an Indian. The disparity is much the same in almost any comparison between Rich North and Poor South. Observant travellers confirm that big spenders in the North show little sign of greater well-being than frugal inhabitants of the South despite their hardships. If this is so, 'amplification' as a goal in life hardly seems to justify the erosion of all Earth's limited resources. From *Earth's* critical viewpoint it is a source of intolerable stress.

Nothing real unless local

Most people familiar with the business world are also acquainted with the principle propounded by the educator and writer, Lawrence J. Peter, which states that we get promoted to the level of our incompetence. So long as we do each job well we are promoted; only when we are appointed to one that is beyond us does promotion cease; in consequence we continue to do that job — and do it incompetently.

Known as The Peter Principle this aptly describes the earthly human predicament, an outstanding violation of the natural principle of 'enough is enough'. We have been too clever by half. In our obsession with over-promoting ourselves we have failed to notice at each stage the consequences of our actions: in other words *the connections*. It is a significant explanation of why the man-made world fails to work properly. This flaw constitutes 'the remoteness factor'. To understand how it operates in daily life, we need to examine its origins.

The primaeval dawning of consciousness was altogether too much for us to handle. We were too immature, too fragile to cope with its immensity. The frail craft of our overloaded neocortex had to throw out some hefty anchors to ride out the stormy winds of change if it were not to capsize and go under. These anchors included the survival devices that had been designed to protect us from assimilating more than we could cope with at any one time. Insulating us from stress, they persist to this day. They assume two principal forms: the protective syndrome of the unthinkable and the remoteness factor — virtually unchanged since its origin within our archetypal survival group.

At that time, lacking surplus, we lived almost exclusively in the present: beyond the next hunting or gathering expedition, no future could be contemplated. Our survival was the hub of our lives. The welfare of each member was the concern of all. Reality comprised everything close at hand: beyond the farther hills lay strange country; beyond them, who knew what? A protective rule came about which, loosely translated, meant 'charity begins at home.' It stuck.

In today's global village where, more than ever before, the actions we take in one place necessarily affect what happens elsewhere, we have acquired an inbuilt resistance to knowing about remote consequences — not only remote in distance, but in time as well. It assumes many forms. We become better and better at specifics, less able to take the crucial overview; ever more obessessed with analysing details to the detriment of understanding the whole. We even mistake the part for the whole. The consequences are myriad. We allow inadequately tested chemicals to be added to our food, from farm to factory, which could cause cancers thirty years hence. In the West we maintain the right of 'first use' as the basis of NATO's 'flexible response' strategy without thinking through its suicidal consequences. We agree to the commissioning of ever more nuclear power stations with little idea of how they may be eventually decommissioned, nor how to deal with their radioactive waste. A similar amnesia about the future haunts virtually all government plans and policies, where a five-year time scale is the accepted optimum.

Businesses too seldom plan ahead for much longer; farmers let their soil erode each year without regard for their successors; MPs have their eyes more on re-election than reform; as dedicated consumers we exhaust oil reserves with no safe substitute in mind for the future. The same mental myopia pervades our attitude to other scarce resources. In nobody's long-term plan does our children's future have any place.

The remoteness factor operates geographically as well. When millions face starvation, Western governments allot less than the equivalent of one day's defence expenditure to fill their bellies. We allow our power stations to discharge noxious emissions, heedless of the consequent acid rain that ruins other lands. As tourists we descend on other countries by the million, oblivious of our effect on their cultures, economies and natural environments. We spend millions on products with microcircuitry ignorant of damage to the eyesight of the distant, desperate assemblers. We fail to appreciate that we too suffer when faraway, ignorant peasants, grasping landlords and conniving governments alike denude mountainsides of trees, so that devastating floods cost lives and soil and irreversible harm.

Yet we should not be too hard on ourselves. Except for those who are more fortunate or unprincipled than the rest of us, the pressures of society allow us precious little surplus energy after we have concentrated on simply coping. For most of the world's people, reality is confined to surviving the next few days. We should not be too surprised then if the realisation that the world is one village is not yet understood. Nor that we write the future today.

Our spurious nature

In industrial societies, the character defects that spring from our uneasiness in the man-made world combine to change our whole nature. We acquire a false nature to see us through. In consequence we behave in ways that are entirely foreign to our *original* nature. There is nothing universal about this acquired nature: just as the man-made world varies from one place to another, so does this false nature. It responds to our surroundings. The greater the threats that seem to engulf us, the uglier the environment, the more unfriendly or violent our neighbourhood or beyond, so our stress increases and our acquired nature become more warped. Under extreme provocation it can degenerate to little more than a grotesque caricature of the kind of people we really are.

We can gain an extreme impression of it by a simple process of choosing antonyms for the qualities listed in the earlier summary of our original nature. Anyone who happened to conform totally to the results of this exercise would almost certainly be either a committed recidivist or a suitable case for treatment, unduly influencd by the lurking psychopathic genius. Nevertheless, it is disquieting to notice how much of it fits identifiable people in prominent walks of life — from politics right through commerce and industry to show business.

In our spurious nature we are seen to be indifferent towards people except in the way they serve as means to our own ends. Since our usual attitude is one of suspicion, we look for the worst in others, always prone to invent enemies when no real ones exist. We are always ready to commit ourselves to causes that add to our power, status or wealth, and to devote more time and concern to them than to our own families. We usually put our own interest and welfare first. We treat others as inferiors except when flattery seems likely to gain us approbation or other advantage.

Competition and acquisition dominate our lives, as also does an urge to pursue everything to the limit. Although most of us already have more than we need, we covet it and even seek more, rather than share it with others who have less. Sincere in our belief that the pursuit of wealth leads to greatest well- being, we are unashamedly greedy and acquisitive, content to spend our days in getting and spending.

Although we like to keep on the move, we can be exceedingly territorial where our property and possessions are concerned. Aggressive whether threatened or not, we condone and even relish violence, happy to kill for the pleasure of it. We expect to win every dispute. It is very difficult for us to admit we are ever wrong, or to apologise if found out. We accept that fear must be a dominant feature of life and do our best to conquer it, even if this involves implanting it in others.

We respect those rules and values that suit us and disregard those that do not. As women we consider home and family less important than an emulation of men in pursuits considered to be their exclusive domain. As men we are obsessed with achievement for its own sake, and we are similarly fascinated by organisation and gadgetry.

Sex is chiefly for pleasure, adventure and 'ego massage'. Forced to stay put for most of the time, we compensate by worshipping mobility for its own sake. Nature, though pleasant to drive through or fly over, exists essentially to be tamed, 'sanitised' and above all exploited.

In certain ways this spurious nature corresponds to the 'shadow'. Many of its features represent the qualities needed in order to rise to positions of influence in the kind of society that we have allowed to happen over the years. They are not illegal. They are not unrepresentative of the rules and values which dominate society: the covert ones, rather than the pious declarations of intent that emanate from most politicians, many columnists and some church leaders. The qualities that make up our spurious nature may only motivate a minority of those severely stressed or over-motivated to reach the top, or both. Yet they filter down to infect the rest of society. They are the qualities that fuel the current world crisis, responsible, directly and indirectly, not only for its prevailing poverty, hunger and injustice, but also for much of the destruction of the natural living world. They ignore Earth's needs, exactly as they deny our own true needs.

The next chapter returns to the human story, showing how colonisation spread the European way of life throughout the world with far-reaching, adverse consequences to people and Nature alike. Science supplanted religion, and technology brought us to the brink of Nature's tolerance.

9: The Event that Dwarfs any Ice Age

The essence of man's situation is slowly becoming obvious . . . He has seemingly 'discovered' the secrets of the universe. What need then to live by its principles!

Fairfield Osborn,
Our Plundered Planet (1948)

The continents have not always been arranged in the familiar pattern of Mercator's projection. Until 200 million years ago, all of them were enmeshed as a single vast supercontinent. Then, over a period of some 20 million years, intense strains and stresses to Earth's crust relentlessly broke up this single land mass; the seams of its composite parts split asunder, and the resultant pieces separated to make their slow journeys across the oceans to assume the present day pattern of continents and islands.

Geologists have called the original supercontinent Pangaea. Before its disintegration it was the only habitat for all the land animals in the world. As the sole arena for competition between species, it held nothing like the variety of flora and fauna that fills the world today. Pangaea was chiefly a reptile world, dominated by the dinosaurs. Once its parts became separated from each other, however, new flora and fauna unique to each area evolved independently. From then on, the natural world rapidly acquired the familiar diversity of life that has helped to preserve the balance crucial to her well-being.

The story, which had begun 180 million years ago with massive geological upheaval, seemed to have ended with this efflorescence of disparate life forms. Yet it had not. A mere 400 years ago, after successive failures, the vanguard of European mariners succeeded in crossing the deep water oceans that had once been the original seams of Pangaea. In so doing they ushered in Pangaea's ecological reunion. The rest of the story is all too familiar: as the living world's diversity subsequently suffered, so too did its crucial balance.

By drawing together the the seams of Pangaea, the first mariners initiated a revolution destined to wreak changes to the living world even more profound than the mass extinctions of the last Ice Age. Makers of history, heroes of fiction and paragons of zestful male enterprise, these naive sailors, explorers and merchant adventurers take on a very different hue once we are able to see them from Earth's viewpoint. The consequences of their exploits help to explain why our future no longer carries a guarantee.

They were not the first people to cross Pangaea's drowned seams. When the Ice Ages lowered the oceans' level our ancestors walked across the Bering land connection from Siberia to North America, eventually reaching South America. Migrants from South East Asia similarly crossed to Indonesia, and later others made the crossing to Australia. Except in fire-smitten Australia, as hunter-gatherers, they created relatively little disturbance to the ecosystems of their new homelands.

Not so the fifteenth century mariners. They were not making hazardous journeys just to acquire a tan on the nearest beach. As the historian, Alfred W. Crosby, has chronicled, they went to acquire wealth, spices and slaves: to explore the hinterland, to trade with its people — and to conquer them. In short to exploit whatever the New World might reveal. They and their numberless successors took with them not only the *values* of the city and the rest of the man-made world, but, perhaps even more disastrously, their Old World weeds and diseases.

The crucial staging posts for voyages to and from the New World were the Canary Islands, the Madeiras and the Azores. The Canary Islands, only a few days' voyage from the ports of Europe, were the first to encounter the outward bound European mariners. The people that the Spanish invaders found there at the beginning of the fifteenth century were some 80 000 Guanches, refugees from European Imperialism from no further back than 2 000 BC. They had brought with them grain and pulses, goats, pigs and dogs, but no cattle or horses. They made pottery but no metal artifacts, for the islands were without ore. In consequence their impact on the land had been slight. The affronted Guanches possessed nothing more than stones to hurl at the invading armies and their formidable artillery. Yet for almost a hundred years they held out, trapping their would-be conquerors in ravines, and driving them into the sea in a succession of bloody massacres on one island after another.

Conquest attained, the Spaniards promptly set about 'Europeanizing' the islands. Among their importations were the rabbit, the ass and the blackberry, all of which promptly went wild and, helped by deforestation and the plough, laid bare most of the islands' scarce good land. With their tropical climate softened by the trade winds, the islands' key export crop was sugar, in insatiable demand among the well-to-do of the Renaissance. For labour to work the cane fields and mills, this crop sucked in thousands of immigrants, as well as most of the islands' non-exportable trees to fuel the mills. The islands produced one more valuable export 'crop': the surviving Guanches. They were required, either as slaves or 'voluntarily', to open up uninhabited land on Madeira and The Azores, and later to augment the 'uncooperative' Amerindians of South America.

The remaining Guanches were equally doomed. Having lost their land and their culture they lost the will to live. With no immunity they soon succumbed to syphilis and other imported diseases. Today their genes live on only in the mixed blood of the new settlers who poured in to all the archipelagos of the eastern North Atlantic. Of the pure Guanches and their culture nothing survives save a few semi-fictional relics and legends that help to entertain the tourists who have replaced slaves and sugar as the Canaries' chief 'crop'.

If the rabbit gnawed at the ecosystems of The Canaries, it completely destroyed those of previously uninhabited Madeira. One doe which had given birth on the voyage from Europe was set loose with its young on arrival. Its successors not only ate every native plant they could get their teeth into, but all the crops the settlers planted. Defeated by their ignorance, the settlers left. When a second wave returned some years later, they found that the rabbits had totally destroyed all the vegetation within reach, and that most of the native animals had perished for lack of food and cover. The sole survivors were trees, so prolific on the island that the Portugese settlers named it after the word for wood: *Madeira*. It provided a valuable export, but so impatient were they to farm that they set fire to the forest. The ensuing unexpected inferno very nearly forced them to evacuate the island. It is said to have burned for seven years before it was finally extinguished. With this ecological arson man achieved destruction where the rabbit had been frustrated.

The settlers set to work planting the bared lowlands, first with sugar then tobacco. Their prime need was labour: to construct extensive irrigation channels and to work the land and mills. The need was met by slaves, imported from Africa. It was on Madeira that the Portugese began their heavy involvement in the slave trade that was destined to kill and tyrannize millions of Africans when later it embraced the Americas.

The world encompassed

As the Europeans improved both their navigation and the design of their ships, the oceans that straddled Pangaea's widening seams became less of an obstacle to their curiosity and avarice. At each place where they landed — America, Australia, New Zealand and the islands of The Pacific — they treated the native people, animals, birds and plants just as sympathetically as they did on Madeira and the Canaries. The mariners did not always encounter the hostility shown by the culturally advanced Guanches. In some places, especially in South America, the natural friendliness of the natives prevailed and for a while, where sexual hospitality was the custom, the first sailors had a jolly time exchanging strains of venereal disease and other gifts. Only when the real, one-sided objectives of the newcomers became apparent did the frolicking turn to fighting.

Whether opposition to the invaders was immediate or delayed, bloody or pathetic, no place could resist forever the superiority of their weapons or their guile. The human toll was immeasurable. In the conquest of Tasmania, the British wiped out every man, woman and child in an island-wide man-hunt, and an entire sub-species vanished. On the Australian mainland, the Stone Age aborigines were hounded from their spiritual homelands of the fertile coastal forests to languish without hope in the alien, barren interior. The minority who remained were reduced to third class status.

Throughout the world, untold millions died from the diseases the Europeans brought with them — far more than succumbed to their bullets. Tuberculosis, syphilis, dysentery, German measles, whooping cough, meningitis, mumps, influenza and the common cold all took their toll, but smallpox was the most effective killer of them all. It first crossed the seams of Pangaea at the beginning of the sixteenth century, and for the next four centuries it proved as essential as gunpowder in ensuring the spread of white imperialism, especially in the conquest of the Americas. It was a faithful ally: indigenes frequently learned to use the intruders' own muskets against them, but smallpox rarely fought on their side. In Australia an estimated one third of the aboriginal population succumbed to the disease. No place escaped the bacterial baggage of the intruders. Into the earthly paradise of the Pacific Islands the Europeans introduced the mosquito, and with it malaria and the hideous, terminal disease, elephantiasis.

To the toll of gunpowder and infection must be added the element of cruelty. In the export of slaves from Africa to the Americas, millions died in transit — often more than survived the voyage. These could be counted among the fortunate: they were at least spared the fate of surviving indigines in every violated territory. Stripped of land and cultural heritage, coerced to accept alien values, denuded of dignity, forced into unwelcome sexual relationships, crippled by disease and extreme stress, men, women and children of every hue and belief were everywhere degraded to the status of objects: things that either stood in the way of exploitation or might be employed to achieve it.

The fate of animals, birds and plants has been no better. Well documented though they are, since they lack our human feelings and aspirations, their demise is even less well known. In much the same way that we decimated human populations with our diseases and bullets, so we played havoc with virgin ecosystems with those two fatal European importations: weeds and the plough.

From the days of the early mariners, settlers clustered where the climate most suited their temperament, their farm stock and their crops. They ventured into the steamy tropics and arid deserts too wherever the pickings were promising, and many who stayed amassed fortunes. However, for most migrants the climates of such regions were too inclement and sooner or later they moved on.

Tropical Africa, more than any other colonial arena, has suffered from European exploitation. In prehistory, after our early predecessors migrated north, those who remained in Africa preserved the continent as an intact ecological system. Within it, thousands of tribes lived for millennia in balance with each other and with their surroundings. Eventually the north of the continent fell victim to the depradations of The Romans and other northern invaders, and later the coastal hinterland suffered the incursion of slave traders. The mysterious, forbidding interior and the remote South remained undisturbed until the end of the nineteenth century, when Europeans invaded in the guise of civilizing missions. Into this splendid matrix they blundered, bristling with guns and an evangelical brand of Christianity in which God was a European. They left Europe to do good, and many of them did extremely well. Inserting their alien values and institutions, they proceeded to loot the continent for its metals, precious stones and natural wealth to satisfy the bourgeoisie and their factories, rapidly multiplying back home. The price that Africa paid was the eventual extinction of its tribal system and natural excellence. Today the evidence of this disaster exists as the insoluble human problems of poverty, disease, starvation and violence, together with the relentless disappearance of wilderness, jungle and forest, with its resplendent wildlife . . . all this sadness in the land that had been the cradle of Earth's consciousness.

In the language of the invaders, success was purely economic. Ample evidence of it was soon to be found in the fast-growing cities and thriving farmlands of the new lands — the 'Neo-Europes'. The invaders created these cities in South Africa, in North America, in the cooler and drier regions of South America, in New Zealand and in favoured coastal areas of Australia. Everywhere they recreated the cities and societies of their origins and treated the land as if it were home.

The immediate effect on the land was impressive. The resultant cheap food, which flowed both to the Old World and to the regions' new cities, paid for the imported goods that these cities urgently needed. For this bounty however the newly opened land was to pay an intolerable price. Not until the winds and torrents of these neo-Europes had ravaged their fragile soils did many of the transplanted farmers realise that the farming methods of their native Europe might not be similarly transplantable. Blind to connections, it was not until they ran out of farms to ruin that many of them learned the lesson.

Vast tracts of the farmland of the world's neo-Europes were soon reduced to desert or so degraded that they could no longer yield an economic return. In Australia early sheep graziers and wheat farmers settled in thousands on promising tracts of land that sprawled over the margins of the continent's vast and arid heart. Yet, when they had ringbarked the trees or their sheep had destroyed the native bushes, those unable to move on were forced to retreat to the cities in the face of successive droughts, dust storms, deepening erosion gullies, crop failures and stock losses.

Nevertheless, from the neo-Europes' favoured areas of easy terrain, deep soil and accommodating climate — notably in the corn belt and wheat lands of North America — food continued to flow in spectacular abundance. In such areas the fertility was so prodigious that the soils seemed able to withstand the punishment of relentless mono-cropping and attendant heavy machinery. Yet even here, where the land has been consistently 'mined', its output has only been maintained because of its apparent richness: sustained largely by chemical fertilizers, it is a resource that cannot last forever.

It is away from these favoured areas in the rest of the Neo-Europes and in most of the tropical regions of the New Worlds that the greatest damage has been inflicted on the living world: on her ecosystems, individual species and life-giving soil. Meanwhile it is in the Old World that power station and factory chimneys, effluent pipes and exhaust pipes inflict the greatest damage to Earth's once-pure air and water. And ironically, the wealth that spawns and nourishes the offending industries could never have come about without the plethora of 'cheap' food and raw materials, imported from the New Worlds at so great a price.

The human 'monoculture' initiated by colonisation has cost Earth dearly in lost diversity: flora, fauna and human alike. In some ways even more alarming than soil erosion, this genetic erosion jeopardises the stability of the biosphere. It is one of the most cogent reasons why the man-made world does not work. The failure shows most graphically as the poverty afflicting most of humankind; as the huge, irredeemable debts owed by their countries to the banks of the North as a consequence of stupendously inappropriate aid programmes; and as the widening gap between over-rich North and hungry, pauperised South.

Far from being the achievement that history books and contemporary Western politicians extol, colonisation has been a man-made, global disaster on the scale of an Ice Age; a legacy from the past that we are obliged to confront as part of our collective shadow if we are to regain our future.

Religion versus nature

As Chapter 5 stressed, our survival in prehistory depended on our ability to sacrifice our own narrow self-interest to the wider interest of the group. Religion provided the justification, the means and the motive to do so. In meeting our universal need for meaning and explanation, religion satisfied our curiosity and calmed our fears.

Based originally on Nature gods, religion was never free from the excesses of our wild imaginings. The greater the degree of stress that consciousness and subsequent city life engendered, the more desperate became our need for the anchor of meaning. In the cities of the Fertile Crescent especially, which eventually saw the rise of Judaism and Christianity, the cleavage was most pronounced. No longer experiencing our gods in Nature, we moved them up into the sky.

Beset by constant change, religion eventually evolved into the commanding faiths that were crystallised and revealed during a remarkable period of history, between 1 400 and 2 600 years ago, when seven influential seers offered profound and immortal insights intended to bring us to our senses. In turn, Zarathustra of Iran, Deutero-Isaiah of the Syrian tradition, the Buddah of Kapilavastu, Confucius of China and Pythagoras of Greece, who all lived around the same time, were followed some 500 years later by Jesus of Nazareth, and some 600 years after Jesus by Muhammad of Arabia. Each of them showed evidence of a direct personal relation with the ultimate spiritual reality of the

Universe; each in his own way was a revolutionary, condemned and repudiated for seeking to change the accepted rules and values of his time. In varying degrees, most of them were to have their teachings misinterpreted or ignored by the power structures of states through the ages. Their teachings were not at fault: they were simply too true to be palatable.

As monotheism spread west across Europe — in contrast to the way religion evolved in the East — we placed more emphasis on the celestial than the terrestial, more on the supernatural in preference to the natural. As we intellectualized religion we reduced our gods from many to one. A monotheistic god had to be *outside* Nature, directing and controlling her. Accordingly we transferred from Nature all our humility and awe to a single, demanding god in the sky. We were encouraged to see our purpose in life under a different light. Instead of seeking communion with Earth, we were called upon to renounce the world and seek a fellowship with some force above and beyond. Our flesh, our senses and the primal driving forces that emanated from Nature were portrayed as obstacles to the perfection we were expected to attain. To overcome the temptations of the world we were given two choices: to ignore Nature or master her. This was in sharp contrast to the principle of oneness with her, common to the religions of the East that have subsequently been embraced by the majority of humankind.

In heeding the call to 'replenish the Earth and subdue it', while ignoring other less violent, more humble exhortations from the same source, Europe set both the cultural direction and the pace that were to culminate in world crisis. The self-centredness that city values had imposed on us asserted itself. Nature existed solely to serve us, while God was increasingly experienced as 'out there' rather than 'in here'.

As Professor William Macneile Dixon has explained, Christianity did not, as is commonly supposed, convert Europe. On the contrary, Europe transformed Christianity: an Eastern, ascetic creed, and accepted as such in its early centuries. The energies of the Western races, however, were too unsubduable to submit to abandoning the world's conflicts and competitions, and so it came about that Christianity came to terms with the West. Yet was an uneasy compromise, for to the lovers of life and the world, Christianity had no clear message. It had much to praise about celibacy, but hardly a word on sexual love, or anything very pleasant about women. As to our relationship with Nature it maintained a virtual silence. No rights were accorded to the whole of the rest of creation apart from man, and we were given no specific duties in respect of it.

Not surprisingly, over the years, Western culture legitimised greed and acquisition and focused its energies increasingly on the production of wealth. The means to acquire it justified the end, irrespective of whatever the means might do to the natural world or to people who stood in the way.

As Nature ceased to exert her restraining influence over our lives, it fell to organised religion to fill the vacuum. The powerful churches of Europe, however, were slow to respond. For by then they had encountered a problem: having acquired inordinate wealth and property themselves, they had drawn closer to the power structure than to the people. Increasingly distanced from the common touch, they either silenced or disregarded protest of the kind voiced by St Francis of Assisi. The pursuers of power and acquisition were then able to achieve their goals unchecked. Meanwhile ordinary people were encouraged to accept their poverty and its attendant suffering and see both as the surest way to gain entry into heaven — an exclusive reward, denied to their less fortunate leaders.

When the colonisers knitted together Pangaea's seams, they encountered people who still embraced the reverence for Nature they had forsaken. To all the indigenous people in America the soil was sacred. Earth was the Mother-goddess of all things from the beginning. It was not only a view held by the continent's hunter-gatherers and primitive farmers, the 'Red Indians' of the north. In the southern Inca civilization, where large scale irrigation works and terracing had transformed natural landscapes, the people continued to worship Earth in defiance of the imposed state religion of Sun worship. Throughout America, in various forms, the Mother-goddess of Earth remained enthroned. When the European invaders toppled her in favour of their own interpretation of God, it was not only the irrigation works that collapsed; the soil of the continent, from north to south, began the familar, deathly decline which culminates in desolation. As we shall see in later chapters, alienation from Nature emerges as a prime cause of the present crisis.

Science versus Nature

Nearly 500 years ago Copernicus, a Pole who had studied law and medicine in Italy, published the fruits of a lifetime's heretical doubting. In a mathematical description of the heavens, he challenged the biblical view of Earth as the centre of the universe, and proposed instead that Earth was merely one of several planets circling a minor star at the edge of the galaxy. At this time of the Renaissance, an age of religious upheaval, he had no illusions about the stir his work would create. It was from fear of reprisals that he kept his work secret until the year of his death at the age of seventy. Even so, it saw the light of day only as a hypothesis.

A succession of scientists and philosophers — Galileo, Newton, Bacon and Descartes — followed Copernicus and paved the way for a view of a universe in which all phenomena could be explained, and indeed foreseen, on the basis of mechanically operating laws of Nature. The medieval concept of Earth as nurturing mother, in an organic, living and spiritual view of the universe, gave way to that of a world-machine which must be reduced to its parts, understood, manipulated and exploited.

Science revolutionized the way that people looked at life: technology changed for all time the way they would *live* life. Together science and technology created the new values of progress and growth to replace those of religion. The old values had stood for contemplation of reality unaccompanied by any overwhelming desire to change the world: yin. The advent of science sealed the end of this increasingly fragile view. For humankind to assume power over the natural world, knowledge had to be put to work. Science regarded knowledge not as an end, but as a means to attain this mastery. The means was to be expressed and applied in technology: yang. If Nature would not reveal her secrets willingly, then she would have to be treated as an antagonist and 'bullied' if necessary to yield them.

The human intellect became divided against itself, concentrating as it did on achieving specific goals or purposes without applying its critical gaze to the end or purpose. The fundamental approach of the scientist was to divide Nature into two separate and independent realms: mind and matter. This enabled him to treat matter as if it were dead and completely separate from himself. He could then understand the physical world as a multitude of different objects assembled into one huge machine. Moreover if objects in reality had a separate existence 'out there', independent of the scientist who observed them, several observers could then corroborate their findings and so conduct experiments that could yield unassailable conclusions.

This led to the principle of analysis, in which scientists observed selected parts of reality to learn the connections between them. In the process they made the assumption that knowledge of the whole could be steadily gained by understanding the relationships between the parts and the laws which governed their working. The outcome of this was a view of reality as though it were fragmented. They were unable to see the parts of the whole as they really are: dynamically integrated in an infinite web of interconnectedness with neither beginning nor end. Instead they saw the interactions between parts as merely mechanistic, devoid of either mystery or purpose. Scientists then became highly susceptible to 'the searchlight effect' in which a beam of intense light might permit detailed knowledge of a specific part of reality, while plunging the rest into ever deeper darkness. It was a failing with its origins in 'the remoteness factor' of failing to see connections. It was magnified by the practice — still current — of dividing science into separate disciplines with less and less willingness to talk to each other.

As so often happens in all fields of human endeavour, this syndrome obscured any understanding of the whole of reality. Nevertheless it did lead to spectacular advances in *specific* areas such as medicine, agriculture and engineering. Predictably, since these advances were made without concern for wider connections, they were not won without cost: as the respective record of iatrogenic diseases, soil erosion and nuclear accidents alarmingly testifies. Yet this is not all. While the analytical approach, as applied to one specific area after another, may have given us, however temporarily, the apparent mastery over Nature that we sought, it has done so without giving us any assurance of escaping severe repercussions. It has brought us no closer to understanding the mystery and meaning of life: instead it has given us, for the first time ever, the knowledge and power to annihilate all life on Earth — conceivably for all time.

Since the rules and values of today's industrial societies are firmly based on mastery of Nature, the aims of science are synonymous with those of the state. Any attack on science is therefore seen as subversive. This ensures that science remains the only source of true knowledge and any 'facts' that lack scientific backing have little value. This closing of options amounts to a restriction of human liberty that can be expected to intensify until state and science have been separated in the same way as state and church.

Since science addresses itself to the solving of technical problems, most scientists insist that questions of value have no place, and that science is neutral and value-free. Yet, as a growing minority of dissenters from the mainstream have warned, a science concerned primarily with technical control must inevitably serve the interests of some people more than others and, similarly, some sections of society more than others: which invariably means the better off.

Technology, as now directed, chillingly implies not just control over Nature, but ever more effective control and domination over humankind itself. In the light of our inherent flaw of suggestibility, this is a matter of gravest concern. Yet, as the dissenters point out, it need not be. Once we rediscover that humankind is irrevocably not separate but part of the Nature that we attempt to dominate and control, we shall realise that any abuse of her is an abuse of ourselves. In Chapter 12 we shall see that such a rediscovery promises to be aided by what has come to be called the 'New Physics'.

Point of departure

A little over 200 years ago an unknown man sent a troublesome steam powered water pump to Glasgow University for repair, and there James Watt applied his engineering genius. His decisive improvements to the rudimentary apparatus led swiftly to widespread steam-powered traction and industrial production. In one quantum leap, he hurled us, unready and disarrayed, into the industrial age.

On the sixth day of August in 1945, at 8.16 in the morning, a hitherto unknown American released the first atom bomb into the clear blue sky above Hiroshima. The near-instantaneous destruction of the unsuspecting city heralded the nuclear age and our next quantum leap: limitless energy and with it the power to destroy the natural world we know.

The Industrial Revolution, which was to give birth to the nuclear age, was the child of Mother Earth's mineral wealth, newly penetrated by the rapacious sire, technology. Powered initially by coal, later to be joined by oil, it held the promise of two immense benefits to all humankind: machines would release us from degrading labour; and an outpouring of cheap commodities would end the poverty of deprivation and make us all happy. Since it has not turned out quite like that, perhaps we should take a fresh look at its origins and consequences.

Steam engines granted us an unprecedented increase in power, over both human beings and Nature. By marrying social innovation with its technological counterpart, new power over human beings was achieved first. By the time James Watt had perfected the steam engine, poorly trained armies throughout Europe had been replaced by disciplined professionals. The same regimentation was then applied to the manning of factories. In this cunning synergy lay the real essence of the Industrial Revolution: a vastly magnified re-run of the Sumer syndrome

Power over Nature arrived within the span of a few generations, when technological innovation was applied to agriculture and livestock breeding. Until then the natural world had tolerated our presence, but with this dramatic new intervention we were trespassing beyond acceptable limits. By then we had subverted the biosphere to our own whims and needs, eventually endangering all familiar life, ourselves included.

The Industrial Revolution rapidly spread from Britain to Europe, to the recently colonised neo-Europes, and from there in time to the rest of the man-made world. Its innovators' aims however were not those of meeting the collective need of rapidly rising populations; their aims were primarily to benefit themselves. They increased wealth, but they also increased not only the already unequal way the wealth was shared, but the unequal distribution of the land and plant that were the instruments of production. In consequence, cottage industries and small-scale subsistence farming declined and were replaced by large-scale units. In Britain and elsewhere a long-standing programme of enclosing common land merely hastened the exodus of people who had already been deprived of their livelihood by the competitiveness of the burgeoning city factories. On arrival in the cities they found themselves subjected to the regimentation of factory work. There, living on less than subsistence wages, they were forced to renounce all semblance of any previous independence.

In countries overtaken by the industrial revolution, gross national products were substantially increased, but only at the cost of immeasurable injustice and suffering. As in Sumer, the concentration of surplus in the hands of a distanced, power-hungry minority resulted inevitably in its wholesale abuse. The waste and chaos of greed-inspired competition created a huge landless and disenfranchised social class, sentenced from childhood until old age to unremitting work, banned even from joining together in order to improve their lot, and cruelly punished whenever any natural leaders among them were caught trying to do so.

The initial, overall consequence of the Industrial Revolution was less the spread of universal wealth than the creation of vastly more victims than victors. Irrespective of class, material gain was largely offset by spiritual loss. In Britain at the end of the nineteenth century, after a 100 years of bountiful production, 30 million or more impoverished workers and their families were effectively keeping in luxury a ruling class of some 30 000.

In this century, technology has acquired a momentum of its own, beyond the control of any nation, group or individual. By means of it we in the West have harnessed the atom, cracked the genetic code of life and sent missiles, people, probes and platforms into Space. Yet we have consistently pressed such achievements into service for ourselves, regardless of their effects on either the rest of humankind or the rest of life on Earth. The goal of achievement has become value-free, acquiring the status of an end in itself, rather than a means to an end. Yet if the word 'end' is to lose its more sinister meaning, the might and genius of technology must be re-directed from destroying the natural world to the task of rescuing it. Only then can we be assured of a future for our children.

The next chapter shows how the inherent drives, flaws and limitations of humankind, identified in earlier pages, have brought on the present world crisis.

10: Earth in Crisis

Where man goes, nature dies

Richard Jefferies, nineteenth century writer, farmer's son

This post-Hiroshima era of ours is a time of increasingly, widespread and disturbing occurrences. All of them stem from human interference with Earth's natural systems. High above us the protective ozone layer is thinning, letting through more of the Sun's dangerous rays: over Antarctica a hole in it is spreading, already the size of North America. Carbon dioxide and methane in the atmosphere are rising too and the Earth is showing signs of warming up. This, the expected 'greenhouse' effect portends serious climatic disturbances. Every continent has already been visited by droughts, floods and storms of an intensity that confounds experts.

Our interference has played havoc with the living world. Dutch elm disease has killed countless millions of trees, and other species now face similar threats. Acid rain has crossed frontiers — even seas — to devastate virtually every forest and lake downwind of industrial centres. While the long-term lethal effects of DDT on countless bird species persist, other pesticides and herbicides still take their toll.

The Vietnam war demonstrated how chemical warfare could lay waste vast areas of jungle. In the 'mutually assured distrust' of the arms race, nuclear bomb tests persist, ever more nations develop nuclear capabilities, and ongoing wars continue unabated. The sinking of the Greenpeace ship 'Rainbow Warrior' by the French Secret Service, DGSE, demonstrated the unscrupulousness of 'civilized' nations, unhesitatingly jeopardizing the natural world in reckless pursuit of national interests.

Mass poisoning of people and habitat has escalated. At Seveso, Italy in 1976, 30 000 people were put at risk from long-delayed carcinogenic dioxin poisoning, 10 000 times more deadly than cyanide. It was at Bhopal, India in 1984 that nearly 3 000 people died of isocyanate and phosgene nerve gas poisoning and tens of thousands were injured. Only luck prevented the 1986 accident near Basle, Switzerland from being Europe's greatest catastrophe ever. Chemicals that were spilled from a factory blaze rendered 200 miles of the Upper Rhine dead for at least the next decade, while 12 tons of organo-phosphates, similar to nerve gas, narrowly missed exploding. These disasters made headlines. All the time, however, lorries spill toxins, other accidents continually poison our habitat, and few of them attract attention.

The hazards of nuclear power have been highlighted by the three major disasters of Windscale (Sellafield), Three Mile Island, and Chernobyl, with their ensuing invisible but deadly pollution of radioactivity. Background levels of radioactivity everywhere are increasing, while the growing worldwide traffic in radioactive equipment, fuel and waste offers untold opportunities for accidents, terrorism and theft, as illustrated by the horrifying consequences of the 1987 robbery in Goiania, Brazil. As background levels of radioactivity continue to rise, deaths from cancer, which in Britain now accounts for a third of all deaths, are predicted to rise still more. The sudden onset of AIDS has served to remind us of the ravages that can be inflicted on *any* species by constantly mutating viruses. Immune to natural antibodies and antibiotics alike, these spread unnaturally by swift, worldwide travel.

As with everything else on Earth, all these seemingly disparate events are in fact connected: all are manifestations of the way our original nature has been warped by cultural evolution. Together they represent the muted stirrings of global disaster of proportions far beyond our limited understanding. On the horizon of time, in the shape of our species' extinction, the Unthinkable has materialised to haunt us. If we can make radical changes in our relationship with Earth soon enough, our children may still escape this horrifying scenario. If we fail however, the crisis can only worsen and — at best — they can expect to inherit a future of intolerable bleakness.

Predicted by one eminent authority after another, the fearful prospect should come as no surprise. Increasingly over the years we have deranged the hidden flows and forces that maintain Earth's stability. We have polluted her three vital elements of air, land and water, and dangerously depleted the physical and living resources that make life possible. Reeling under the impact of artificial systems that are ousting her sustainable natural cycles, our mother Earth is seriously ill: suffering from severe disequilibrium, poisoning and exhaustion. No less vulnerable than any other living organism, Earth can only take so much: critical breakdown is now a real possibility. Her illness could prove terminal.

Earth's principal enemy is humankind's unholy trinity of lawlessness, misguidedness and obsesssion with material growth. Together they ride roughshod over natural principles. Before consciousness visited Earth in the ape-like guise of humankind, there was no possible way that these principles could be defied. Since the beginnings of life they have been all that has stood between order and chaos. Every species, humankind included, observed them. Equipped with consciousness and our new-found knowledge, however, we ignored them and used our ensuing power, not for the benefit of the whole, but solely for our own ends.

At first Earth was able to heal the wounds that humankind inflicted. Even when the first cities intensified our power and our cultural evolution took the wrong path, she still tolerated us. The actual moment when we exceeded her tolerance may never be known. Certainly colonisation and the spread of European culture played major roles. Science, technology, the Industrial Revolution and the rapid doubling of human population too doubtless strained Earth to the limit. Yet not until the present post-Hiroshima age, with every restraint abandoned, did our power and its abuse manifestly outstrip all reason. The global spread of misguided, Western-inspired cultural evolution is now almost complete. Even if the threshhold of Earth's tolerance has not after all arrived, the increasing incidence of widespread disturbances strongly suggest that it is imminent. This is the essence of the crisis.

The needs of Earth and those of humankind long ago ceased to be synonymous. The further we travelled along the road of exploitation, the more they diverged, the more inevitable that eventual crisis became. As a species we are now at the turning point. We can exercise the ultimate choice and change our cultural evolution. Or we can continue as we are and plunge deeper into crisis. Each carries a cost. We have to choose between the two. This is the dilemma that eventually leaves the arena of academic debate and returns to haunt each one of us. It unites us all with Earth in a single locked embrace.

Nature defied

In a perceptive analysis of the causes of crisis, the one-time diplomat Ronald Higgins identified the six chief threats to Earth, ourselves and the future as population explosion, food crisis, resource scarcity, environmental degradation, nuclear abuse, and science and technology unleashed. Along with the blindness and apathy of humankind — 'the Seventh Enemy' — they subject the living world to undue stress. In the next two chapters, all six will be discernible, with environmental degradation identified as posing the greatest threat of all to the excellence of natural design.

When we quit our hunting and gathering niche, we opened up myriad opportunities that would have been impossible in a life dominated by a single occupation. At first all promised well. Our new skill of farming qualified as an alternative niche — as does the subsistence farming on which millions still depend. Over time, however, we turned to other occupations. As our ancestors settled down in one place, as leisure increased and surpluses accrued, so needs multiplied. To meet them specialisation was born, and a host of trades and professions came into being: potters, weavers, smelters, administrators, priests, soldiers, healers, prostitutes... The variety grew and grew, so that in places where cities sprang up, their numbers surpassed those of farmers. This represented a turning point, for these new activities failed to qualify as true niches and in our pursuit of them we began trespassing on the niches of other species. We were disregarding natural principles.

As we disturbed other species, so their numbers collapsed, balance was upset and stable ecosystems fell apart. The frenetic onslaught of firestick and axe, later to be joined by chainsaw and bulldozer, transformed the surface of the globe. Wildlife retreated to the shrinking wilderness to dwindle, even to perish. European flora and fauna, transported to distant lands, became opportunist and supplanted native species. Under the plough, fragile foreign soils eroded, blown or washed away beyond recovery. For aeons, tiny organisms had helped create soil, maintaining and adding to its fertility: yet as soil structure suffered widespread collapse, they too joined the multiplying legions of lost and threatened species. Rivers that had once flowed cleanly now murkily carried to the sea the soil from vast stretches of land laid bare. Deserts proliferated and as they spread, so climates altered: untimely rain fell on areas beleaguered by excess, while needy regions suffered unprecendented droughts.

Under the hand of man, the crucial cyclic flow of birth, death and renewal was broken and everywhere Earth's previous fecundity and diversity steadily diminished. Here and there at times the influence of wiser, enlightened people briefly reversed the trend, but any such local improvements made no significant difference to the whole. It is a pattern unique in Earth's long history. The excellence of her natural design has survived massive cosmic, geological and climatic disturbances for over 800 million years. Yet within the 10 000 years since we quit our niche it has all but disappeared.

Earth has only so much room, only so much wealth to give

and share around: hence the principle of adequacy which states that 'enough is enough', and any excess of power that threatens the whole must be neutralised. The check applies within ecosystems, limiting the numbers of each of its species: the locust swarms that so devastatingly sweep across tropical farmland eventually die out through lack of suitable food; if vermin populations rise dramatically, so too do their predators and balance is restored. The growth of each individual too has a limit. Birds that grow too big and heavy become unable to take off. If predators do likewise they can no longer run fast enough to catch their prey. At every point in the web of life, constraints operate to protect the whole from the vagaries of its parts.

The same principle applies to surplus. According to natural principles, no individual or group can claim the right to any excess beyond its needs: once this point is reached, a state of imbalance occurs, the excess is deemed to belong to others and it is promptly shared. In Nature there is no such thing as waste: anything that one organism discards soon becomes food or shelter for another. By the same principle, no species takes all, but invariably leaves something for others. Rather than leave enough for others in the web of life, however, we take all. By amassing ever more surplus, we ignore the principle of adequacy and the constraints that circumscribe the rest of life.

As a species our appetite for food, artifacts and energy is prodigious, Consumption by the wealthiest amongst us — nations and individuals — has reached a scale that challenges credibility. Within our niche, as an unusually ingenious creature we enjoyed a wider variety of food than any other omnivore, but that indulgence apart, we were spartan. Our nomadic life style allowed no yen for unnecessary belongings. Today we scour the world for every creature or crop that could conceivably satisfy our needs and wants, whether real or imagined. Not merely to eat and drink, but to smoke, inject, wear, live in, sit on, lie on, move around in, burn, look at, listen to, play with, or merely own. As Herbert Girardet has suggested, we are virtually a new species: 'amplified man'. When we have no further use for our artifacts, we treat Earth as sewer or dustbin.

In our 'throughput' societies the concept of renewal is not one we readily take on board. As we push our heavily-laden trolleys from supermarket to carpark we would be as puzzled as we would be angry to be called 'looters'. It is not part of our ethos to query how the bounty was produced, nor to worry about the sewage systems and dustbins that are its initial destination. Arnold Toynbee summed up the consequences of throughput when he wrote: 'Any species that overdraws on its renewable resources or exhausts its irreplaceable resources condemns itself to extinction'.

The principle of renewal, that sustains the life cycle of birth, death, decay and re-birth, is perhaps the most crucial of all those we repeatedly ignore. By doing so we are treating Earth's capital as income, a universally accepted formula for bankruptcy. Barry Commoner has reminded us that we have broken out of the circle of life, and in place of endless cycles we have introduced linear events. He points out: 'Oil is taken from the ground, distilled into fuel, burned in an engine, converted thereby into noxious fumes, which are emitted into the air. At the end of the line is smog.' Everything has to end up somewhere and anything we discard that does not fit into the living world threatens its natural cycles. Interruptive pollutants such as toxic chemicals, sewage, garbage and radioactive waste are worse than merely nasty or poisonous for they propel the living world to critical breakdown.

If each of us were to examine our own lives and compare what we take from Earth with what we return, we could find it a useful, even humbling, experience. It might make us less comfortable about assigning all the blame for the way things are to 'Them'. Sometimes such an exercise can act as a trigger for welcome changes in the way we work and generally run our lives.

Nature ignored

For most of us, surrounded all day by bricks and concrete, Nature is little more than scenery. We may feel angry when a favourite beauty spot is threatened, or saddened when yet another furry creature faces exinction, but for the majority of us who live in cities the living world is so remote that it is easily ignored. Bombarded constantly with propaganda on our dazzling high-tech achievements — from sub-atomic physics to outer space — we can hardly avoid the alienation from Nature which is the heart, core and root of the global crisis.

'Nature' is not merely some trivial romantic concept. Nature can be defined as the condition that prevailed on Earth before we became self-aware and consciously altered our surroundings for our own benefit, to the detriment of countless other species and their ecosystems. In other words, naturalness is encountered wherever we have not yet interfered with the *unconscious* homeostatic cycles that sustain life.

This being so, it is not surprising that we tend to have woolly ideas about the natural world: in most over-developed countries there is virtually none of it left! Nearly all original tree cover has long been felled and the vestiges are too small to support unharmed ecosystems. Downs and moorland, now sought by escapists for their bleak, mysterious beauty, were once rich with trees and shrubs and the wildlife they sheltered: now they are man-made disaster zones. There is nothing 'natural' either about today's farms and market gardens: breeding practices over centuries have completely transformed animals and crops to suit our special needs. Even where bulldozer and chainsaw have spared a traditional landscape of fields, woods and hedgerows, any tranquillity is illusory for it conceals the tons of chemical fertilizers thrown out each year that seep into our drinking water, as well as countless gallons of toxic crop sprays that kill friends and foes alike. Farming and gardening have never been 'natural' activities, but until recently they did give Nature a sporting chance.

In short, the dice are loaded against naturalness. In schools, natural history has a low priority, and ecology is usually absent from curricula altogether. 'We are what we eat', but by the time food reaches our plates it has been added to, subtracted from, processed and cooked beyond all resemblance to the natural goodness we were designed to hunt and gather. The closest encounter that most of us ever have with 'nature red in tooth and claw' comes through books or TV screens. Yet excellent though books and wildlife programmes can be, most of them are forced to be simplistic to the point of bias, for their prime aim is generally to entertain, rather than educate or unearth any awkward truths. Nature abounds with paradoxes: apparently cruel yet necessarily merciful, seemingly complex yet miraculously simple, as reassuring as she can be terrifying and more invisible in her workings than apparent. If we never draw closer to her than an input of TV documentaries, we are as likely to penetrate her secrets as to breathe the heavenly scent of frangipani or be stung by a scorpion emerging from the screen.

Although her immense forces impinge unnoticed on every aspect of our lives for as long as we draw breath, our ignorance of Nature is overwhelming. If she means anything at all, to each of us it is something different. To many who see her as a threat to their faith in science and technology she is little more than a sentimental irrelevancy standing between mastery of this planet or colonising space. As if to justify the shortcomings of the man-made world, some of us think of her as little more than bloody chaos. Others call to mind an array of cuddly, furry creatures, gazelles and butterflies, robins and roses: a Disneyfication that not only takes the 'Mickey' out of mice but trivialises all that is aloof, mysterious and timeless outside our own narrow worlds.

We have come so far from the natural world that blissful ignorance of her realities can swiftly erupt into hatred. It is not hard to see why. Raw nature is too stony or prickly, too full of biting, stinging creepy-crawlies for our thin-skinned, almost hairless bodies and vivid imaginations. We prefer parks to pathless woodland, gentle meadows to teeming swamps. Millions of us consider the peak of naturalness as a sterile sandy beach where we can take off our clothes and briefly re-live our ancient post-forest savannah era before flying back to the city. There, hiding our shame with clothes, we can roll back the living world to where she belongs and re-live our fantasies watching TV.

That eminent writer on the human predicament, Arthur Koestler, once graphically observed that 'ever since the first cave-dweller wrapped his shivering frame into the hide of a dead animal, man has been, for better or worse, creating an artificial environment and an artificial mode of existence without which he can no longer survive. There is no turning back . . .'

This desire to push Nature away is not something created by Newton, however much he may have contributed. With its origins in prehistory, it inspired the earliest city builders. It is a goal we have deliberately sought since then in order to protect ourselves from her vagaries. We perceive Nature not only as primitive and consequently restrictive, but also — the ultimate offence — boring. She is strictly for the birds and the bees; the antithesis of our urge to amplify ourselves and extend every sense to the utmost. Once Nature is deemed an unwanted restraint on ambition and progress, any idea of subordination to her becomes repugnant, while that of actually loving her counts as ridiculous sentimentality. Yet we need contact with her, not only to remind us of our roots, but to affirm that we can break the chains of our own conditioning and climb to inspiring new heights. We should do well to note that the workings of her remote life flows are synonymous with those of our own bodies. However much we reject the primaeval animal within us, Nature could scarcely be closer or more deserving of respect.

City values

Apart from a space platform there can surely be no environment more artificial than a modern city. In times past, for all their shortcomings, cities at their best have been life-enhancing springs from which have flowed statesmanship, justice, tolerance, debate, knowledge, philosophy, literature, architecture, the arts, music, theatre . . . all that serves to lift the spirit, nourish the intellect and delight the senses. In the hideous giantism of contemporary mega-cities however, such qualities are submerged and sucked into the ever-rising floodwaters of industrialism, now speeding us blindly on its course to who-knows-where?

As Anthony Stevens has perceptively commented: 'In the West, our technological triumphs, economic miracles, redistributed wealth, planned cities and welfare states have not noticeably coincided with greater personal happiness or any apparent flowering of the human spirit. . . . Delight in the glory of human existence is not what strikes one . . . rather disenchantment, resentment, an obsession with material possessions, and an insatiable appetite for more.'

When Gandhi had been a while in Britain, a reporter asked him what he thought of British civilization. His immediate reply was 'I think it would be a good idea.' Apart from Gandhi, there has been no latter-day leader of note to advocate fresh ideas, free from city orientation; yet even his teachings were early casualties in the wake of his assassination.

The cultural imperialism of urban orientation has become self-perpetuating. Virtually all major leaders, whether revolutionary or wedded to the status quo, are held so fast in the city's assertion that it is the sole, rightful and effective representative of human hopes and aspirations that they can conceive of no alternative. Its power infiltrates every crevice of thought, feeling and action, acting like a drug until body and mind progressively adjust to its alien unnaturalness. In this mode the reality of existence recedes and any attempts to escape are thwarted in withdrawal symptoms of isolation and insecurity. As if by conspiracy it numbs us into a state of planned helplessness. Its spurious imprint has become imposed upon our whole culture to the point where we are trapped. To stand against it is to invite pity, ridicule and contempt. Yet despite all this some of us still do, and for some time their numbers and influence have been growing.

The wealth machine

Alternatives to what is already established are not always easy to bring about, however desirable they may clearly be. 'The immovable object' has an awkward way of surviving 'the irresistible force'. Particularly in human society.

The power structure within our culture has progressively assembled a global 'Machine' for generating and defending wealth, based on the premise that the way to attain well-being is to acquire ever more material goods and ever more opportunities to escape from the dissatisfaction of doing so. In short, acquisition plus distraction. The 'Machine' determines priorities for wealth generation and distribution, not according to need but through the operation of the market place: in other words, investment flows to where the highest return can be obtained. Spanning the world as it does, its 'components' — nations, corporations and individuals — are all fully committed to perpetuating its output and ensuring that it retains its built-in protection against being superseded, whether from internal collapse or external force. The game that it plays is all-out competition for Earth's vital resources such as minerals, energy and food, along with the human resource of technology. It is the 'Sumer syndrome' up-dated for the demands of the twentieth century. Programmed by networks of value-free computers, the Machine is the most sophisticated means ever devised for extracting and misappropriating surplus.

It boasts at least one curious feature: although at lower levels its participants may be fiercely competing, at successively higher levels, where activity becomes more covert, it forms blocs in which competition is replaced by co-operation. Thus rival firms may compete for domination of the marketplace, yet connive to maintain prices at a profitable optimum. At the international level, nations defer agreement on, for example, pollution control measures for fear of losing to rivals within the Rich North, yet combine through bodies such as the World Bank and International Monetary Fund to permit poverty in the Poor South to continue. This has the effect of prolonging the world's limited stocks of material resources, which only the rich can buy in the quantities they desire. Within the the Poor South, rulers and wealthy fellow travellers openly align themselves with their opposite northern numbers to share in the spoils.

The Wealth Machine possesses an ingenious ability to ensure continuing inputs: when exhaustion threatens a source of any input, the Machine seeks and until now has invariably found substitutes. It is from such structural flexibility that the Machine largely gains its awesome efficiency.

As with most machines, in addition to intended output it also generates waste. In this, people figure prominently, for it discards as waste those people who can no longer be made to fit in, either as components or beneficiaries. Such victims may be located within highly developed societies close to its centre, or, more often, on the periphery, chiefly in the under-developed South. Waste also exists as countless human psyches, irredeemably damaged in the spiritual emptiness of over-competitiveness and pointless work, or in the absence of available work and an ensuing erosion of personal value. Young people are prime victims. In Britain especially, having largely downgraded education to vocational training, the Machine effectively conditions them to join the Faustian bargain of selling their souls as 'machine fodder'. Waste is also generated in the form of pollution, degraded environments and disrupted natural systems.

The Machine has never been more eloquently and poignantly depicted than by Sir Charles Chaplin, in the pathos of his classic film, '*Modern Times*'. With his portrayal of the universal 'little man', subjected to the time-saving feeding machine, caught up in its giant cogs and eventually driven crazy, his genius comically revealed the impotence of ordinary people emeshed in its unstoppable momentum. That was over fifty years ago. Today the Machine seems still virtually unstoppable, even by the beneficiaries who operate it. Yet it has weaknesses, not least the nervousness, even panic and collapse, that are liable to erupt in its world-spanning stock markets.

The Wealth Machine is heavily dependent on continuous growth, with emphasis on throughput of materials rather than social benefit. In this it exhibits another serious weakness. As it runs up against inevitable limits to growth it is bound to encounter the combined strains of resource shortage, mounting wastes and a resurgence of the human spirit. Without major re-programming, the Machine will eventually self-destruct. Long before then, however, wastes may accumulate so fast that they cancel out any wealth produced, even when appropriated solely for a surviving elitist core.

Up to now the Machine has responded to the demands of our misguided culture. If however, as its ultimate consumers, we noticed that it was failing to deliver its promised well-being, we might realise that its premise, 'happiness is owning things', was dangerous nonsense. Again, only major re-progamming would save it.

To the Machine, environmentalists are a spanner in the works. Pollution control measures add to production costs; scares about radiation or safety hazards undermine public confidence; sanctions against oppressive regimes interfere with the free market. Make no mistake: if the ecological imperative — whether expressed as 'Earth awareness', Green politics, the 'peace movement', or in any other form — were to pose a real threat, the Machine would muster every means at its disposal to stifle it, as Ralph Nader experienced to his discomfort in the Sixties during his successful campaign for safer cars. Faced with wider challenges, it would identify with the State, with the fight against poverty, with patriotism and freedom. Branding its opponents as 'subversive and dangerous', it would manufacture emotive evidence of Communist or other undesirable involvement and enlist appropriate support: in the USA as the FBI, CIA and the Defence Intelligence Agency; in Britain as MI5, the Special Branch, Defence Intelligence or any other agent of the status quo.

Throughout all levels of the Machine it is the almost surreal isolation from the real world of cause and effect that enables dog-loving family men to make weighty judgements and far-reaching decisions with minimal risk of ever being emotionally involved in any possibly distressing outcome. For years, heavily advertised baby food exports contributed to countless infant deaths because Poor South mothers had no means of sterilizing bottles: despite irrefutable evidence, manufacturers persistently refused to withdraw products until forced by pressure groups. In Britain, the Central Electricity Generating Board steadfastly maintained its innocence over acid rain damage until a 1988 two-year study forced Government admission of responsibility. Manufacturers of CFC gas have hitherto similarly disclaimed resonsibility for atmospheric ozone depletion.

Yet to assume that those who run the Machine are necessarily evil would be to fall smartly into the trap of Jungian 'projection'. Blessed with a surfeit of push and cunning, so apt for their jobs, they behave little differently from the way any of us would in similar circumstances. If the Machine is 'evil' it is not because the people who run it are, but because, value-free and responsive to markets and political expedience, in no way can the Machine be anything else. In few activities is this more apparent than the arms trade. Whether in preparing for war, 'insuring' against it or waging it, the consequent hardware is a source of untold wealth for all who operate the Machine. Ensuring that money and power continue to flow from planet and poor alike to those who are already wealthy and powerful, the Machine enables the Top Twenty per cent to use up Earth's limited resources, while the Poor South fruitlessly tries to catch up. Effectively spreading Western values across the globe, the Machine dictates the cultural evolution of our human species as totally as it infiltrates our private lives.

For our children's sake, the task — as later pages will elaborate — is to free Western culture's great body of knowledge and beliefs, along with all its ensuing values and rules, from the Wealth Machine's steely embrace.

Technological might, human frailty

'Civilization has never yet been an accomplished fact, but has merely been an endeavour or aspiration that, hitherto, has always fallen far short of its ambitious target.' So wrote Arnold

Toynbee, who went on to attribute the shortfall to 'our horrifying and humiliating experience of the atrocities we have committed'.

Atrocities spring from our defects; the man-made world derives from our endeavours and aspirations. It palpably reflects these defects. The Wealth Machine could only have arisen in a society whose rules and values emanated from brains dominated by the masculine attributes of the left hemisphere. The work ethic came about only because people were too easily swayed to 'follow my leader' in the regimentation factory life demanded. Consumerism thrived on our inability to accept the natural principle of 'enough is enough'. With this we lost all sensible restraint. As Marshall Sahlins, has observed: '. . . it was not until culture neared the height of its material achievements that it erected a shrine to the unattainable: *infinite* needs.' Limited by our difficulty in seeing connections, little of this has so far worried us. We may have known about it in our heads, but we did not feel it in our hearts. Attaching most importance to what is nearest and most immediate, in our eagerness to dominate Nature we have failed to notice her plight.

When the earliest farmers wielded antlers to cover their seeds, they were innocently planting a crop of technological progress, destined to flower as the science, philosophy and arts with which the pages of orthodox history abound. Yet the rest of humanity, along with Nature, paid a terrible price for this flowering, reserved as it has been, expressly for the fortunate. Carried away by our cleverness, believing that more of what seemed good would be even better, we not only ignored the skewed distribution of technology's benefits, we let it get out of control. We have awakened to a disturbing role reversal: technology has become master; we are now its slaves.

Characteristically the genie is reluctant to return to the bottle. Rich and poor nations alike have need of technology; not 'high-tech' but appropriate and sustainable. For that, however, the Machine is no more willing to be reprogrammed than the rulers of poor nations are prepared to adopt what they perceive as second best. For technology disturbingly resembles a drug: in the short term a shot or two makes us feel better, but as the side effects escalate, we need more of it merely to achieve the same effect until eventually it only makes us feel worse. Our dilemma is absolute, for we know that to stay hooked is to court death, yet the agony of withdrawal is more than we can bear. Since technology makes us all dependent, neither rich nation nor poor is likely to change attitudes until the full extent of its hidden costs becomes apparent. This will come about only when the crisis has deepened enough. As we have seen, these costs have no place in conventional accounting. Knowingly or apathetically, often ignorant of their origins, most of us simply adapt to the lower quality of life they thrust on us: pollution, noise, ugliness, dirt, stress, ill health, medical bills, cleaning bills, long hours of pointless, often harmful work, commuting, inflation, erosion of freedom, and the probability of yet more nuclear catastrophes.

There are other costs too, more serious, less apparent. Living in the rich North, we remain unaware that for most of humankind in the poor South the benefits of industrialisation have passed by. They are still living in the neolithic age. Yet they do so with one important difference: no longer do they have access to our forebears' untrammelled open space and wilderness, nor to the abundance of food that an undisturbed Earth once yielded for an appropriately small human population. For the past 5 000 years they have been increasingly saddled with the burden of our attempts at civilization. As these attempts become more feeble, so these women, men and children are obliged to shoulder more of the costs of our failures — costs which render our own trivial by comparison. With the gap between Us and Them irredeemably widening, so are they forced to quit their farms and villages and migrate to the shanty towns of the bursting mega-cities where they will look for work that does not exist.

It is because of our inherited flaws and limitations that our sense of responsibility has failed to keep pace with our technological innovation. Anthony Stevens sees the fatal imbalance exemplified in '. . . the economic slavery a man is prepared to embrace in order to compete for consumer goods, and . . . the money, care and attention he is willing to invest in his car or his home rather than in his mind and body.'

Real men don't eat quiche

In all the world's societies, men not only write the rules but also ensure they are carried out. From the outset, men have made the most of their superior physical strength, first as protectors, later as hunters. When our ancestors took to living in cities, warfare supplanted the hunt as the respectable outlet for men's inherent need of excitement and danger. In today's societies, even though TV delivers surrogate violence daily, the ancient need remains unassuaged. Through virtually all this time, the submissiveness of women has been as universal as men's domination. Throughout the Poor South, women do most of the work, yet they are generally treated as men's property, they eat last and have few rights.

Men everywhere have set society's rules and values. Notwithstanding the efforts of pioneers, from the Suffragettes to the camps of Greenham Common, women have failed to counter men's pandemic yang imbalance with their own potentially effective yin. Instead of moderating yang, too many have been dazzled by it, succouring men exhausted by it, healing their self-inflicted wounds — and as mothers of boys — even encouraging them. Where women have eventually broken the mould and rejected their submissive role, instead of asserting their yin, many have rejected it and set out to emulate men, determined to beat them at their own game. In so doing they have accorded their crucial relationship with their children a lower priority. No sensible observer would propose that women should be tied to the home while men pursue exciting, rewarding careers. Instead, men need to be liberated from the work ethic. They need help to find balance in their lives, and to do so by sharing in the caring occupations where women already excel, at home and beyond. Earth has a need to be cared for, just as people do. For any kind of a future, *caring* has to become a 'growth industry'. All the evidence points to the need for balancing the yin and yang principles. No valid argument exists for either reinforcing the present lethal yang dominance, or for a violent swing in the other direction.

There is no single, handy explanation for the universal 'Daimon' in men's nature, the obsessional, restless and unnecessarily aggressive behaviour that has helped to precipitate the crisis. In part it can be understood in terms of frustration through inability to enact the inherent drive to hunt, in cerebral imbalance, in superior physical strength, in response to women's archetypal passivity, and as a manifestation to the lurking psychopathic genius in us all.

Throughout history it has been the kings, emperors, politicians, officers, churchmen and captains of industry who have made up the ruling elites. Since each new generation has been recruited predominantly from the same ranks of the well-to-do, all would have been conditioned in childhood to accept the values of a household headed by a strong father as their role model. But this is not all. Rearing the children would generally have been taken out of the hands of their natural parents and handed over to armies of wet nurses, nannies, servants, governesses and tutors. As Chapter 5 explained, inadequate mothering can lead to an unhealthy preference for things rather than people, who consequently tend to get treated as objects.

Women know full well that many men are still boys at heart, never happier than when playing with their new toys: computers, guns, bombs, supersonic aircraft and space ships, or simply pushing other people around. Just as puppies romp to prepare their reflexes for the hunt, and kittens play with mice the better to kill them, so men play through life the games they were given as boys. It would be the height of naivety to expect sensible decisions and a sane world so long as it is ruled by mavericks, many of whom may have got where they are chiefly because they are psychologically unbalanced.

The work ethic

It will be recalled that an ecological niche is primarily an occupation. All species pursue their respective occupations with a fervour only occasionally surpassed by copulation. Seen in this light the current phenomenon of 'workaholism' is easier to understand. Having left our niche we have substituted work for work's sake. Whether our occupation is demolishing buildings, making TV commercials, running poodle parlours or tinkering with genes, we are basically escaping from the stress of nichelessness. In our highly competitive industrial societies, men, deprived of the hunt, suffer most of all. Work helps to satisfy their inherent need for achievement in groups away from home.

As a compulsion to go on working long after the need to do so has evaporated, the work ethic is a singularly Western aberration that has now become pandemic. It wastes human lives but it extracts even greater sacrifices from long suffering Earth. As an opening gambit to conversation 'What do you do?' is now more common than 'How do you do?' for in our materialistic society, the work we do determines our relationship to it. Most of us are haunted by a fear that without work we would be non-people, for an abyss yawns beneath meritocracy, and into it people have been known to disappear, sometimes for ever. In general, our well-being demands that we *become* our trade or profession. The extreme specialisation of work today exacts a further spiritual toll, for it overdevelops one aspect of our nature to the detriment of the rest. We become psychically lop-sided and our capacity for full human development is impaired. We become strangers to ourselves.

In a more enlightened age, our successors may marvel that we might spend more than 100 000 precious hours of our lives working and travelling to and from our workplace with so little to show for it at the end. And even fight for the right to do so. Deep down, many of us know we were made for more than such a strange detachment from reality. Occasionally our consciences may stir, for much of it can be seen as not merely pointless but demonstrably harmful. Many older people may envy the young, not so much for their youth but for their growing refusal to subscribe to the ethic.

In the market economy of the Wealth Machine, the prime importance of work is not its social benefit but the contribution it makes to economic indicators such as Gross National Product, Balance of Payments and Unemployment Statistics. The Machine needs work as a means of tax collection, not least for the vast sum required to maintain the many who cannot work and the few who prefer not to. Since the lack of it can be so devastating, the words 'work' and 'jobs' have acquired an emotive content no government can resist when the need arises. If, for example, enacting overdue pollution control measures were to render an industry less competitive internationally and, in so doing to threaten jobs, then jobs would take precedence. If it were politically advantageous to increase, say, defence expenditure, or build some tunnel under the sea, the government of the day would be certain to use the jobs created as a major justification.

To the average male ego a job is vital. If it damages the remote natural world or jeopardises the future, any such thought must be promptly tucked away in the 'shadow'. Total apathy about the wider connotations of work is essential if good citizens are to satisfy the pressing needs of the Wealth Machine.

Nevertheless, work in a sensible amount, work that enriches the spirit, work that meets the genuine needs of people or planet — that all this is desirable must be obvious. Yet many concerned people, with a well developed sense of responsibility and no wish to aggravate the world crisis, have difficulty in discriminating between acceptable and harmful work. The author Theodore Roszak threw light on the problem when he wrote:

> 'Work that produces unnecessary consumer junk or weapons of war is wrong and wasteful. Work that is built upon false needs or unbecoming appetites is wrong and wasteful. Work that deceives or manipulates, that exploits or degrades is wrong and wasteful. There is no way to redeem work by enriching it or restructuring it, by socialising or nationalising it, by making it "small" or decentralised or democratic. It is a sow's ear that will yield no silk purses. Is the job honest and useful? Is it a real contribution to human need?'

The book's closing chapters will throw more light on this problem with a discussion on changing life-styles and an agenda for personal action.

Giantism

Wherever Western culture extends its influence, runaway growth soon takes over: as technology out of control, as irresponsible multinationals, faceless bureaucracy, exploding megacities, escalating arms race, and as planet-depleting consumerism. It is the Peter principle exemplified. We manage things tolerably well on the human scale for which we were designed because on that scale the consequences of our flaws and limitations are constrained. But as size or numbers grow, our incompetence reveals itself and ill effects multiply. The distinguished academic Leopold Kohr has explained in his numerous writings that nothing is immune from the overgrowth disease of giantism: '. . . love turns to possessiveness, trust to fear, freedom to tyranny, symbiosis to exploitation, while harmony gives way to rigid conformity, instability or collapse.'

The giantism we practise not only exposes our inadequacies, it also defies the natural law in which constraints impose optimal limits to growth. Throughout the universe, countless mobile parts are able to co-exist in a self-regulating, law-abiding way, without the supervision of a master, because none of them accumulates enough mass to disturb the harmony of the whole. Earthly evolution has followed the same pattern. In the natural world, as in physics, any part that poses a threat to the whole as a consequence of undue growth is automatically destroyed. Such a drastic solution is perfectly acceptable in the realm of physics. In the natural world too, where the stability of the whole may demand supreme individual sacrifice, drastic measures may be demanded. Yet, given a choice, it is not a solution we would wish upon the human family.

Our aim should surely be to accomplish a rather more *humane* solution. To be valid, it must take account of our original nature and the lessons of the past. The folly of combining into ever larger unmanageable groups would then stand out. It is chiefly because we have ignored this approach that our dominant position as a species has been achieved at so great a cost. From the earliest days of giantism, ordinary people have found themselves increasingly distanced from their leaders and kept in the dark about affairs of state. With censure and constraints virtually gone, rulers have had carte blanche to amass wealth, tyrannise, wage war and absorb neighbouring small nations into their own empires. In our own time, the Wealth Machine has enabled them to shift their chief means of aggrandisement from military conquest to economic infiltration. Its decision-makers possess power of unimagined proportions.

Leopold Kohr has identified a principle under which the bigger any group grows the more emotional, irresponsible and even insane the actions of its leaders are likely to become, and the more apathetic, submissive and even suicidal will its members be. Through the operation of this principle, crimes that would otherwise have been condemned as unconscionable have been committed under a concealing mantle of respectability. The list includes colonisation, slavery, witch-hunts, and religious and political persecution all the way to the Holocaust; it takes in the curtailment of freedom and suppression of knowledge, and in addition the pursuit of wealth, the institutionalising of poverty, and the fighting of patriotic wars of aggrandisement.

The leaders of small groups, past and present, have always numbered tyrants among them, but at least they did have faces, their victims were relatively few and face-to-face confrontation tended to curb excesses. Nowadays the real leaders of gigantic groups are not necessarily even the faces we see flattened into the TV screens and newspapers that constitute the chief sources of our world views. All too often they are merely the fictional figureheads enrolled to do a professional public relations job for the invisible manipulators of wealth who hold the reins of power.

The overriding aim of the real leaders is to uphold the status quo, the body of knowledge and beliefs with their values and rules that make up our prevailing culture: to maintain the present distribution of wealth and influence. Since they carry the major responsibility for our present predicament, they are demonstrably not the people to whom we should turn to find a way out of it. Instead, that initiative will necessarily involve changing the objectives of the Machine and the power structure that commands it.

We are all victims of our conditioning. The difference between powerful leaders and ordinary people is less than we might want to accept. To pretend they belong to some other species is to fall into the trap of projecting our own inadequacies onto them. Outside Utopia there will always be some of us born with a head start in life, while others stagger on with deserved or undeserved handicaps. Most 'top' leaders are simply *us*, but operating in positions where the checks that normally restrain the rest of us are missing. In their shoes we would probably behave much the same.

As the columnist Katharine Whitehorn has pointed out, it is tempting to categorise people into labelled compartments, believing that we know 'Who good guy, who bad guy', to use the words of *Time* magazine. Life is not that neat. Someone who is Good in one context may be Bad in another. 'For some, too,' she adds, 'dedication to a cause is not only something that runs side by side with rotten behaviour on the personal plane: it's the excuse for it. . . . It is very disorientating to discover that someone whose views you detest does not, after all, have horns and black fangs.'

The exhortation to 'lead us not into temptation' is singularly apt. Tempted enough — and provided that no one is looking — how low would most of us not stoop? Unstoppable as we tend to be whenever a welcome free-for-all is on, as on the career ladder, it is hard to resist the temptation to ignore the Peter principle and attempt the climb to the top: even though we may have to climb over the corpses of our principles, if not those of our competitors.

Leopold Kohr has proposed a 'power theory of social misery' which says that everyone having enough power will, in the end, commit the appropriate atrocities. His theory states that at a given size and density the *human mass* not only generates the ideal conditions of anonymity without risk of detection, but it becomes so spontaneously vile that it begins to produce a quantum of its own, a wickedness that bears a relationship to its size but not to the 'human molecules' composing it. Everything then becomes predictable and nothing preventable. A moral numbness paralyses us; in effect we condone even the ultimate immorality. The theory helps to explain how we have been able to ignore our original nature and not only create the Bomb, but possess it and necessarily declare our willingness to use it. In this time of world crisis, 'The problem is not wickedness but misplaced bigness, and not the thing that is big — whatever it may be — but bigness itself,' as he puts it. If this is so, prospects for solving the crisis hinge on our success in trimming giant social groups to human scale. It should help us to escape the consequences of critical mass, whether nuclear fission or otherwise.

A plague upon the Earth

Our relationship with Earth has seen three distinct stages. Before The Fall, we were a part of her. Afterwards, as farmers we were parasites. Now that we swarm over her, destroying her, we have become a plague. Edward Hyams expressed the relationship in similar vein nearly 30 years ago when he wrote: 'What for thousands of years have been nothing worse than ephemeral and insignificant sores upon the face of earth, become permanently septic sores. The sickness spreads. Man, from being a mere source of irritation, like lice on a dog, has become a mortal disease, like *Pneumococcus* triumphant in the human bloodstream.'

The ecologist, Norman Myers, perceived humanity as '. . . a super-malignancy on the face of the planet, spreading insidious effect and fomenting ultimate crisis in covert fashion.' Cancer cells, he wrote, are exceptionally stupid for they kill the host on which they depend, yet unlike them we can, if we wish, recognise what we are doing.

Whichever analogy fits best, the overwhelming problem of overpopulation belongs unequivocally to the realm of the Unthinkable. As such we tend to put it out of sight in the hope that it will go away. Moreover, when millions who observe a major religious faith are conditioned to adopt such an attitude, not only do they prove the point that the larger the group the less responsible is its behaviour, but they also enhance the likelihood of early collapse.

Although the Top Twenty per cent are largely responsible for raiding Earth's resources, the twin problem, overpopulation, which also puts Earth in jeopardy, stems chiefly from the Poor South. Each person there consumes on average a tiny fraction compared with his Northern counterpart, but the total effect is alarming. Their already prodigious numbers are rising so fast that the reasons why need urgent consideration.

First of all, there is poverty: with no state pension to look forward to, old age for most people is a bleak prospect. Since their children are the only hope they have of being looked after when they can no longer work, the more they have, the better their prospects promise to be. The promise cannot be fulfilled however, for as long as everyone else does likewise their total number increases and so does their poverty: typical Catch 22!

Second, ignorance: even if people know about contraceptives, even if supplies are available, even if they can afford to buy them, and are not constrained by their religion from using them, frequent 'accidents' through ignorance and natural impulsiveness are bound to happen.

Third, machismo: to men, children signify virility, boy children most of all, and so in many countries they will keep on trying for a son, or even better, for sons, whether or not children are needed. Men moreover are usually the ones to take the sexual initiative. In the Top Twenty we tend to forget that for people without television, mobility, literacy, money or hope, children give meaning to life, while sex may be one of their few affordable pleasures.

Fourth, governments: most countries in the Poor South, with the possible exception of China, are in the grip of oppressive regimes, obssessively worried about being oustripped by menacing neighbours or industrial rivals. A rising population fills empty territory, ensures both factory workers and army recruits, and also enhances rulers' crucial prestige in international conference chambers.

Fifth, hygiene: The North has exported hygiene, chiefly as medicine, insecticides and education, without exporting the means to cope with the obvious social consequences: lower infant mortality, higher life expectancy and hence population increases.

Last, all this adds up to an excessively high proportion of young people: in some countries over 40 per cent of the population are under fifteen. Even if birth control maintains each family at only one or two children, numbers still rise inexorably.

To add to the threat of numbers, the South is under intense pressure to 'catch up' with the North as a consumer of resources: on one hand from its own prestige-hungry rulers and business leaders; on the other from eager Northern exporters of aid tied to industrial contracts. In the ensuing squeeze, the problems of city shanty towns, pollution and land loss multiply, while ordinary people suffer helplessly. The living Earth suffers too, for in the North, those who run the Machine exploit the opportunities offered by the South for industries that are unpopular or unprofitable at home on account of their dangers or the pollution they inflict. In general the South has neither the wherewithal nor the political will to deal with such pollution, at source or afterwards.

Like many other causes of the world crisis, the population explosion is the result of our species ignoring natural principles. What a family sees as best for itself is not necessarily what is best for the rest of humanity, let alone what is best for the rest of Nature. However understandable this may be, it is another instance of failure to see connections. What is more, it contradicts a principle in Nature that creatures of higher intelligence generally raise the optimum number of babies that will achieve the best chances for their survival. With too few babies born, their line risks dying out; with too many surviving babies for the food available, fewer than the optimum will live long enough to breed, and all will suffer.

The gift of language endowed humankind with the unique ability to pass on learning without the need for it to be encoded in the genes. In this way, over years sexual taboos and other conscious restraints encouraged people to limit the number of children to what they thought they could afford to rear. For over a million years this 'Darwinian breeding strategy' effectively kept human numbers down to levels compatible with the space, food and other resources that were available. Then with technology, resources dramatically expanded and population rose accordingly. People were no longer aware of old taboos and restraints and even less aware of connections. Because more and more parents *thought* they could afford bigger families, overall numbers not only rose, but they did so geometrically. Yet even technological ingenuity had its limits. Resources had rarely expanded faster than arithmetically, and, under increased pressure, they began to tail off. Since there was then not enough of everything to go round, the Machine ensured that those who already had enough should have even more, and the strain on the planet became acute. In the last few years the rate of increase has begun to decline, but nevertheless the overall total is still rising faster than Earth's ability to cope. Paul Colinvaugh points out that while some parents may choose otherwise, as a species we operate the Darwinian breeding strategy of optimum children; however, since we are not constrained by any lasting niche of our own but poach on the niches of others, we rear more children than Earth can eventually support.

Seen in this light, the population explosion is both a cause and a dimension of the world crisis.

In addressing the dimensions of the overall problem, the next chapter brings it to life with revealing statistics and examples of the most striking ways in which the crisis is erupting.

11: Dimensions of Crisis

Every animal leaves traces of what it was; man alone leaves traces of what he created

J. Bronowski

In the past decade few serious subjects have excited the writers of books, documentaries and articles more than humankind's assault on planet Earth. And few subjects have ever fallen on so many deaf ears. If words could save trees, Earth would not be losing 40 hectares (100 acres) of rainforest every minute and all temperate forests would now be free from further acid rain damage. If rhetoric could rescue threatened species, they would not be disappearing at the rate of one every half hour, and the threat of extinction would be lifted from 25 000 endangered plant species — a tenth of world stocks. Neither would Earth be losing each year fifteen tons of topsoil for every human inhabitant; nor, with deserts laying waste a further 21 million hectares (52 million acres) each year, would a third of her surface face gross degradation or worse within a mere 75 years. There is no shortage of information: only goodwill.

Limited as our species is, we not only attach little importance to what is most remote, and consequently least urgent or obvious, but we relegate what is unacceptable to the realm of the unthinkable. Yet for our children's sake if for no other, the scale of the crisis must somehow be brought home, and so here it is, stated yet again. Unlike the rest of the book, however, there is little that is new in this chapter. The sadness is that a general disregard for these non-revelations should make it necesssary to repeat them.

The soil is a good place to begin. Our own lives, along with most other lives in the world around us, depend on the soil, and yet of all Earth's elements we abuse it most. We simply do not comprehend. The soil is not 'dirt'. It is a living community of interdependent creatures large and small, above and within the soil. Even though we have changed our status within it from contributing member to parasite, we still belong to this community. Yet only in a few places in the world are soils fertile enough to support a parasite such as ourselves indefinitely. In favoured places throughout the world, such as parts of Britain and Europe, ancient soils could sustain agriculture indefinitely if nutured by organic farmers, as they traditionally were till recently. Certain rich volcanic soils in the world, and the deep soils of the US grainbelt could also be sustained if farmed with that objective. Throughout most of the world however, soils less fertile and more fragile, upon which the great majority of humankind depends, are steadily succumbing to the way we poison and pulverise them and constantly take from them without adequate replenishment. As each soil's vital community of minute organisms dies, so it loses the spongey texture that prevents it from washing and blowing away. So too does it lose fertility. Adding chemicals may temporarily boost crop yields and sustain humankind living *above* the soil, but it will seldom revive the dying community within.

A dog can continue to host a number of parasitic fleas just so long as it remains healthy, but if their numbers rise too far, it sickens. It may even die. If so the fleas must move to another dog or they die too. Similarly, since we cannot conveniently move to another planet, we would do well to restore and nurture Earth's soil.

Normally it takes from 100 to 2 500 years to build the one inch depth of fertile soil that human interference can so easily destroy within a decade. Technology can cut the rebuilding time dramatically, but it is a costly process. Moreover, so long as land will still grow crops, the world's agribusiness farmers find they can make more money by 'mining' the soil, often growing the same crop year after year with chemical fertilizers, rather than investing in its replenishment. Uninterested in the more distant future, they know that at present it makes economic sense to buy replacement land elsewhere while it is still available.

Worldwide, the degradation of land due to soil erosion is expected to reduce food production by fifteen to twenty per cent by the end of the century. Even the best land cannot stand up to agribusiness for ever. In the USA, soil erosion is on the increase. In just two centuries of intensive farming, one third of its topsoil has been lost. Until now the nation's long-term environmental and social cost of erosion has been estimated as $43 billion, but new findings put the true figure at several times this already alarming sum. Fresh calculations from Cornell University puts the annual USA soil loss at 18 tons per hectare (2.5 acres). Other calculations show that a third of USA croplands are now so affected that unless exploitative policies change, within fifty years their grain harvests will be cut by 50 to 75 million tonnes.

Elsewhere in the world the outlook is even grimmer. Topsoil is eroding at the rate of 25 billion tonnes every year; that is about seven per cent of the world's soil every decade. If we continue to treat farmland like a factory floor, to farm by the balance sheet and poisonous sprays, then soils everywhere — even those in much of Britain — will eventually become liable to critical collapse.

Erosion is not the only cause of loss. Throughout the world already we lose six million hectares (15 million acres) each year through toxic chemical contamination and the spread of deserts. Short of catastrophe, world population is set to double within 100 years. By then, on present trends, our grandchildren could inherit a global Sahara.

Soil protected by trees is stable, but trees are incompatible with high output farming. Humankind and trees have never got on well together. Today the world's trees are disappearing faster than ever before: an area of rainforest equal to the British Isles is lost every year. In addition, acid rain damage inflates the global total. Yet it is not only trees that are disappearing: we are destroying the rest of Earth's green mantle: shrubs, grassland and all.

As the well-travelled botanist, Anthony Huxley, reminds us, since flesh is only plant life secondhand, without plants hardly any kind of animal can survive. Plants alone have the ability to tap the sun's energy and make edible starch from carbon dioxide and water. Through this miracle of photosynthesis, they feed the world. Yet we are destroying their habitat at an unprecedented rate. The world has known previous 'extinction spasms' when the estimated loss was one species every 1 000 years; now it is building up to one *every hour*. For every plant made extinct up to thirty non-plant organisms may go with it. Each lost plant is a loss to ourselves.

If we were to imagine Earth's history condensed into a single year, life appears in August, humankind not until late evening on 31 December and the industrial revolution with all its ensuing destructiveness at two seconds to midnight. The next 50 years amount to half a second, and in that time, on present trends, we may well eliminate a third of all Earth's species.

Death comes by poisoning, hunting and interrupted breeding cycles, but the chief cause is vanishing habitat as we wipe out forests and wilderness for timber and human settlement. As Anthony Huxley puts it, the major loss of the world's natural vegetation comes from 'the paving over, digging up, ploughing under, overgrazing, chopping down, poisoning, flooding, burying, blasting and trampling of natural ecosystems.'

The greatest single source of plant loss is destruction of the world's rainforests. Their loss is running at ten times the replanting rate. These vast but vanishing areas of unbelievable beauty are home for up to half of all recorded species. Here humankind's most urgent direct interest is medicinal, for half of all prescribed drugs originate from plants found chiefly in rainforests. Despite the growing need for new drugs to cope with cancer, AIDS and the alarming spread of other mutatating pathogens, nothing of consequence is done to halt forest felling. As always the problem is one of politics and economics. Backed by the far distant World Bank, South American governments encourage their urban slum dwellers to settle in rainforest clearings and raise cattle; the beef is then sold to the USA, chiefly for hamburgers. Because the tropical soil is so thin, the cleared land on average supports productive pasture for only about seven years before it has to be abandoned.

Japan buys half the world's total rainforest timber at market prices that undervalue this irreplaceable resource and ignore the ensuing environmental damage. Two thirds of the land in Japan itself is forest, but this is protected by the Shinto religion which reveres trees! Throughout the tropics, desperate peasants fell trees to grow food and for scarce fuel. Soil from the denuded Himalayan foothills and mountain slopes of Nepal is steadily building a 5 million hectare (12.5 million acre) island-to-be in the Bay of Bengal.

Yet the world's stock of species is not confined to plants, nor is it disappearing solely through loss of habitat. Because we do not know when to stop, many species of mammals, fish, cetaceans, birds and reptiles have already been rendered extinct and ever more are joining the endangered list.

Whales, the world's greatest living creatures, are a special case. After the International Whaling Commission had resisted lobbying, public opinion and economic common sense for decades, its members finally agreed to a moratorium. Yet initial delight soon faded, for the agreement contained a loophole allowing killing to continue 'for scientific purposes'. Consequently commercial interests in Iceland, Norway and Japan continue to slaughter hundreds each year, with the full backing of their governments.

As species of all kinds decline and approach extinction, survivors become increasingly valuable and the trade in wildlife — as items to wear, eat, or simply collect — gets brisker. Rhino horn, the alleged aphrodisiac, can fetch £4 000 per lb, while the rest of the animal is ignored. With poaching rampant and unstoppable, the total trade is now worth billions of pounds a year. Although posing no direct threat to our survival, this unconscionable trade is a poignant indicator of technological achievement unmatched by responsibility.

Normally extinction is simply part of the natural order of

renewal. Now, for the first time in the history of humankind, the number of species in the world is in decline. It seems there is no stopping us.

Playing games with Earth's climate

Plants do more than stabilise the soil. Since they also stabilise climate, reducing their numbers can have both local and global effects. Deforestation in Brazil, for example, is creating deserts in Peru and may already be affecting the USA grain belt, where 1988 manifested the worst drought this century.

All the ecosystems on Earth combine to form one giant system which maintains the atmosphere in its critical, present form. By tampering with them and constantly destroying them we are upsetting the air's vital balance. Even though the sheer volume of oxygen in the air is considered enough to postpone the effects of depletion for centuries, we are nevertheless living on capital; unforeseen cicumstances, moreover, could shorten the safe period. According to Theodore Roszak, the greatest threat Earth faces is ocean pollution and the resultant annihilation of the phyloplankton that renews so much of the atmospheric oxygen.

With carbon dioxide the situation is entirely different. When we burn oil and coal, we are releasing within the period of a century or two all the carbon dioxide that has been locked up since these fuels were formed from the plants that slipped out of sight millions of years ago. This sudden imbalance is more than Gaia, through the oceans or plant life, can foreseeably regulate. The greenhouse effect, apparently already under way, may intensify or it may be reversed by the screening effect of mounting industrial pollution. Either way, according to Paul Colinvaugh, 'We are embarking on the most colossal ecological experiment of all time, doubling the concentration in the atmopshere of an entire planet of one of its most important gases; and we really have little idea of what might happen'.

In the highly probable event of all-out nuclear war, and its aftermath of a thick mantle of radioactive dust and subsequent prolonged 'nuclear winter', the carbon dioxide problem would fade into obscurity. All stability of ecosystems and climate would be wrecked for an indefinite period — possibly for ever — and any human beings with the misfortune to survive would lose their reason.

Less spectacular, but already endangering us is the human-induced thinning of the ozone layer in the upper atomsphere that absorbs the Sun's damaging ultraviolet radiation. Without it life on Earth cannot flourish. The thinning means that more radiation is getting through everywhere. Since 1969, atmospheric ozone has decreased by as much as three per cent over densely populated areas of Europe and North America. Each percentage point of decrease could lead to a five to seven per cent increase in cases of skin cancer. The decrease in ozone is also adversely affecting other life forms, including food and fibre crops and marine organisms. Moreover by accelerating the 'global warming' it is expected to disturb climate and dependent vital ecosystems. Yet thinning of the layer is not the whole story. Over Antarctica instruments have detected a hole in the layer the size of North America. And it is growing.

Chief culprits are chemicals called chlorofluorocarbons (CFC), widely used in industry and as propellants in aerosol sprays. Once up in the atmosphere they can persist for up to 100 years. CFCs release chlorine, a single molecule of which can destroy 100 000 molecules of ozone. The amount that has been entering the atmosphere is six times more than can be absorbed. CFCs were banned as aerosol propellants in the USA back in 1978, but despite constant lobbying in Britain ever since then, neither the British Government nor industry has followed suit. Finally, in 1988, alarmed by public concern over the Antarctic hole, major UK aerosol manufacturers announced plans to phase out CFC 'as soon as possible, and by the end of 1989 at the latest'. Lobbying was then targeted on aerosol manufacturers in the rest of the world, and on eliminating the use of CFCs for foam-blowing, fast-food containers and other industrial purposes. For how long the momentum of damage will continue, despite industry's tardy action, remains in doubt.

The pollution legacy

The waste from New York City each year is enough to cover all Central Park to a height of eleven feet. Every Top Twenty nation city generates its own statistics. As natural law asserts, everything has to go somewhere, and the waste from our misappropriated surplus is no exception.

All pollution is unwelcome, much of it dangerous. One source of mounting concern is the residue from the thousands of synthetic chemicals, unknown in the natural world but introduced to the environment in the past few decades. The annual rate of production of new industrial and agricultural chemicals is generally put at 350 a year with no signs of abating. In the USA alone more than 60 000 different chemicals are currently in use. The world total is at least 65 000. Data for health hazard evaluations are available for only ten per cent of pesticides and eighteen per cent of drugs. The hazards range from accumulating poisoning to cancer and genetic mutations, any of which may take up to 30 years to manifest. With rising manufacture and accumulation, eventually the toxic effects will reach a critical level overall. In some areas, where ecosystems have collapsed, this has already happened to wildlife — the DDT effect is only one instance. Later, unless checked, people too will be the direct, rather than indirect victims.

No large scale studies of the effects of pesticides on humans have been carried out and incidents of poisoning are grossly under-reported. Many old formulae in use are highly dangerous with effects that will take 50 years to clear. Already an estimated 10 000 people in the Poor South die each year from pesticide poisoning and another 400 000 suffer acutely.

Of all the new chemicals, PVC (polyvinyl chloride) is reckoned to be the most widely used: in building and construction, in hospitals, in the home, as packaging, records, toys, clothing and cars. It is made from vinyl chloride, a highly carcinogenic gas that produces tumours that can take up to 30 years to manifest. The gas is trapped in the plastic and released slowly. When PVC is incinerated, however, the gas is immediately discharged into the air we breathe. Some dangerous substances in common use, such as asbestos and the heavy metals, lead and mercury, occur naturally. The biosphere and the human body alike have adapted to natural levels, but not to the concentrations achieved by industrial processing.

Disposing of chemicals by incineration is not necessarily a solution to the problem. Some by-products may be rendered less nasty, but all simply rise into the air and descend somewhere else. Burying is only a short-term answer, for containers corrode and rainwater carries the toxins first into the subsoil and from there to streams and eventually to the sea. Dumping at sea has the same end result. Despite restrictions, much illicit disposal still takes place.

Whether through the atmosphere, the land or direct, the great majority of pollutants end up in the oceans and there, carried around the world, they remain for ever. Billions of tons of contaminants arrive there every year: eroded soil, domestic and industrial pollutants, radioactive waste, and a million and a half tonnes of oil spilled from tankers. All of them upset ecosystems and either injure or kill living organisms from plankton to fish and whales. The seas are in trouble.

Of all the toxic legacies that we are leaving future generations, radiation is without doubt the most serious. Low-level radiation occurs naturally all the time. It arrives from the Sun and it is emitted from rocks at a 'background' level to which we have adaped along with other species over millions of years. Now however, man-made radiation is being superimposed on this safe level at a rate that rises every year, and the safe level is being dangerously exceeded.

The global increase that followed atmospheric testing of the Bomb has now been amplified by nuclear power generation in two forms: as continuous 'leakage' into the air and oceans, and as accidents in nuclear power stations and reprocessing plants. These range from unreported 'incidents' to full scale disasters as at Sellafield in the UK, Three Mile Island in the USA and Chernobyl in the USSR. Nuclear power generation carries additional risks in the disposal of radioactive waste, its transportation from place to place and susceptibility to terrorist attack.

Critics of nuclear power say that it carries a risk and cost out of all proportion to the tiny contribution it makes to the world's energy. They say that production should be halted until operational safety can be guaranteed and the problems of waste disposal and decommissioning power stations have been solved. Yet no engineer can *guarantee* no accident risk, while even a one-in-a-thousand risk to the world's expected five hundred reactors means one accident every ten years.

Neither is there a solution in sight to the nuclear waste problem. It is all carcinogenic. The least radioactive waste product is xenon 133, with a half-life of five days; strontium 90 chalks up 28 years, while plutonium tops them all with 24 000 years. Since every land dumping site raises swift local opposition and a sea dumping moratorium has been in force since 1987, radioactive waste is temporarily stored *in situ*. In the UK, 40 years of nuclear waste — a thousand cubic metres — has already accumulated and increases by 50 lorry loads every week. Over the next 100 years the volume of low level waste will rise to three and half million cubic metres, and intermediate-level waste to nearly 700 000 cubic metres: an awesome prospect, compounded by the task of decommissioning ageing power stations. The world's first decommissioning job, an early Magnox station, is imminent and the indications are that the cost may exceed the cost of building the station in the first place.

As a pollutant, radiation threatens ominously with a kind of hi-tech authority that mere sewage lacks. Yet each is unthinkable in its own way, each poses its own brand of danger. Sewage spreads disease: 70 per cent of India's water is polluted, causing over 65 per cent of illnesses there. Sewage kills fish: 'oxygen sag' in watercourses, lakes and inland seas causes breeding losses. The nine million tonnes of sewage from New York and New Jersey dumped each year have degraded all marine life over an area of 12 000 square kilometres.

Sewage is a spectacular example of the abuse of surplus. In the natural world, carrion and animal (including human) faeces decay and are converted by bacteria and fungi into humus for plants to feed on. Without this process, land life on Earth would end in a matter of months. In this light sewage can be seen as a vital asset, feeding vital soil organisms, improving fertility and spreading seeds. Yet in the man-made world it turns into costly waste, a dangerous pollutant and a seemingly insoluble problem.

The whole subject of pollution bristles with misconceptions. It is still regarded as the small price we have to pay for the colossal benefits of technology, to be accepted chiefly because the cost of reducing it would render any offender uncompetitive: a factory would lose out to competing factories, a nation to competing nations. In each case, jobs would be lost and the cost of living would rise. Government and commercial interests alike procrastinate unashamedly. Corrective measures are therefore nearly always 'too little too late'.

It is not generally realised that pollution has neither the need nor the right to be there in the first place. It all began because no one took any notice of the connections. Smog, noise, illness, filth, ugliness, degradation, all grew from small beginnings until they became part of the scene, accepted almost as sacrosanct, with a status approaching acts of God. What started as a local irritant now threatens the whole living world. DDT, aerosols, nuclear power, X-rays, cars, plastics, coal fires, flush toilets . . . in a world where everything is connected, most man-made products and many human activities generate a hidden 'knock on' effect that the living world, people included, would eventually be better off without. In our throughput societies we treat the air, land and water as if they were repositories created for the waste that is unknown in Nature. Lacking adequate means of coping with it, Nature suffers.

Playing at god

Most of pollution has arisen by default. We never intended it; pollution was simply an unwelcome by-product of wealth creation that took us by surprise and subsequently got out of hand. Even though we knew about radiation long before developing the Bomb, our inherent problem with connections prevented us from foreseeing the dangers in store.

With genetic engineering — or biotechnology as its proponents prefer it to be known — we can claim no such defence. Well before May 1987, when scientists in California released the genetically engineered bacteria, *Pseudomonas syringae*, into our habitat, the risks were fully known. They make chillingly disturbing reading. By comparison with them, the effects of chemical pollution appear trifling; in some respects the risks even surpass those of radiation. For such reasons as these the subject tends to be put to one side as unthinkable. For chemicals there is a science of toxicology by which to estimate their possible effects. For genetically-engineered organisms there is no parallel science, no means of risk assessment, because living organisms reproduce, disperse and even mutate into different forms. Once released they cannot be recalled. Radiation may have a half-life of 10 000 years but genetically altered microbes may survive indefinitely

To assess risks, laboratory tests are useless, while in the real world outside we are little better off. Our knowledge of the way organisms interact in ecosystems is severely limited. The relationships are fantastically complex; we do not fully understand even such a simple system as a pond, let alone the whole world. Let it be made clear: biotechnology is big business, nothing less than *creating new forms of life*. There is no way of accurately assessing the long term-risks of playing at God.

Jeremy Rifkin, Director of The Foundation on Economic Trends U.S.A, in papers and seminars on both sides of the Atlantic, has spelled out the implications of initiatives such as agriculture, biological warfare and human eugenics. Genetic engineers accuse him of being a Luddite; others less financially involved treat his warnings with more respect.

In the USA, if a gene from another organism is introduced into the genetic make-up of an animal, the 'new' animal (termed transgenic) is now considered a human invention and can be patented. By introducing human growth hormone genes into mice and pigs, US experimenters have produced abnormally large and fast-maturing animals. Jeremy Rifkin warns that transgenic animals that escape from captivity may out-compete natural forms of their species, disrupt wider ecological relationships and become pests. As Chapter 9 depicted, colonisation resulted in many plants and animals becoming opportunistic in their new habitats and becoming unforeseen pests. This new technology promises even worse disruption.

From an ethical viewpoint he regards the patenting of animal life as hubris: 'It reduces all animal life to the status of a commodity for human consumption; transgenic animals are a violation of species integrity.' Genetic engineers can create crops and livestock that are faster growing, higher yielding and more disease resistant, though not without exacerbating existing problems caused by the so-called 'Green Revolution'. Since genetically engineered crop varieties can be tailored precisely for a given habitat, or even be produced as clones, further loss of genetic variety is inevitable. Yet without genetic variation, plants and animals cannot easily adapt to changing conditions. Since monocultures are vulnerable to any disease or pest attacking a particular strain, the likelihood of widespread crop failures increases.

Systems to regulate biotechnic products are under review, but with thousands of products eventually coming up for consideration either a backlog will develop or else controls will have to be relaxed. Moreover no regulatory body has yet considered the malignant release of a dangerous organism from a research centre. This could easily happen. Terrorism apart, any student or disgruntled employee could manufacture a pathogen and walk out of a laboratory with it.

A ten-year project under way to map the human genome promises to isolate and eradicate the genes responsible for hereditary illnesses such as haemophilia and cystic fibrosis. However, eugenics — the refinement of human offspring by improving inherited qualities — implies that someone has to decide which are good and which are bad genes. Since all decisions are likely to be culturally biased, whoever makes the decisions, whether scientists, governments or regulatory bodies for the gene pool, will be altering the direction of our cultural evolution according their *own* standards rather than for the common good. The effect on the rest of life on Earth, moreover, is likely to be accorded a low priority.

Genetic engineering also has applications to biological warfare. Despite an international convention banning the use of biological weapons, several countries are undertaking research on them for 'defensive purposes', possibly with aggressive systems in tandem.

Conventional scientific wisdom dictates that if something can be done it should be done, and nothing should get in the way of progress. Yet up to now far more has been said about the benefits of this dramatic technological revolution than its enviromental costs. Its enthusiasts pose the question: 'Since we have already destroyed umpteen species why should we not compensate now?' They forget that it took over 800 million years to create the excellence of what now supports us. The world we know is the outcome of countless risky experiments — one of them us — spaced at intervals over millions of years. Between each successful introduction, Earth had time to redress any disturbance of balance. Flawed as we are, we cannot assess the connections or repercussions of whatever we introduce, whether by accident or design. We are already at risk from imbalances arising from natural introductions: recovery from any one of them could take years. For the sake of our children, surely we should not countenance further hazards by deliberately playing at God.

If the bio-scientists and their powerful commercial lobby get their way, our technological brilliance will leave our sense of responsibility trailing still further behind. Our track record implies that we shall abuse this new power as we have virtually all others, and employ it to manipulate Nature as never before. It is a prospect that ensures this 'science that frightens scientists' a major role in the world crisis.

Future theft

There will come a day when children in Britain will ask us whatever became of all the North Sea oil and gas that came and went in a few decades. How shall we answer when they ask what there is to show for it? How shall we explain the way we squandered *their* property, piping it ashore and burning it as fast as we could without thought for them? Do we expect them to be reassured by the menacing hulks of ageing nuclear power stations? These are the kind of questions to be faced eventually by our successsors in one country after another.

The threat to our future posed by disappearing resources, unlike pollution, is remote and invisible. It neither chokes us, makes us sick or offends the eye. Since it belongs to the future we can pretend it doesn't exist. Using this trick of the 'remoteness factor' we are able to steal from our children, squandering finite reserves in an infinite orgy.

This continuing wastage of Earth's limited stocks of metals, fossil fuels and fertile soil menaces the living world less directly than pollution, but it makes a formidable contribution by powering the Wealth Machine chiefly reponsible for all these threats. It does not jeopardise the survival of our entire species: it simply means that the rich in the Top Twenty per cent enjoy better prospects of surviving at the expense of the rest. For as minerals run short, so miners must expensively dig deeper, and so must technologists incur extra costs in extracting fuel and metals from poor seams and deposits or by inventing and making pricey substitutes, if they can! Either way the bounty is placed tantalizingly beyond the reach of those who need it just to live, which is not asking much.

Squandermania takes many forms. It may be expressed as an obsesssion with consumer goods, prematurely discarding goods, cars especially, a mania for new clothes, needless travel or needlessly energy-guzzling (supersonic) travel: all of them wants dreamed up by 'the persuaders'. Or waste may be governmental: space exploration, 'overkill' and the rest of the arms race. All combine to deprive our children tomorrow and the Poor South today. The implication is clear: the way we live now — each one of us — deserves close scrutiny with a view to understanding connections and making appropriate changes before it is too late.

After President Reagan took office, one of his acts of statesmanship was to instruct the Administration to disregard a document drawn up at the instigation of President Carter aimed at continuing where the Limits to Growth project left off. The document, entitled *The Global Report to the President: Entering the Twenty-first Century*, comprised 750 pages of statistics, computer model results, graphs, diagrams and tautly written text. It confirmed what any concerned, thinking person already knew: continuing material economic growth spelled disaster. The new President's brief was to the point. All environmental and development aid projects were to be downgraded. In short: 'overturn it'. In 1984, the year of Reagan's re-election, a book, *The Resourceful Earth: a Response to Global 2000* came out in an attempt to do just that.

Nothing could have been more timely nor more welcomed by the US power structure. Its top members had long been worried that ever since the ideological unrest of the Sixties, with the guilt and frustration spawned by Vietnam and the rise of the Counter Culture, the Wealth Machine had been under attack. Despite the mysterious assassination of President Kennedy the rumblings continued, fuelled by Carter's reforming zeal. Enough was enough. With the election of Reagan and impassioned appeals to patriotism, the Red Menace, Motherhood, Fundamentalism and plain old fashioned greed, an unparalleled American spending spree began which sucked in the rest of the Top Twenty, further impoverished the Poor South and planet Earth alike, and effectively put the clock back to the pre-Sixties.

The statistics speak for themselves. The average American uses twice as much energy, chiefly as oil and coal, as the average European and six times as much as the average person in the Poor South, who depends largely on dried dung and brushwood. Each American uses nearly twice as much metal to maintain his life style as a European and 50 times as much as an African. The US boasts almost one car for every two Americans; West Germany, top of the European economic league, has a car for every three; a better-off poor country such as Turkey, one for every 65; while for most of the world a car is a vehicle driven by somebody else. Let it be clearly understood: Americans are neither better nor worse than anyone else. By accidents of birth, history and geography they merely have more opportunity than others who would behave likewise. Free of the constraints that fetter others, they act as pace-setters in a man-made world where some twenty per cent of its people already consume roughly eighty per cent of Earth's resources.

The controversial Limits to Growth Report assumed that five times our present known mineral reserves would eventually be found. If world population numbers and economic growth were to continue roughly as now, most of our basic metals would be exhausted within a century — aluminium, lead, manganese, molybdenum, nickel, platinum, tin and tungsten. Iron might last for 170 years, but it is doubtful whether copper, gold, silver, zinc and mercury will last fifty years. Such precise figures have been the subject of ongoing dispute, but the principle behind them remains incontrovertible.

Also indisputable is Earth's limited supply of water. As Ronald Higgins has reminded us, Earth may be an ocean planet, but of the five per cent that is non-saline most is either permanently frozen or locked underground. Only about an eighth of the rain falls on land and most of this on inhospitable terrain where it cannot be used or economically collected. Water tables in many areas are sinking fast, while industrial wastes are poisoning rivers and underground reserves. Yet it takes about 60 gallons to produce a pound of wheat, 1 000 for a quart of milk, at least 2 500 for a pound of meat and around 100 000 to make a car. In an era of deforestation, climatic uncertainty, intended doubling of economic growth and unintended doubling of human population, it is proper to question where all the extra water is to come from. And the same question might be asked of the oil-dependent chemical fertilizers on which modern agriculture now totally relies.

In this crisis of resource shortage, virtually certain to confront our grandchildren and generations beyond them, apart from peddling the dubious concept of substitution, most people simply don't want to know.

War, a species disorder

Except when the occasional headline crisis makes another World War seem likely, most of us confine the prospect of global war strictly to the realm of the unthinkable. This is understandable: if we failed to put it out of our minds we would probably go mad. In a state of sanity the facts defy comprehension.

Humankind's nuclear arsenal equals the combined firepower of over a million Hiroshimas. Just one solitary Trident submarine carries a nuclear payload equal to *eight times* the total firepower expended during World War Two — enough to destroy all the major cities of the northern hemisphere in a few minutes. In this unique post-Hiroshima age, we live each day with the insufferable certainty that within minutes, remote and unaccountable people, just as fallible as ourselves and almost certainly under greater stress, can kill or maim everyone on Earth and destroy the world we know. Living in the shadow of such obscenity, we may be expected to behave, if not with a lunacy to match, then at least a little oddly at times.

At any time, somewhere on Earth, men are sure to be engaged in war. And any war anywhere has the potential to escalate and and 'go nuclear'. According to the 1987 World Commission on Environment and Development, of all the threats facing the natural world, war is by far the greatest. Yet to be such a threat, war does not even have to break out: merely preparing for it is cost enough. Running at close on a trillion dollars a year, the global investment in arms exceeds the *total income* of the poorest half of the world's people. Such a staggering sum effectively assures that they stay poor. Though not a shot may be fired in anger, the arms industry not only absorbs limited stocks of raw materials and energy, but it diverts labour and research away from projects to save life and improve living standards, at the same time that it fuels the inflation that hits poor nations hardest.

Half a day's gobal military spending would be enough to implement a proposed five-year, $6.5 billion Action Plan for Tropical Forests. Two days' spending could implement a United Nations Action Plan for Desertification that calls for $4.5 billion a year until the end of the century. Lack of clean drinking water accounts for 80 per cent of all Poor South disease, yet ten days' arms spending would end the scourge for all time. A substantial part of global military expenditure consists of the $61 billion-a-year arms sales that the Top Twenty make to the Poor South. In the decade ending 1982, arms imports by the non-oil producing countries of the South were the cause of a fifth of the crippling external debts acquired within the period.

In humankind, evolution has suddenly produced a unique form of life which, as the American psychologist, Stephen Kull, puts it, '. . . intentionally sacrifices itself in the name of abstract principles.' Such behaviour contravenes the deeply entrenched and universally held goal of survival that pervades all other species. Hardly ever does any animal deviate from pursuing the course that offers the best chance of survival, both for itself and its species.

Stephen Kull maintains that war cannot be dismissed as a natural manifestation of our instinctive aggression — there is too much evidence to the contrary. No other animal makes war. War is a species disorder in the same way that a person's self-destructive behaviour is a sign of individual disorder. 'It can be regarded as aberrant not only because it is a deviation from previously established behaviour patterns, but because it is a behavioural mutation that is maladaptive in that it presents a potential threat to the survival of the species.' Stephen Kull points out that so rarely does any other species kill even one of its own kind that if ever it does happen, the incident can be dismissed as either accidental or as a serious one-off deviation caused by sudden, excessive stress. Clearly evolution selects out mutations that fail to conform to the principle of respect for the life of one's own kind. In the light of all this, war must be regarded as the ultimate example of our inherent paranoid streak.

Until farming and later city life enabled our ancestors to acquire surplus, war was as unnecessary as it was improbable. J. Bronowski too maintains that organised war is not a human instinct. He writes: 'It is a highly planned and co-operative form of theft. And that theft began ten thousand years ago when the harvester of wheat accumulated a surplus, and the nomads rose out of the desert to rob them of what they themselves could not provide.' And he points to the walls of ancient Jericho as testimony.

Our ancestors found that violence became easier to contemplate once their improved weapons reduced the need for close face-to-face encounters. Even the primitive bow and arrow may have been enough to lower the threshold. As weapons and tactics developed, so the distance between attacker and attacked increased. By World War One the connections between the two had become so remote that generals safely behind the front lines were able to sentence men to certain death by the million — not just in one battle, but in repeated waves of futile carnage. Only the men's readiness to submit to leaders and die for a cause made the slaughter possible. In different ways the phenomenon was re-enacted on the Russian front and by the Japanese in the Second World War. In the nuclear war for which we prepare today, missiles effectively remove decision-makers from appreciating connections and the probability of war is raised accordingly.

To override our instinctive abhorrence of killing women and children we deprive our victims of their humanity and so render them at best a sub-species, at worst some kind of animal. In time of war, men are afforded the legitimacy of leaving behind a life of intolerable monotony and pointless work to find excitement and danger again in groups of other men. Once the move is made, it becomes difficult to return except as a hero. The trap snaps shut and the killing begins.

When wars first began, our ancestors had just begun living according to new rules and values in unfamiliar city states. The future we now seek to rescue offers the prospect of equally sweeping change. Out of it new rules and values for society may well emerge, powerful enough to supersede those that have not only brought this species disorder into existence, but have enabled influential elites throughout history to profit from it. Our study of the past, leading as it does to an understanding of the present, offers a glimpse of hope for the future.

The poverty factor

The principal concern of this book is the danger facing tomorrow's children. Remote though it is, poverty is part of that danger. It is also a part of our collective shadow, which we relegate conveniently to the unthinkable. The absolute poverty of extreme degradation is the way that a billion of us are forced to eke out each day. It is not life, just existence. Lesser poverty with the attendant suffering that still afflicts most of the people alive today is a also part of the danger.

Statistics on children's suffering may bring it closer. In the Poor South one child in seven dies before his first birthday. Every minute ten children die and another ten are disabled by diseases for which cheap immunisation exists. Each year 12 million die because of unsafe water. Out of the 1 000 million each year who suffer acute diarrhoea, 5 million risk death for the lack of a simple solution of boiled water, salt and sugar costing about a penny a dose. Every day 40 000 children die needlessly simply because they are so weakened by hunger that they cannot fight off common diseases; measles has become a major killer.

Their parents are among the 730 million people who do not get enough to eat. Yet food is not their only shortage. The world has a glut of oil, all of it beyond their means. Wood to burn is scarce in most of the Poor South, even the brushwood gleaned from bared hillsides. For millions the only affordable fuel is their animals' dung — burned when it should be returned as fertilizer to land crying out for renewal. Yet its smoke causes chest and eye diseases, often blindness; and so the people and their land both suffer. If preaching could cure poverty none of this would happen.

Poverty in our time, much like pollution, has been accepted as an inevitable concomitant of the modern-world: proof if any were needed that it does not work. Poverty drives a third of humankind to ravage the environment in a desperate struggle for livelihood. Poverty breeds disease. The South, where its people lack food, clean water, hygiene and literacy, is an area plagued with disease. As AIDS has shown since its African origins, in an age of mass travel, microbial pathogens are subject to rapid spread and mutations. Epidemics are no respecters of frontiers. If for no other reasons than these, poverty is a major dimension of the world crisis.

Most of us in the Rich North are able to dismiss this dimension because it seems remote. Yet it is not. In 1986 over 16 million people in Britain were living on or just above the poverty line; every night in London 50 000 people sleep rough. Hunger, so much harder to bear in the midst of plenty, is poverty's constant companion.

The proximity of the two extremes renders each of them unconscionable. During the early years of the ongoing famine in North Africa, when Band Aid had raised £76 million and the British Government gave £285 million for the starving, mountains of surplus food remained locked up in Europe for fear of destabilising world markets. In 1986 stocks of food in EEC warehouses (measured in tonnes) were: wheat 9.5 million; barley 4.7 million; and butter over 1358 million (a lot of butter!) skimmed milk powder nearly a million; beef over 600 000, olive oil 260 000. In the year before, the EEC Commission had put forward a desperate plan to turn million of tonnes of surplus grain into plastics. It is not generally realised that surpluses as large as these exist only because of cheap livestock and other feedstuffs imported from the hungry Poor South.

Although future food prospects are uncertain, at present there is neither a shortage of food or land on which to grow it. The cause of hunger is poverty. Like other forms of surplus, food 'flows' not to where there is need but to where there is most money. And so, while many eat too much, even more eat too little. With fairer distribution and less waste, everyone could have more than enough. Throughout the South the best land is often farmed not by small, local farmers but by wealthy landowners and multinational corporations, chiefly to grow export cash crops. Apart from non-food crops like cotton, rubber, jute, coffee, tea and tobacco, the exports include fodder for Northern farmers' livestock at prices hungry locals cannot equal. Indigenous farmers of the South are frequently ousted to the poorest land which is soon farmed out. In desperation they clear slopes of trees and so induce erosion. In time they are forced to migrate to the city and join the queues for work that seldom exists. Instead of proud assets to their country they become pathetic liabilities. Thanks to the world's crazy economics, the Poor South as a whole is a net importer of food from the North.

In the international money markets, the North sets the rules that ensure that the poor stay poor. In fact they do more than that: they get poorer. Paradoxically, development aid has helped to widen the gap. Financial columnist Harford Thomas is one who has drawn attention to the way aid to the South has seldom been either humane or wise. Much of it, he points out, has been spent on 'jumbo schemes' to please governments, whether local or donor. These tie ambitious engineering projects, mostly inappropriate, to donor country's manufacturers — a practice for which Britain has become notorious. Such trade has many perverse and perhaps unintended ramifications. For trade has become locked into the debt crisis where countries have been saddled with interest and repayment obligations that can never be met. Facing reality at last, banks in the North have made contingeny plans to wipe off irredeemable debts. Throughout the wretched saga, hardly anyone gained except the manufacturers and construction companies concerned and the sundry middlemen who arranged 'gratitude' payments. Many however lost.

The aid debacle has been a prime example of misguided city thinking. As The World Commission on Environment and Development noted, cities in the North have real problems, but most have vastly superior means and resources for dealing with them than do their counterparts in the South. These lack all the basics: clean water, housing, schools, sanitation and transport. In their ever-growing shanty towns ever more people suffer from preventable disease caused by their surroundings: tuberculosis, intestinal parasites, dysentry, hepatitis and typhoid. Of India's 3119 towns and cities, for example, only eight have proper sewage facilities.

Aid to the South that should have renewed farmlands and villages has been funnelled instead into the cities. Even though the North, with all its resources, cannot get its cities to work properly, the South has tried to imitate them. Predictably they exhibit all the North's worst features: everyone's air fouled by the cars of the rich, city centres and residential areas gashed by motorways, high-rise living quarters, polluting and noisy factories cheek by jowl with houses, unsewered slums and ribbon development, lack of parks and playgrounds, with mounting ill-health, violence and stress. They just do not stand a chance.

In more and more countries the trend towards a dominating capital city compounds the problem. As the seat of government, the nation's rulers perceive this megalopolis as the nation itself and its economy is then hopelessly skewed. Decision-makers become so remote from the countryside that they regard it as existing solely to maintain the capital. As the task becomes increasingly impossible, economic and social collapse ensue. A victim of runaway giantism, the nation re-enacts the fatal 'Sumer syndrome'.

The next four chapters show how Earth awareness could rescue the future. In the first one we encounter some of the chief obstacles.

PART FOUR

Reclaiming the future

12: Lions in the Path

It will ever remain incomprehensible that our generation, so great in its achievements of discovery, could be so low spiritually as to give up thinking

Albert Schweitzer

As earlier pages have shown, today's children and those who follow them can expect a future only if we abandon our policies of rampant exploitation and, in all our thinking, feeling and behaviour, begin to accord Earth's needs a priority at least on a par with our own: expressed simply, 'to put Earth first'. This is the essence of Earth awareness that the rest of the book will explore.

Never has there been a more compelling need for the vigorous, worldwide change that Earth awareness implies. Yet we should not delude ourselves that simply because something should happen it necessarily will. The way ahead is strewn with obstacles. Some of them lie within ourselves as our flaws and limitations; others come from outside, chiefly as opposition from the institutions we have created. If the hope we cherish for a future is to be more palpable than illusory, we have to identify and overcome both kinds.

Enemies within

Most of us prefer to leave things just as they are. We may have the required knowledge, we may experience concern, but for most of the time, gripped by inertia at the prospect of anything beyond what is familiar and immediate, we stop short of any kind of effective action to make changes. If pressed to think about the likelihood of nuclear war, another Chernobyl or our children's future, our inventiveness knows no bounds, our excuses no limits: 'It's all too awful; worrying will only bring on the worst; it's highly exaggerated; it's too far off; it won't happen; I've enough problems already; something will turn up; it's being taken care of by technology (or by 'them'); we first need more research; and there's nothing I can do anyway.'

Yet we should not be too hard on ourselves. It is natural to feel trapped. Our defects are aggravated by the stress our industrial society induces. At the very least we are tainted by it, at worst irreparably damaged. The younger we are, the more we are distracted by our distractions. The older we grow, the more we become possessed by our possessions. Mesmerised by our reflected images, we see only what we expect and want to see. As if agoraphobic, we fear the open spaces of the mind. Like someone long institutionalised, we stand transfixed before the open door of opportunity. In the presence of infinite possibilities we remain inert.

Yet all this is only to be expected. We are little different from any other animal. Within the muted competition of the natural world where fitness counts most, swift reflexes are paramount, dithering fatal; neither the numbed, the neurotic nor the arthritic can long escape being eaten. When faced with a situation for which we are not programmed, as would any efficient computer, we flash an appropriate warning signal: 'Go away, stop bugging me!' Only by clinging to whatever reassures us can we forget the fears stirring in the realm of the unthinkable. Rather than break down, we switch off.

At the end of the last century, Amerindians in North America faced total defeat in their 300-year struggle with the invading Europeans. To help them live with this unthinkable prospect they fashioned a new religion: in a whole new world their dead would come alive again and the buffalo and wapiti and all the game wiped out by the whites would come up from the west in their former profusion and slide over the surface of the present world. The Amerindians who were dancing the Ghost Dance would be carried upward by their sacred feathers and would then descend to alight on this renewed world. After four days of unconsciousness they would awake to find everything just as it had been before the coming of the Europeans. In this way they were able to live a little longer despite their fate.

Normally fear is a survival device that triggers either fight or flight: whenever challenge generates response, equilibrium is restored — usually swiftly. In this way, fear can be positive. Safe within their respective niches, other creatures are spared the constant, debilitating fear unique to modern humankind. Our solution is to switch off. How much we do and in what way depends much on our view of the world and our beliefs and values. If our job depends on the Wealth Machine, we are likely to believe that it is here to stay and that 'the creation of wealth in a world of want is a moral duty'. If in the process the environment has to take a knock or two, then this is the price we pay for the pursuit of the greater good. Within this pattern of beliefs, we are happy to pit *our* morality against that of an environmentalist any day of the week.

Sociology professor, Stephen Cotgrove, has given such optimists the name 'Cornucopians' and called the pessimists 'Catastrophists'. In recent research he found that radical environmentalists concerned about the future were on the whole young, well educated, politically Left, and employed outside the so-called 'market sector' in activities such as teaching and studying, social work, health care and the arts. Overwhelmingly they were Catastrophists; on the other hand industrialists, whose values inevitably coincided with those of prevailing industrial culture, were equally dedicated Cornucopians.

Environmentalists, he found, blame the ecological crisis on our society's commitment to growth and domination of Nature, and its shortcomings to the giant cities and over-sized, impersonal institutions that deny deeper human values. According to them, modern man has paid too high a price for his Faustian bargain: in exchange for power and wealth he has lost his soul.

Industrialists in contrast, seeing wealth as a moral imperative, define the rules of the game as rewards for enterprise and risk within a free market and a climate where individuals are motivated to look after themselves rather than turn to others. They see respect for authority as providing the essential context of law and order, and the task of politics as ensuring that the game is played according to the rules without interfering with the players. The goal is mastery and domination over Nature, with the right and ability to use her for our own ends and purpose — science and technology furnishing the means to do so.

The two camps might as well be living on different planets. Each sees only what it wants to see: whatever accords with its own interests. So long as each holds such totally opposing beliefs and values, any prospect of dialogue between them remains pie in the sky. Moreover, for as long as the beliefs and values held by our existing culture are identical with those of the industrialists, the prospects for change are slender.

An examination of this long-running impasse, reveals the inherent flaws and limitations of our species: our yang imbalance, our misplaced aggressiveness, and our tendency to be easily swayed and lose ourselves in causes irrespective of their aims. It also highlights our allegiance to groups, in this case the two 'camps' of Environmentalists/Catastrophists and Industrialists/Cornucopians.

In the USA, a psychiatrist and educator, John E. Mack, has observed a similar pattern in discussions with young people about their fears and anxieties on the issue of nuclear war. He writes: 'Our minds and hearts cannot grasp the meaning of a million Hiroshimas or the possible deaths of hundreds of millions, if not billions of human beings, so we turn away in a kind of benumbed horror and address ourselves to problems of a more manageable scale.' He has also detected a sense of betrayal. No longer can people see the nation as a powerful, autonomous, protective institution that can secure survival by military means, for the Bomb has turned out to be unusable. To be credible it requires 'the willingness to annihilate most, if not all, of human life in the service of national goals — a piece of societal self-knowledge that is potentially devastating to our self-regard.' We become identified with a kind of collective mind, allying, often quite unconsciously, our individual selves with the values, purposes and prejudices of the larger group, which functions as a parent to whom we surrender authority and our powers of discrimination. And he continues: 'To raise questions, to challenge and confront, creates anxiety and revives ancient fears of being cast out of group or family.'

All of us have difficulty in perceiving the connections between our seemingly harmless behaviour as individuals and our collective behaviour as the world's dominant species. Each of us has been accustomed to think of himself as an asset to the world, in stark contrast to the debit entry in the environmental balance sheet that we have now become.

In our defence, we absolve ourselves from the accusation that humankind is at war with Nature. We have become conditioned to enjoy the benfits of life in an industrial society without much idea at all about what unpleasant practices might go on in the forests, farmlands, tea, coffee and sugar plantations, mines, power stations, factories, research laboratories, military establishments and rubbish dumps on which our society depends. Bulldozer, chainsaw, flame thrower, herbicide, pesticide, fungicide, growth hormone, toxic chemical, vivesection, biotechnology, nuclear device, missile and biological weapon — each one violent in its own way, all of them in the hands of strangers far from the High Street — are some of the facts of life we prefer not know too much about.

Slimbridge Wildfowl Reserve in Avon attracts 200 000 visitors a year. Everyone has to pass through an exhibition hall where there used to be a notice: 'Look into the frame below and you will see a specimen of the most dangerous and destructive animal the world has ever known.' Mounted directly above an eye-level mirror, it was probably the hall's least popular exhibit, for it is no longer there. The threat nevertheless remains.

Until we become aware of our own contribution to the problem we remain part of it. We may be a competent provider, loving parent, great lover, supportive companion, skilful worker and respected member of our local community. Yet if we withdraw into these roles to the neglect of wider issues, we become one more obstacle in the way of change. We also impede change when we use our brains and energy chiefly to make money or unnecessaries, while the problems of the crisis, crying out for our intellectual resources, remain unsolved.

Many of us fear that something is dreadfully wrong. We may even sense the distant murmur of the approaching storm. Yet for most of us it is still too remote, not enough to get in the way of having a good time. Life — we justifiably remind ourselves — is for living. If Earth were invaded by aliens from Space, all humankind would doubtless forget the differences that divide us and unite in her defence. There is an enemy, of course, yet he is neither remote nor invisible: in fact he could not be closer, for as author Ronald Higgins has identified, he is none other than ourselves. Most of us are all for promoting ecology and abolishing poverty, but invariably with the one small proviso that we never have to forego anything we enjoy. This promises to be one of the more formidable obstacles. It stems from our flaws and limitations, aggravated by the way city life separates us from Nature. Research shows that most city dwellers claim they would like to move to the country, but if only a minority of them realised their dream, the countryside would vanish even faster than now. Only a programme of education coupled with plentiful opportunities to meet Nature face to face seems likely to close the gap.

In the work we must do on the psyche we shall find that the 'shadow' fools us constantly. Along with inertia it is the commonest inner obstacle to change. Generally unable to tolerate the unconscionable aspects of ourselves, we repress them within the 'shadow', and project them onto social systems, political institutions and each other, rather than accept full moral responsibility for them. These are the convictions of Anthony Stevens, who declares, '. . . the problem of dealing with the Shadow exists for each and every one of us — particularly if we care that our children should survive to bring up another generation.' The only alternative to global catastrophe, he insists, can be a collective refusal to project shadow qualities in this way.

In consigning the future to the 'shadow' we run the grave risk of 'thinking' ourselves into demise. All prospect of changing direction then vanishes. Yet this need not happen. We have the equal capacity to 'think' ourselves into reclaiming the future instead. Hope lies in working to expunge, not the future, but the iniquities that haunt and paralyse us. There is nothing to hinder us but ourselves: our future knows no other enemy.

Resistance from without

Subversive as it will doubtless be branded, Earth awareness can expect few friends within the Wealth Machine. Once the Machine's faceless men perceive the new consciousness as more of a threat than an irrelevance, they will rise and fight it to the last 'Yuppie'. In the activities of MI5 in Britain and the CIA in America, the Machine has already shown its mettle. Insistence on excessive official secrecy, accusations of BBC 'left wing bias', covert staff vetting, photographing demonstrators, telephone tapping, persisting inadequacies in data protection measures, refusal to reveal evidence of pollution offences . . . disparate though these examples may seem, they have one common factor: the power structure is determined to stand no nonsense. In Britain, as in France and countries behind the Iron Curtain, efforts to muzzle the media began as the Cold War started to warm up, and nuclear power stations were commissioned to provide the plutonium needed to make nuclear weapons. When the world crisis worsens, such efforts can be expected to intensify.

The Press, for all its 'thundering', has been increasingly obliged to ally itself with the Establishment as it has realised that profits are inextricably linked to advertising revenue. As radio and television too find themselves increasingly dependent on advertisers' money and government goodwill, they join with the Press in their reluctance to challenge prevailing assumptions.

Any conservationist warnings of mankind running out of resources are interpreted by committed politicians as 'loss of nerve'. Provided that we believe in ourselves, they say, the market forces of free enterprise will discover how to create limitless energy and synthesize limitless resources. The strong reservations held by conservationists about the merits of living in such a society are met with contempt. Suggestions that Earth has needs we must respect or that nuclear is anti-Nature are dismissed as romantic nonsense: they merely impede the wealth creation necessary for all to benefit from further stunning scientific discoveries yet to be made. Only in this way can poverty be abolished. Nature exists solely for our benefit. The technological imperative is sacrosanct!

In this context Green is easily portrayed as costing jobs, impairing development, cutting living standards, risking national security and even as curtailing freedom. In times of recession governments plead they have no cash to spare for reducing pollution or environmental protection. Jobs must not be put at risk, nor international competitiveness impaired. In boom times when no one must rock the boat and political debate declines, the Green threat is all the more easily subdued with overdue 'cosmetic' solutions that change little. Doubts from any quarter on the ethics of prevailing values are dismissed as 'party political'.

In 1987 the renamed Green Party in Britain issued a Manifesto. It abounded with good sense: work alternatives, guaranteed basic income scheme, conservation taxes, wealth redistribution plans, resources and pollution control, sustainable agriculture, a charter for women, Poor South debt relief . . . and yet it was destined to gather dust. In the ensuing general election the party's 1.36 per cent share of the vote invited association with the 'lunatic fringe', and failed to represent the electorate's considerable concern for Green issues. In spite of pre-election eco-hype, all the main parties focused on old perennials: health, jobs, education and defence. As a political issue, ecology never even got off the ground — a common scenario enacted virtually everywhere except in West Germany.

The political facts of life are stark. Most voters are all for 'green' values so long as they make no inroads on their material standards of living, and pollution problems seem capable of solution through technological fixes. Once the word gets around that a sustainable society with emphasis on human scale calls for nothing less than a revolution in values, electoral enthusiasm wanes. Yet this is not the only obstacle to green politics. As ex-senior civil servant Clive Ponting reminds us: 'The greater the chance of [their] success the greater would be the effort to thwart real change from those who benefit from the existing structure and who consequently are powerful and have easy access to the media'. And he quotes the sums spent by industry to support the British Tory party, by the tobacco industry to stop anti-smoking legislation or by the food industry to encourage unhealthy eating. These prodigious efforts indicate the scale of resources that would be mobilised '. . . to counter the spread of ideas that would strike at the very core of the way in which industry currently operates and is organised.' Any programme of political change, he emphasises '. . . faces even more massive hurdles at each stage of the game — the electoral system, then the Parliamentary system and eventually within Whitehall and the wider world of political "realities" and power, both national and international.'

For any genuinely Green party to gain power, not only would its radical programme have to survive the scepticism and possible hostility of the bulk of the electorate, but the party would have to resist the tempting expediency of compromise with other parties when it gained power. Even so it would still confront the inertia of bureacracy and meet a head-on clash with the power structure that is the Wealth Machine. Clive Ponting poses the key questions: 'Where are the levers of power to alter the way in which big business operates; to alter, or even remove, the profit motive or stop the exploitation of non-renewable resources?' And citing huge multinational corporations and world-wide financial markets, he asks 'How could [a Green government] isolate the British economy from the impact of the world economy still run on conventional lines?' Apart from dealing with the European Economic Community, such a government would have to influence transnational institutions such as the IMF and the World Bank, and find an acceptable way of redressing the built-in subordination of the Poor South within the world trading pattern.

Although for any truly Green initiative to work it must eventually grow political teeth, it seems highly improbable that political processes themselves will bring about change in the first instance. The nearer any party comes to power the more 'respectable' it has to become and the more its policies and values have to conform to the existing pattern. The system offers the choice between ideological purity and ineffectiveness on one hand, and compromise with the existing system and some form of power on the other. The type of person attracted to the party changes as it gets nearer to power and politicians move from being radicals to power seekers and therefore inevitably become preservers of the existing system. The most that a reforming party can expect is cosmetic change.

Even if a simultaneous Green movement were to spread through Western democratic countries, Earth would still have to contend with the polluting materialism of the Communist world and the emerging consumerism of Russia and China. Moreover the party would also have to persuade the Poor South where its dominating dictatorships share a common goal of development to the levels of the Top Twenty. A sustainable society could only be acceptable in the rest of the world if there were a massive redistribution of resources in its favour. And Clive Ponting asks tellingly: 'What political party in the developed world is going to win power and keep it on that basis?'

Even if support for a Green initiative were to grow within the major parties, the prospects for radical change promise to remain bleak for as long as the Wealth Machine is able to keep up deliveries. For when the system finds itself attacked, its response will not be to reform but to increase the level of exploitation, to go harder in the direction it is already going. As he puts it: 'The system is in fact on auto-pilot.'

The prevailing economic system seems set on a course that is bound to lead to disaster, probably within the next century. Any challenge to the powerful will be resisted by them. Clive Ponting reminds us that the demands of those who advocate Earth awareness in a sustainable society are revolutionary: 'Perhaps they could only be implemented by a revolutionary party prepared to act ruthlessly — but that would of course involve a level of authoritarianism and violence that would destroy the very values the movement enshrines'. Whatever happens, we can expect an increasing degree of authoritarianism and social control designed to support the existing system as its contradictions increase and the difficulties of maintaining it become ever greater.

Only when the crisis deepens and the current contenders for government prove even less able to cope than now, are the prospects for an effective reforming party likely to improve. Throughout history, all reforms have been the result of demands on governments from the people, not the other way round.

The dominant System is maintained by political expediency, which in turn is characterised by inertia and conspiracy. As has been shown already, the bigger the group, the greater its inertia. Post-Chernobyl bureaucratic delaying tactics in Russia and White House paralysis after the 1987 Wall Street crash are classic instances of inertia. Tacit conspiracy is strongly suggested by the conspicuous failure of Top Twenty governments, the World Bank and the International Monetary Fund to alleviate Poor South poverty. And yet this should come as no surprise. As we approach the limits of what Earth can produce and the human population that she can support, it becomes less in the interests of the Top Twenty to stimulate domestic economic growth in the South. Any extra consumption of resources there could lead to a smaller slice of the cake for the Top Twenty.

It is the familiar Sumer Syndrome, for as Paul Colinvaugh reminds us in the context of the population explosion: 'Once the numbers of people begin to catch up with the resources, the leaders will find that even thir own ways of life are threatened. They must look to their own privileges, becoming a repressive ruling class.' His words have a chillingly prophetic ring.

Earth awareness asks that people think globally. Yet inherently obsessed as we we are with all that is local, we find understandable difficulties in grasping the concept. For the growing number of people worldwide now living in cities, Nature means little more than occasional scenery; in the poor South where the exodus from the country is greatest, abject poverty concentrates minds and energies exclusively on sheer survival, and Nature becomes a mere irrelevance somewhere 'out there'. When some three quarters of humankind are locked into a struggle to survive that consumes all their energies, wider issues soon fade. So long as the Top Twenty continue to deprive the Poor South of Earth's resources, Earth awareness confronts one of its greatest obstacles.

Revengeful Earth

As Chapter 2 explained, the living Earth has ways of protecting herself. Since nothing within the web of life can keep on growing for ever, constraints serve to limit the growth of individuals and the species to which they belong. Natural principles state that if any one species becomes so dominant that it poses a threat to the rest, the whole eventually takes action to reduce or eliminate it. Now that humankind has arrived at this threshold, we would do well to see what may be in store for us if we fail to apply constraints of our own accord.

The most cheering scenario rests on the somewhat self-indulgent idea that Nature herself will soon benignly intervene to rescue herself from our excesses. She will then endow our species with the sense of responsibility that evolution omitted at the primaeval time when we became self-aware. This implies that some 'miraculous intervention' will implant Earth awareness in our collective unconscious without our having to lift a finger to achieve it. As a kind of divine revelation or 'second coming' it will relieve us of doing any work on our psyches. Yet just because 'miraculous intervention' might be a handy spiritual short-cut is no justification for dismissing the idea out of hand. 'Instant spirituality' after all is nothing new. Revelation is common in orthodox religion. Miraculous intervention is also implicit in the contemporary New Age movement with its conviction that because the Age of Aquarius is newly upon us things will go right for a change.

There may well be something in these well meaning expressions of hope within the crisis. All the same, even though a motorist may have taken out a comprehensive insurance policy, he has no valid excuse for driving like a fiend. It would be imprudent for us merely to carry on demolishing Nature much as before while we wait for something nice to happen inside us. Better to start making improvements, both to ourselves and to society, encouraged by knowing we are on the side of the angels and that help is on the way. In the loneliness of our quest, in the rebuffs we shall endure, faced with the obstacles to surmount, we need succour from *any* quarter.

If the doubters should be right and 'other worldly' help is not to be forthcoming, then we must expect Earth, acting as a single living organism, to reject a 'body cell' as foreign and malignant as humankind. She may adopt one or more of many ways.

The damage we do stems both from our numbers and our behaviour. In order that our numbers may be reduced to manageable proportions we may expect plague, genetic breakdown, famine or war — or all four. They are predictably connected. Plagues such as AIDS may arise from breakdown of the immune system, through trans-species infections, or from escaped genetically engineered viral mutations. They may not be new plagues: familiar epidemics may be intensified by mass starvation. Increased radiation may give rise to mass cancer outbreaks to trigger unimaginable mutations. These could stem from global nuclear war, through the collapse of the already thinning, disintegrating ozone layer or by the addition to the environment of thousands of inadequately tested synthectic chemicals. Or as a result of all three. As in the past, plagues may lead to famine simply because the dying find it difficult to farm. Soil abuse, stemming from greed as much as from overuse, may force hungry people to acquire fresh land by declaring war. The aftermath of all-out nuclear war will not only kill most of us more or less quickly, but will possibly bring on plague, genetic breakdown and famine to exterminate the rest.

The idea of a world without people is so strange and repellent to us that it belongs strictly to the unthinkable. Even a world of vestigial survivors from the three chief threats is a bearable prospect only so long as we can keep our minds away from imagining the horrendous minutiae of what life in such an aftermath would be like. This being so, we are likely to carry on as before in the hope that something will turn up and make the problem go away; or alternatively to fret about it in an agony of helplessless and, by 'thinking ourselves' into demise, risk creating a self-fulfilling prophecy. Either course, however, amounts to an open invitation for the sheer momentum of our exploitative societies to propel us inexorably to extinction. The only way to escape from such a Catch 22 dilemma is to acquire appropriate knowledge and concern so that we may take decisive action before Earth pre-empts us.

No attempt to rescue the future can succeed unless we confront the two major issues of war and overpopulation. Together they are widely regarded, not only as the most serious threats of all, but also the most intractable. It is not enough to declare that war should be outlawed. We cannot dis-invent the Bomb or for that matter the rest of the War Machine's obscene paraphernalia. So long as we insist on banding into over-size groups of nations numbering millions and living in a man-made world of stress-inducing cities, war will remain to haunt us. And for as long as it does so, we shall continue to 'think' war into existence.

Overpopulation is of the same order. Even if humankind were able to plan families of one or two children, to implement such a plan and cope with the ensuing problem of a preponderance of old people, the sheer momentum of the problem would ensure that it persisted long afterwards. The reality of it presents agonising choices that we all shirk. The seemingly harsh methods by which the natural world controls its numbers have no place in our thinking. While abortion and contraception continue to provoke heated debate, most of us are no more ready to extend to the terminally ill and the afflicted old the voluntary option of an early death before all joy and dignity have gone, than to volunteer to be first for the gas chambers.

War and overpopulation are desperately urgent problems that call for resources of intellect and resolve as great as the transfer of resources necessary to heal the Earth and alleviate pandemic hunger and poverty. Until they are accorded their proper priority, war and human numbers will remain supreme obstacles to meaningful change and incalculable threats to the future that all children expect and deserve.

Why things may have to get worse

Many of us only stop smoking when an x-ray shows a shadow on our lungs, or someone close to us dies of lung cancer. Until then the statistics that 30 000 people a year in Britain needlessly die from smoking mean little. Similarly, even though on average over 800 people every day are killed and injured on British roads, many of us continue drinking and driving recklessly until we hit someone or either kill or nearly kill ourselves. In each example the gruesome connections only become apparent when it is all but too late. Our inherent defect similarly prevents us from facing the world crisis. The Chinese have another word for crisis: it is *wei-chi*. The first part means 'beware, danger', the second part 'opportunity for change'. Too often in the West we ignore this positive approach. In the face of crisis, as if seized by a death-wish, we become bogged down in doom and gloom predictions that help to bring on what we most fear. The Chinese approach would begin with a constructive analysis of what caused the crisis and continue by searching for the way out of it. We would do well to emulate them, for challenge can trigger enormous resources. As author Peter Russell reminds us: '. . . crisis may be an evolutionary catalyst in the push towards a higher level.'

Arthur Koestler has noted that crisis may require us to 'draw back to leap forward'. Throughout evolution this process of undoing before re-doing has been a favourite gambit. Progress in any field rarely follows a steady upward path. The history of science shows that each of its repeated revelations has occurred as a timely way out of a blind alley. Great surges in creativity come after times of stagnation and regression when we seem to have lost our way. Knowledge evolves in similar fits and starts. After any breakthrough there follows a period of consolidation and elaboration which degenerates into a downwards spiral of rigidity, orthodoxy, over-specialisation and the inevitable dead end. Crisis then ensues, and with it a way out of the blind alley. Any resultant new vision or theory is rarely built on top of the previous edifice however, but branches out from the point where progress went wrong.

In drawing back to leap forward we are able to recognise the worsening world crisis and, instead of lapsing into despondency, we can tap creative potentials which normally lie dormant and unrecognised, stifled as they are by conditioning. At such times, cherished beliefs may have to be abandoned, but in the ensuing emptiness, creativity may stir and blossom. No longer able to reach out for what had previously lent support, we gain an openness for new visions. The chaos of emptiness can be the cradle of change.

As artists, writers, philosophers and research scientists alike can testify, the effect can be electric. Not so much the exhilaration of a surf rider at the breaking of the wave near the end of his run: more the suppressed excitement of a prisoner released from long captivity, rapturous at the prospect of freedom, opportunity and fulfilment. Sometimes it is only when everything we value seems to be disintegrating that we awake to reality. So it is with society: it may have to be buffeted by surpassing crises before we see the fallacy of seeking infinite progress and growth in a finite world.

Theodore Roszak has forecast that one day this wasteland of abandoned principles that we mistake for civilization may be exposed as no more than a stage we must pass through on our evolutionary journey. Meanwhile most of us will continue to shun radical change until we find that we can no longer be lulled by all that has hitherto spoonfed and comforted us at so great a price.

When a culture faces new circumstances that impede its continuation and growth it is liable to 'critical breakdown'. If around the same time new ideas and values arise and gain critical mass the breakdown is likely to be accelerated. This new force he calls 'the rising culture'

The rise and fall follows Arnold Toynbee's model of cultural dynamics which states that: 'During the disintegration of a civilization, two separate plays with different plots are being performed simultaneously side by side. While an unchanging dominant minority is perpetually rehearsing its own defeat, fresh challenges are perpetually evoking fresh creative responses from newly recruited minorities, which proclaim their own creative power by rising, each time, to the occasion. The drama of challenge-and-response continues to be performed, but in new circumstances and with new actors.'

As history shows, the same melancholy drama has been re-enacted with minor variations by one civilization after another, Sumerian, Egyptian, Mayan, Greek, Roman, Mongol . . . and there is no reason to suppose that the future promises anything different. If this prospect seems alarming, we may console ourselves with the likelihood that the eventual collapse of industrial civilization does not necessarily mean the demise of the entire human species: it may be followed by another civilization of a different order, possibly 'the meek'.

Whatever form post-industrial society assumes, the model depicted by Arnold Toynbee offers hope that Earth awareness may metamorphose from the concern of a few to an irresistible worldwide movement capable of becoming the new life-affirming culture to rescue the future. The normal leisurely progression of political, economic and social change alone is not enough. Without such a phenomenon — or some miraculous intervention to equal it — we should not delude ourselves that the necessary radical change will happen within the time that is left. The obstacles of inertia and self-interest are too immense.

Some 3 500 million years ago, life itself faced a serious crisis. At that time, since the atmosphere contained no oxygen, the only life forms were simple anaerobic bacteria. Before life could become more diverse Earth had to find a way out of the impasse. She found it by encouraging bacteria to use a new process, photosynthesis, which released gaseous oxygen from previously unassailable water molecules. As the oxygen content of air subsequently rose to its present level the effect on anaerobic bacteria was catastrophic: with their atmosphere poisoned by this new gas they survived only in oxygen-free habitats, chiefly in subsoil, ooze and the ocean depths. Aerobic life in contrast was able to make the quantum leap that led to the richly diverse forms we know today, ourselves included. Paradoxically, anaerobic bacteria are now contributing to the downfall of their aerobic competitors. For as Chapter 2 observed, so long as they maintain their vital work in our own guts, so will they also ensure we live to persist in destroying the aerobic world we inhabit.

In our concern about our children's future it is not enough to think in terms of their lifetimes alone. They will not experience well-being if they feel uneasy about the future for *their* children — our grandchildren. Moreover, they in turn need the same assurance. The chain extends ad infinitum. The message is unequivocal: in making decisions about the future we are fatefully influencing not merely a few score years but a period that could span centuries.

The pattern of reform through history suggests that Earth awareness is unlikely to come about until it is universally perceived to be not only in our own self-interest, but potent enough to remove the threat of extinction. Timing hinges on unforeseeable events. A few more 'Chernobyls', a rash of 'Bophals', more disasters such as acid rain, further depletion of the ozone shield, another epidemic of AIDS proportions, widespread crop failures triggered by the greenhouse effect, or a limited nuclear war could be challenge enough to cause humankind to respond as never before. Chilling though the thought may be, one or more such disasters could be the very catalyst we need to galvanise us in time.

Hope within the crisis

The world is not the place it seems to be. That which is apparent is not necessarily real. All that is real may not be apparent. There is another dimension to reality beyond and within material things, where unpredictable, improbable and inexplicable events take precedence over the logical rationality that we have come to revere. We would be negligent in our quest for an assured future if we denied this dimension. Although it would be unwise to rely solely on its potential to help us surmount our predicament, we should not create such a hostile climate for its workings that we either ignore its manifestations or deter their ever arising. In the presence of such immensities we should feel humble, our minds and hearts open to all possibilities.

The growth of knowledge this century exceeds all that humankind has previously ever learned. The more we know, the more we realise there is to know. Or to put it more significantly: the less we know of what there is to know. In perhaps no field is this more apparent than science. In the nineteenth century, it was thought that Newton and others had adequately explained the workings of the universe in terms of a machine. To this century's scientists, however, reaching out to the frontiers of knowledge, the universe is filled with paradoxes and mysteries.

The New Physics has shown that the experiencer changes that which he experiences; that atomic particles sometimes behave as waves, and waves sometimes as particles; that particles appear to be 'aware' of each other and seemingly able to communicate this awareness instantaneously across vast distances. Suddenly only the whole is real and dualities such as cause and effect, subject and object, part and whole, all collapse. The emphasis shifts instead to the interrelationship and interconnectedness between all things. In reality, any reference to the part must mean reference to the whole. Once we probe beneath the thin surface of life as we experience it in the material world, we begin to see the delicate patterns and relationships reflecting the underlying microscopic reality that lies beyond the immediacy of consciousness.

Physics is not alone in such encounters. Psychology and medicine too are late developing nineteenth century sciences where, however much its practitioners discover, they learn that more remains unknown than is yet known. Neither mind nor body is a machine. Ecology, newer still, is confronted with just as many mysterious immensities, if not more.

In the rethink imposed chiefly by the New Physics, scientific infallibility has been shaken so much that phenomena which scientists once ridiculed because they could not be tested and repeated are now becoming increasingly respectable. Homeopathic medicine for example, in which minute quantities of substances often succeed where powerful drugs fail, is growing rapidly. Healers too have made undeniable and inexplicable cures in countless cases. Now that water divining has been actually found to work, highly paid 'diviners' are being employed to locate mineral seams. Relevant to our subject is the hypothesis of Formative Causation proposed by scientist and author Rupert Sheldrake, who has observed, among other phenomena, that when people and animals in one place learn to solve problems or acquire new habits, others isolated by distances up to thousands of miles may quickly do likewise. Transcendental meditation has been shown to improve synchrony between the two sides of the brain. Thelma Moss, a medical psychologist who has made an exhaustive, worldwide study of extra-sensory perception, writes that the scientific examination of meditation could lead to our finding ourselves '. . . approaching the next rung of the evolutionary ladder, a different dimension of being, transforming material man into man of the spirit.' For a scientist now to admit that the surrounding world is full of unaccountable mysteries is no longer tantamount to committing professional suicide. It was, after all, the scientist James Lovelock — still respected — who propounded the Gaia hypothesis of Earth as a single living organism.

We walk a tightrope. Short of the unpredictable, only a worsening of the crisis is likely to engender worldwide Earth awareness, and by then it may be too late. Since there is no guarantee that the expected synergy of critical mass will come to our rescue, the dimension of the inexplicable gains significance. Even so, it too offers no guarantee, for although time and time again its remedies and solutions have conclusively been shown to work, unlike their scientific counterparts, they are not automatically repeatable.

To many of us it may seem unlikely that Earth awareness will ever spread, simply because not enough people will ever act in unison. If so, we may take heart from the examples of 'social super-organisms' that regularly occur in Nature. For example, when the population of a beehive is threatened with mass loss or extinction, all the bees act in complex highly co-ordinated ways to ensure its survival. In certain higher species, huge numbers of individuals act as one unit, either when in danger or to thwart it. Schools of fish and flocks of birds, sometimes numbering several thousand, can change direction within a fraction of a second without a leader commanding them.

The phenomenon of orchestrated mass change is not confined to sudden emergencies. In the debris of woodland floors, microscopic amoebae that constitute a certain variety of singularly unprepossessing cellular slime mould normally forage independently. If food becomes scarce however, they first cluster into small groups and then combine in thousands to form a single light-seeking 'slug', which slithers across the woodland floor in search of food. If successful it disperses, if not it again changes to an erect shape and casts off myriad spores which scatter in the wind so that some may eventually land on food and begin the whole process again.

Encouraged by such exhibitions of unified social behaviour, Peter Russell has explored the possibility that human society may be approaching the emergence of a new evolutionary level. Drawing on knowledge of the origins of life, he predicts: 'Just as matter became organised into living cells, and living cells collected into multi-cellular organisms, so might we expect that at some stage human beings will become integrated into some form of global super-organism.' This he envisages would be as independent and complete in itself as a single biological organism, possessing the capacity to act as a social super-organism which anticipates danger. On this propsect he pins his hope for the future.

In our search for hopeful portents, the current 'information explosion' may prove to be an unlikely ally. Today's world is criss-crossed by electronic arteries and freckled with satellites of communication. For the first time ever, people worldwide can contact each other by telephone, Telex, fax, computers, satellite television and radio. Sadly most of the messages that the network now carries are inconsistent with the needs of Earth; moreover the vast majority of computer terminals are sited in the governments and commercial institutions of the Top Twenty nations where resistance to change is strongest. Nevertheless, whatever the form that global unison may eventually assume, a valuable infrastructure is now in place, ready for the time when such a technological miracle may be needed most.

If our predecessors could visit us they might be amused to find that we are admitting there is more to this world than can be seen, touched and scientifically tested. They knew that Nature, on whom they totally depended, is as mysterious as life itself. This they experienced not least as a sense of incompleteness unless they could serve something greater than themselves. In this way — as we do — they testified to the existence of the human spirit. Despite the materialism that dominates today's values, the same imperative prevails. Any overview of humankind reveals the universal nature of religious belief. Yet for many, especially within industrial societies dominated by science, religion in our time seems no longer appropriate, as empty churches and scant congregations testify. When we are unable to enact this ancient image, we deny our spirituality. We are unfulfilled, and knowingly or not, we transfer our attachment to whatever may come to hand: it may be scientific, national, ideological or charitable; it may be work, the drug scene or affluence. However, since the inherent image is inappropriately enacted, any such substitututes can impoverish the spirit. This is as saddening as it is dangerous. For ourselves as individuals, as well as for our species and for Earth, we have need of a steadying faith with which we may ease present suffering and find hope for the future. A spiritual vacuum exists that Earth awareness has the potential to fill. The new awareness presents no conflict with most aspects of religious faith.

We live in the time of 'the blank generation'. Where now there is spiritual emptiness there is also room for the concern that the living Earth so desperately needs.

We cannot find fulfilment in the material world that we mistake for reality, any more than we can expect to find a melody solely in the notes that form it. Its essence is in our awareness of *the connections* between the notes.

The next chapter explains how we can encourage the spread of Earth awareness, and the effects it will have on society. New beliefs and values will be needed, but before they can replace the old ones, formidable obstacles, from within ourselves and from the Wealth Machine, must be overcome.

13: Rescue Operation

The needs of the planet and the needs of the person have become one
Theodore Roszak

History's long highway is disconcertingly marked by failed attempts to bring about change. To be lasting and effective, change needs to have three components: knowledge, concern and action. Without knowledge we shall understand neither what it is we are trying to change nor what we are hoping to achieve. Without concern, in the sense of feeling a deep, compassionate and lasting conviction, our motives will be suspect. Without action, nothing is changed. No matter how much hot air may have been generated, and despite a plethora of good intentions, everything stays just as it was. All three must be present, preferably in the foregoing sequence. Knowledge needs to embrace more than mere information: wisdom and sound judgement must be injected. Concern may take many forms, from anger through irritation, to indifference, apathy, tolerance, liking, compassion and, from there, to love.

Action may even mean 'no action', for it is a symptom of human arrogance to assume that all the problems we create remain forever capable of solution: time may run out, and *any* action may then only make matters worse. Attempts to solve the world crisis run exactly this risk, for many of us put forward almost any excuse for doing nothing whenever anyone dares to raise the taboo subject. Above all we need concern, and the perseverance that renders it lasting. Translated into action, this means that as individuals we willingly devote more of our time, energy and, where possible money, to aspects of the crisis than many of us do now. Most of us give nothing at all, but unless we begin to give, we can scarcely be said to care.

The bedrock of culture

United we may all be by our common humanity, yet divided we remain by our different cultures. In this lies our species' strength and weakness. In the event of global threat to our survival the fact that people live in different ways enhances our species' survival prospects. The spread of Western economic imperialism, however, is leading to an over-specific way of life that could prove unsupportable. On the other hand, cultural variety may impede agreement on how to deal with the world crisis.

Each culture has its own great body of knowledge, beliefs, values and rules. This is the uniqueness that principally distinguishes Russian from American, West German from East German, Jew from Gentile, and Australian aborigine from Australian settler. The knowledge and beliefs of each culture originate from two sources; one is its inheritance of early religion, folklore, myth, legend, poetry, magic and intuition; the other is each new generation's rational understanding of the world; this is added to the first source and the two merge to form a single culture. Opinion varies as to which of the two is uppermost. One view holds that since our rationality is shaped by the influence of our long past, a culture's great body of knowledge and beliefs can only be understood in terms of the past from which it has grown. The past is seen as its root, recent additions as its branches. It corresponds with the 'bewildered caveman' view of humankind propounded earlier. The other view, predominant in cultures that have their origins in ancient Greece, maintains that rational understanding is uppermost, the rest irrelevant. This view materialises in Western culture as science and the belief that science can explain everything. It corresponds more with the 'psychopathic genius' view of humankind. Since this second view could explain what has precipitated a world crisis, it deserves our scrutiny.

For the past 200 years of our cultural evolution science has increasingly dominated Western culture, to the impoverishment of all other sources of knowledge. In science, the truth or otherwise of a proposition is determined by corroborating experimental techniques capable of being universally applied. A claim that 'water boils at 100 degrees centigrade' is included within science, whereas a claim that 'God exists' must be excluded on the grounds that no one has yet been able to apply objective experimental techniques to assess its truth. Any proposition that cannot be researched, dissected, measured or quantified with results accepted by appropriate experts is liable to be condemned by them as a technically meaningless value judgement. Since 'reality' is experienced as essentially material, any intangibles such as love, kindness, tolerance, wisdom, intuition, aesthetics and spiritual well-being or dis-ease are either devalued or denied any existence in reality at all.

The knowledge on which the values and rules of industrial, city-orientated societies are based is not so much false as skewed — more a part-truth than a downright lie. The consequences are serious. Limited as we are, conditioned as we have become, we attach too much importance to what is not vital and too little to what is. Because of this flaw, we have come to know too much about specifics, but too little about connections and relationships. We know far too much about how the world works to be trusted with the power that such knowledge endows, and too little about ourselves to wield it safely. As a result, we are not what we think we are, any more than Earth is the place we believe her to be. We do not see reality but only what we expect or hope to see: only what can be quantified, dissected, tested and proved.

With more than five billion people on Earth there are over five billion perceived worlds, each one unique. Scientists tend not to live in the same world as poets, Americans occupy a different space from Russians, men from women, adults from children . . . Not until we have understood the reasons for the illusions and prejudices that account for these differences can there be any hope that our divergent views will ever be reconciled. Not until then shall we be able to work together effectively to tackle a common threat and reclaim our children's future. It is part of the work we have to do upon ourselves. If our *knowledge* of the situation is inaccurate or grossly incomplete, our *concern* will be inadequate and misplaced and our *actions* predictably ineffective, if not actually dangerous. That is why the work is so important.

In industrial societies, examples of muddled knowledge and misconceived beliefs abound. They include the widely held cartesian view of the world as a machine rather than as Gaia 'the living being'; acquiescence to the idea that resources are better devoted to exploring space than alleviating poverty, and a lingering insistence that absence of proof equals non-existence. They embrace the pursuance of causes without due regard to the wider validity of their aims; an opinion of ourselves as misjudged geniuses rather than misguided innocents; the myth that more possessions equal greater happiness, and the belief that vocational training is education. They have led to a conviction that the way to peace lies in proliferating arms; an insistence that traffic problems can be solved by building more roads, rising crime rates by building more prisons, or illness prevented by building more hospitals — in short our acceptance that problems caused by technology should be attacked with even more technology. They also include a belief that in any field, more of what may be good is sure to be better; the pursuit of efficiency and utility that puts means before ends; a preference for reason over intuition, and an assumption that the past is dead. And they embrace the view that Earth was made for man; the assertion that men are superior to women, and the delusion that people have made the world a better place.

If our knowledge and beliefs are misconceived, then so too will be the complex structure of values and rules that grows out of them. Values determine the priorities we attach to emotions, ideas, artifacts and institutions alike. Rules then emerge as conventions, customs and laws to implement and enforce values. The prevailing culture that is their summation then surrounds us, comforting, protecting, conditioning — and stifling us. It influences everything we think, feel and do. Dominant as we are on Earth, all that goes on in our heads and whatever we do with our hands affects all life: even the very land, the oceans, the wind, the clouds and the rain. Earth becomes the casualty of our misguided culture, victim of a collective insanity.

Out with the old

At first sight the scientific acquisition of knowledge appears to have been a spectacularly successful accomplishment. In engineering, agriculture, space research, medicine, mobility and factory output, we have demonstrated that mastery over Nature brings tangible benefits. Or so it seems to the beneficiaries. Closer investigation however exposes the associated crippling costs, upwardly spiralling problems, and self-delusions, generally unrecognised but detailed in earlier pages.

As the writer and sociologist, Alwyn Jones, has made clear, industrial society patently fails to satisfy our true needs. It cannot do this because its institutions are oriented to the promotion, above all else, of material growth and progress. This single-minded attachment to materialism, at the expense of other human needs or purposes such as the spiritual or aesthetic, has become a destabilising influence in the culture as a whole. The worthy goals become efficiency and utility and the outcome is the emergence of specialised bureaucratic institutions, distanced from each other, each preoccupied with highly specific objectives. In these, as in activities outside State control, decisions are made without reference to ordinary people so that each institution becomes nothing more than a rational 'shell' with a void where the heart or human spirit should be.

In such a society values degenerate and the quality of life becomes defined predominantly in terms of quantity. As examples, the philosopher Ivan Illich quotes the way we perceive learning in terms of possessing educational credits; health through numbers of doctors available or drugs consumed;

and our degree of mobility by the number of vehicles on the roads. He continues: '. . . people are conditioned to *get* things rather than to *do* them; they are trained to value what can be purchased rather than what they themselves can create. They want to be taught, moved, treated, or guided rather than to learn, to heal, and to find their own way.' And he adds: 'Man now defines himself as the furnace which burns up the values produced by his tools. There is no limit to his capacity. His is the act of Prometheus carried to extreme . . . Some would like to speak about a mutation of collective consciousness which leads to a conception of man as an organism dependent not on nature and individuals, but rather on institutions.'

Whether through some mutation or simply from misguided cultural evolution, we have nevertheless lapsed into a state of precarious dependency. Knowing that if we were deprived of industrial society's institutions we would soon be reduced to a state of even greater helplessness than now, we understandably resent any criticism that our society is failing to deliver the well-being for which we make so many sacrifices. Spurious or misguided our culture may be but nevertheless it renders cohesive the many facets of our individual being: our deep emotions, religious convictions, self-confidence, reasoning powers, relationships, world view. . . . By means of it we live through each day. It unites us. Anyone among us who dares to reject it, to speak out or behave according to a different ethos risks becoming an outsider shunned or ridiculed by the rest. The challenge inherent in seeking Earth awareness is therefore immense.

In with the new

Born out of crisis, the new culture now emerging is both mother and child of Earth awareness. In our post-Chernobyl global village a growing number of us are beginning to appreciate the connections between existing culture and abuse of Nature. For a limited time the usual 'sticking plaster' attempts to solve the crisis may continue as the Establishment intensifies its already strenuous efforts to discourage dissent. Uninformed optimism will linger on until the challenge can no longer be ignored or effective response no longer delayed. Then as the groundswell of informed opinion and concern grows, so will the need for radical change become apparent. The new culture's knowledge, beliefs, rules and values will sharpen and the nature of its new institutions, political systems, economic models, laws and life styles will take shape.

Today's industrial societies have acquired their distinctive pattern of beliefs and values more by accident than design. Science matters more than religion, the arts languish and materialism flourishes. Our societies are sustained by conquering Nature and our fantasies are filled with conquering space. The technological imperative has overridden the ecological, the brain's left hemisphere has dominated the right, and yang has prevailed over yin. The evidence lies around us in the chaos of the man-made world. Change is overdue.

If the living Earth is to survive, a return to yin–yang balance is crucial. To achieve balance, initially yin must take precedence — a task in which women have a key role to play. Instead of allying with men in work that exacerbates the crisis, they have the opportunity not only to restrain men but also to surpass them in the work of healing and restoring the damage done. Even though it suffers from overtones of 'cleaning up after men', there is nothing demeaning in this. Apart from the obvious fields of education, the arts, journalism, politics, social work and health care, challenging opportunities now exist in the growing industrial sectors of pollution control, resource and waste management, along with environmental planning and protection. Women can exert a powerful influence over children too, boys especially, and so help them bring *their* lives into balance. In this way they may help to break the mould that commits each new generation to repeat the mistakes of its predecessors.

Many parents, aware of what is at stake, find they now have to make a choice between demanding children and demanding careers. Victims of the work ethic, they have become increasingly attracted to the surplus money that two jobs can bring in. Yet if children are to be spared the damage their parents suffered, both parents cannot have full-time careers and children as well. And because women are the better designed to nurture, like it or not, it is upon their shoulders that the responsibility for making the choice falls most heavily.

For the restoration of her health, the living Earth looks to a culture that genuinely cares for people and planet. She needs fewer careerists, more carers. Such a culture will encourage the full expression and exchange of love. Within it, women will have more say than they have had so far. In the swing to yin we shall have to rethink our life styles and home life alike.

Nurturing new values

Earth awareness is a state of being, a personal transformation. Yet that is only the beginning. If the future is to be rescued, this new awareness has to spread throughout the world until it becomes the framework by which other thoughts, feelings and actions are judged. It is no 'counter-culture'. It is the *dominant* future culture: the ultimate choice without which there can be no future: a new culture grounded not in the technological imperative and political expedience that characterises existing culture, but in respect for our universal, archetypal needs and those of Earth. These are the roots from which the culture's knowledge and beliefs will grow and the fruit will be new values and rules.

Universal though the new culture must become in order to be effective, it will eschew the global Western uniformity that smothers regional cultures. As each nation feels the pincer grip of crisis, so will its people turn to the new culture, blending it with the old so that the outcome corresponds with Earth awareness.

As with many other exciting ideas within these pages, the subject of values for a new culture could fill another book. The overriding aim of the culture will be to re-create as far as practicable the kind of sustainable world for which we were designed. With this in mind it is possible to select those which seem most relevant. Values grow out of knowledge and beliefs; rules then reinforce our ensuing behaviour. In the new culture, the knowledge we recognise as valid will be less dominated by science, more open to intuition, religion, the arts and aesthetics. Priority will be given to understanding human nature and the need to confront the 'shadow', to cultural evolution and to ecology, with special reference to understanding connections. Beliefs will include the concept of Earth as a living organism with needs to be met, the influence of the inherited past within us, and the importance of yin–yang balance. For the reasons outlined below, values will chiefly focus on compassion, justice, restraint and aesthetics.

Compassion

Concern for others is not enough on its own. To be compassionate it must lead to appropriate action. Since endemic poverty harms not only people but also the resource base which sustains all life, compassion means that wealth and other resources have to be more equitably shared. Concern must also extend beyond the relief of present suffering to include future generations and other life forms. All are interrelated.

Justice

Although people are not equally gifted, nor all fortunate enough to be born into more favoured parts of the world, everyone has an equal right to be treated fairly. As far as possible, justice must be administered to all whose rights in varying degrees are presently denied: women, children and the aged, racial and religious minorities, the disadvantaged, weak and poor. Other species also have rights. Greed and acquisitiveness are rarely if ever compatible with justice. Justice will reduce the misappropriation of surplus. The new culture must devise more intelligent and compassionate means of settling injustice than recourse to war.

Restraint
To conserve resources and minimise pollution, restraint is necessary to compensate for the lack of natural constraint of the man-made world. To achieve this calls for individual responsibility, supported by the ethos of the whole culture. It will reduce the risk of succumbing to the Peter Principle. Restraint is a response to the natural principle of 'enough is enough'. It curbs excessive competitiveness and work obsessiveness.

Aesthetics
With the emphasis on quality over quantity, on freeing the human spirit, and on establishing vital connections with Nature, aesthetics must assume priority over materialism.

At first we shall fail to meet the values we set. When we do we shall have to resist the self-delusion of making pious excuses in order to evade admission of failure. Values will spring, not from those who seek to maintain privilege, but from Earth awareness.

The economic factor

A society of new values clearly needs new economic and political models. Existing ones have encouraged humankind to exploit Earth's resources to create wealth for a minority, but only by concealing the unacceptable costs of pollution, environmental degradation, climatic disturbance and disappearing resources. In consequence, while conventional capital has accumulated, the value of *biological* capital has declined.

Barry Commoner explains: '. . . if the process continues, the biological capital may be driven to the point of total destruction.' For as we impoverish one, so we erode the other. The apparent buoyancy of industrial systems is then exposed as illusory. 'Environmental degradation represents a crucial, potentially fatal, hidden factor in the operation of Earth's economic system. The total rate of exploitation of Earth's ecosystem has some upper limit, which reflects the turnover rate. If this rate is exceeded, the system is eventually driven to collapse.' The inference is plain: if we are to stop treating capital as income, any new economic model must contain self-imposed constraints to replace natural ones.

The current industrial economic model of the West has other defects too. It leads inexorably to giantism; it focuses only on the short term; it measures the quantity of things yet ignores the quality of life; it depends on the myth of infinite growth in a finite world; its growth measurements such as GDP and GNP lump together all kinds of expenditure as positive indicators of wealth, even crime detection, armaments and road accidents; and, significantly, its main source of income for necessities comes from a plethora of inessential goods and services, without which there would be an insufficient tax base to generate it. The upshot has been to create the Wealth Machine and rob the planet.

A replacement model, charged with respecting the tenets of Earth awareness, would have to distinguish between activity for its own sake and activity that contributes to well-being — whether of people, of other life forms or of the planet. Work that makes things yet destroys people would have no place. It would reward enterprises that are clean and careful in their use of resources, and penalise those that are not. It would recognise that since any resource used belongs to Earth, it is to Earth that it should be returned in a form in which it may be absorbed or re-used.

Fifteen years of research into the fields of transport, energy and health have led Mayer Hillman, a senior research fellow at Policy Studies Institute in London, to believe he has gained a new insight into the fallaciousness of conventional wisdom in these three areas of public policy. He has concluded that there should be a 'needs-reducing' approach to complement a 'demand-matching' one. As he explains: 'If we are to achieve self-sustaining futures, both approaches should be firmly based on societal, life-enhancing goals which command a broad consensus. Resources can only be conserved if government and commercial instititutions adopt such goals.'

One of the areas he has studied concerns energy resources. Whether the coal, oil, gas and electricty industries are state-owned or private, by trying to sell us ever more fuel-based appliances all four encourage us to consume as much as possible. Far more than organised waste, these exhortations amount to little less than legalised theft of resources that belong as much to future generations as to ourselves. A more responsible attitude would be to *reduce* demand. To the macho minds of those who have climbed to the top however, energy conservation has little attraction. A negative concept, it lacks glamour and politicians often mistakenly see it as costing jobs. Few have the vision to recognise it as the 'fifth fuel' that it is, and so even when it is encouraged what usually happens amounts to little more than a token gesture.

The same philosophy applies to other sectors of the economy. With Earth awareness, a successful industry is seen as one that uses the minimum quantity of energy and raw materials. An efficient national economy becomes one in which the need to transport goods and people from one place to another is reduced to a minimum: every demand for a new road would imply inefficiency. Similarly a nation's health would be judged by the smallness of its so-called health service; every hospital closure, every redundant doctor, psychiatrist or dentist would be hailed as a sign that sickness prevention was succeeding. In affluent societies, lower food purchases could suggest that people were eating more healthily. Redundant police would be seen as one more indicator that society was at last recovering from pandemic stress. Higher unemployment would be a sign that machines were at last working to satisfy our needs, rather than the other way round. Necessary work could then be shared and people could concentrate instead on living full, balanced lives.

If applied globally, this revolutionary approach to economics could transform the future. From Earth's viewpoint our success as a species would be judged by how little we disturbed the environment, how little we consumed, rendered extinct, degraded and destroyed. By these standards, its adoption would spell breakdown for industrial economies based on throughput; the aims of the Wealth Machine would have to be changed; giantism would topple.

In the years that it has assembled, The Other Economic Summit (TOES) has done valuable groundwork, even though it has not yet been able to agree on a viable new model. This work has furthered the concept of a guaranteed basic income (GBI). This is in essence an untaxed subsistence income, paid to every person whether in paid work or not, which has none of the stigma of the dole. Under the scheme, those who feel they require extra income are free to work as hard as they wish; those whose needs are small or who opt for unpaid work are equally free to follow a more relaxed life style.

Phased in over a decade or so, GBI would be financed from three sources: higher income tax on paid work; savings achieved by abolishing existing tax allownces, grants and benefits and the cost of administering them; and from higher VAT. Proponents of the scheme reject the criticism that it would mean economic disaster; they claim that it would reduce the wages and salaries paid for many kinds of work, production costs would fall, and firms would become more competitive.

As a perpetrator of crisis, the work ethic must be a central focus of any radical alternative. From Earth's viewpoint, work is broadly of three kinds: benign, neutral or harmful, irrespective of how humans view the activity. If it is to be true to the tenets of Earth awareness, any new economic model will have to take account, not only of these three criteria, but also the principle of setting minimum targets for energy use, transport and other sectors of the economy.

Future scenarios

Five differing scenarios for the future have been succinctly drawn up by James Robertson, one-time senior Civil Servant, now consultant, lecturer and author. As he explains, each is believed by some people to be the only realistic view of the future and the way out of our present predicament.

Business-as-usual
A future much like the present and the past with continuing crises but no dramatic change in humankind's main problems, in methods of handling them, nor in most people's general outlook and attitudes. Seen as the only realistic way of keeping things going.

Disaster
Catastrophic breakdown under way with no realistic alternative to events such as nuclear war, increasing worldwide unrest, famine, pollution, poverty, misery, disease and crime.

Totalitarian conservationist (TC)
Disaster risk averted by authoritarian system of government as only solution to the central problem of too many people competing for too few resources. Based on assumption that in times of chaos people turn towards authority.

Hyper-expansionist (HE)
Acceleration of West's super-industrialism and more effective use of science and technology. Space colonisation, nuclear power, computing and genetic engineering overcome limits of geography, energy, intelligence and biology.

Sane, Humane, Ecological (SHE)
Change of direction to balance: within ourselves, between ourselves and others, between people and Nature. Expansion psychological and social, not technical and economic. Decentralisation plus top priority to living supportively with one another to enable most people to fulfil themselves within a learning and planning, 'trans-industrial' society.

As James Robertson explains, business-as-usual is the only scenario which holds that we do not need to concern ourselves much with the future, and Disaster is the only one envisaging inevitable catastrophe. The last three share a similar serious concern and believe disaster is avoidable, but disagree on methods of doing so. TC recommends clampdown; HE breakout; SHE breakthrough. TC and HE are elitist and centralist, while SHE is egalitarian and decentrialist. HE and SHE are optimistic, while TC is pessimistic. TC and SHE are conservationist, while HE is expansionist.

James Robertson points out that the actual future will certainly contain elements of all five, and adds: 'Although I prefer the fifth (SHE) view, I certainly don't deny that government and technology both have a positive contribution to make to a sane, humane, ecological world society.'

It will be apparent by now that the SHE (Sane, humane, ecological) view corresponds closely with Earth awareness. It may also be observed that if indeed our nature is so evil that, given the opportunity, we are certain to exploit and demolish nature, then the TC (Totalitarian conservationist) option would be the only one to offer any hope. Nothing short of an ecologically benign world dictator, or a league of such dictators in unanimous agreement, would have the power to impose the legislation necessary to restrain us and to ensure, by force if necessary, that it was obeyed.

As portents of what may happen, rather than expressions of our wishful thinking, the five scenarios can be divided into two kinds. One kind implies the continuing pursuit of material wealth at the expense of the poor, the natural world and the future. Within it we destroy other life forms and their habitats, substitute ever more unnatural and dangerous materials and processes to replace dwindling natural resources, and live in a the shadow of a proliferating arms race to protect growing material wealth and power concentrated into fewer hands. The scenario implies increasing control and exploitation of Nature.

The second kind of scenario places less emphasis on materialism and more on the quality of life. It means directing technology and industry to supplying needs before wants, sharing rather than competing for Earth's resources, and conserving them for the future. It involves reducing and cleaning up industrial activity. It implies restoring natural habitats, the soil and — above all — the diversity and fertility of life. It is the reconciliation of our needs with those of Earth.

To achieve such a scenario, society would need an economic model based on equilibrium. James Robertson stresses that this would not involve returning to pre-industrial conditions of poverty and subsistence farming. As he puts it: '. . . by moving towards an equilibrium economy, based on sane, humane, ecological use of advanced technology, mankind will have a better chance of meeting economic needs and achieving a higher quality of life, than by trying to prolong the conventional trajectory of economic growth.'

The next chapter covers the work we can each do, singly and in groups, to help accomplish the change necessary to reclaim the future.

14: Agenda for Action

The unleashed power of the atom has changed everything except our way of thinking . . . we need an essentially new way of thinking if mankind is to survive

Albert Einstein

By now it should be apparent that within the time that is left there is little prospect of radical change emanating from the top. Unless the process begins with each one of us, political gains will lack the conviction to sustain them and economic gains will degenerate to little more than a change of management. Yet personal change does not have to be a spiritual transformation. It implies no 'born again' evangelism, but merely the rediscovery of our original nature and an escape from society's all-pervading conditioning. Its objective is to aquire a sense of responsibility appropriate to the formidable power we each wield, however innocently, as members of the human species.

Much of our predicament stems from misdirected science, but in the necessary work on ourselves, one of the newer branches of science can be put to good use. Although psychology has revealed only a fraction of what remains to be known about the brain and the psyche, it can greatly help us to understand ourselves better. The steps that follow are soundly based on psychological principles, yet stripped of in-words that could get in the way of common sense. Anyone interested in their underlying psychology can turn to the ample books available.

Help in the work may also materialise from other sources. In seeking to rediscover our original nature we are responding to frustrated inherent drives. Deep within our unconscious reside these prisoners, desperately signalling us, asking to be released. Moreover, if by now we can accept that we are still part of Nature and that Earth is a single living organism, we may experience this work as the coming together of a triad: psyche, Nature and Earth. All are one, separated but seeking reunion. It is a profound concept, fundamental to Earth awareness, and — if we are only open enough to grasp it — capable of charging us with unxpected energy.

In the work to be done, we begin by aiming to know

ourselves better. We identify our strengths and weaknesses and make changes in our lives to build on our strengths. We do not aim for perfection, but limit what we do to our ability to do it well. Since a sense of *worth* is crucial, we veer away from what harms our self-respect and move towards what enhances it. We examine how we feel and behave towards ourselves and others, and make changes in our daily lives to help us feel more comfortable with them.

To rediscover our original nature we make changes to remove what causes us stress: what frightens, angers or frustrates us. We make the overcoming of fear a positive force that directs our energies outwards rather than inwards. Recalling what we have read about our 'dark side', we explore and expose what we confine to the unthinkable. This calls for a degree of honesty with ourselves that may disturb us. We should not be afraid of crisis however, but see it as opportunity. Without a measure of it, we risk keeping the work 'all in the head'.

At this point we should be ready to direct attention outwards, interested in wider issues and the connections between cause and effect, the less apparent consequences of the way we think and behave. This includes the discrepancy between what comes into our home and what we give back. We are becoming better informed. If as yet we have little desire to make changes to our attitudes and behaviour, this is the time to enquire why we remain unconcerned about the effects we have on others, either through what we do, or do not do — our inertia. Most probably we have experienced no inner crisis and it is still 'all in the head'. If so we should treat reason cautiously and trust more to intuition.

Either way we need to develop openness. This requires us to be attentive and observant of life around us and willing to listen to other views. We search our hearts and find what issues we feel most deeply about. If we find none, we need to do more work on understanding connections. At some point the work we are attempting should gain a spiritual dimension, manifested at least in a desire to be of service to others. Once we have experienced concern, we are ready to do something about it. Unless convinced we can be more effective acting alone, we are ready to join or start a group of people who share our concern on at least one specific issue. We work to achieve the group's aims in ways that enable us to make best use of the strengths we identified at the beginning.

Along the way, the relevance of Earth awareness should become apparent. When we attain it, we acquire the responsibility to share it with others, informing and inspiring them as best we are able. In carrying out this work we should discover that we do count: that we are each a vital particle of the force that can become the unstoppable critical mass of desirable change. The work we do connects with what others are doing.

Group power

Most of us in our hearts feel concern for at least one issue troubling the world around us. We may be deeply disturbed by slums and widespread poverty, hunger and starvation while others own two homes, overspend and over-eat; we may be dismayed at the relentless disappearance of familiar green countryside under concrete, by the sight of trees dying through acid rain, at historic buildings torn down or precious views defiled by motorways and industry; appalled by ocean pollution from radioactivity, dumping or burning toxic chemicals, discharging sewage or spilling oil; and we may be saddened at the plight of whales, pandas, gorillas, koala bears or butterflies, all facing likely extinction.

The destruction of rainforests may anger us, widespread flooding touch our hearts or catastrophic industrial accidents alarm us. We may be anxious about the dangers of nuclear power, or frightened and frustrated by arms proliferation, the omnipresence of the Bomb and the pervading atmosphere of international distrust. The plight of political prisoners may cause us concern. Drug addiction and alcoholism may prove to be too close to home for comfort. Traffic and aircraft noise may annoy us, even affect our health. Issues such as marriage breakdown, child abuse, wife battering, rape and the unchallenged denigration of womanhood may move us to action. We may object to food additives, chemical farming, the use of animals for testing drugs. Apartheid and other forms of racism may anger us. Or, closer to home, we may resent the tightening grips of government on our children's education — anxious, among other concerns, that it will stifle any burgeoning 'green' aspirations.

To express concern and desire for effective action on these issues and a host of others, people all over the world have drawn closer to each other in groups. For more effective clout, many of them have linked up with other groups concerned with similar or associated issues. The phenomenon is recent. It is growing rapidly. And it is significant for the opportunity it affords to transform impotence into power, apathy into excitement and anger into action. It annihilates the excuse idly to watch evil triumph.

Whether the cause is peace, ecology, conservation, feminism, justice, new politics, health, the abolition of poverty or any other life-affirming issue, a wide range of groups now exists to fight it. Known officially as 'non-government organisations' (NGOs), they assume many different forms: some sensibly limit their horizons to local issues, others range from the national to international scene; some are charitable organisations administering aid; some are political pressure groups aiming at opinion formers and influencers; some are mass movements often relying on huge demonstrations, others find that effective action can be best achieved by staying small; some thrive on publicity and are open to all, others prefer to keep a low profile and restrict membership — as in the case of professional people uneasy with the support their recognised bodies invariably give to the Establishment viewpoint. Some engage only in respectable conventional action, other may resort to non-violent action and, under acute provocation, even to breaking the law.

Harford Thomas writes of them: 'Increasingly they have become a powerful alternative voice to which governments and business find themselves obliged to listen — and, indeed, to which decision-makers listen with growing respect. Some are international organisations able to express something like a global view'.

Understandably most of them are to be found in the West. In Russia and China they are beginning to emerge, while numbers are growing in some countries of the Poor South: in Brazil alone some 300 such groups have been listed. Gathering momentum worldwide, they represent a major life-affirming force to challenge the complacency and intransigence of the status quo. They are a source of hope for the future.

A key word in understanding their origin is 'betrayal'. Common to nearly all of them is frustration at the gaping chasm between what is and what could be. By helping us to satisfy our inherent drive to be part of a like-minded group, they can change the inner world of the psyche, as well as the outer man-made world. They can assist too in bringing home to us the crucial connections between cause and wider effect. Their existence makes us less impotent in the midst of injustice, neglect or ignorance. Wherever a life-affirming group exists, so too does the means of locating one. Where no group is already available to join, any concerned person can bring one into being: either by forming a new local branch of an existing organisation, or by starting a fresh one altogether. (A number of effective life-affirming non-governmental organisations are listed in an appendix.)

In becoming involved with NGOs an element of caution is advisable. Some groups focus on the *causes* of life-destroying problems so that lasting solutions may be worked out; others merely hide symptoms so that causes persist and little if anything changes. We need to spot the difference. Crash programmes in times of disaster have their place, but as Oxfam has long warned, continuing handouts allow the perpetrators of injustice to carry on as usual while rendering the aid recipients ever more dependent and demoralised. All too often problems demand a political solution which has minimal appeal for those who really only want to salve their consciences by 'playing lady bountiful'.

Life-affirming organisations have their counterparts within the System. As in ancient Sumer, today's ruling elite must ensure that the populace keeps working for their benefit. Whereas Sumer relied on superstition and armies, their modern counterpart — while not always averse to these aids — has developed a powerful armoury of trade associations, guilds, lobbies and pressure groups to press home their limited interests. While some of these can play a valuable social role, others exist to ensure that surplus and power continue to be abused so that wealth may flow to where wealth already is. In response to the challenge of deepening crisis, such organisations can be depended to proliferate, frequently posing as the life-affirming groups they seeks to oppose.

Some NGOs are closer to the heart of the world crisis than others. Among the best known are the international organisations Greenpeace and Friends of the Earth (FOE). While Greenpeace has attracted the limelight for its risky and dramatic actions at sea over whaling and waste-dumping, the two NGOs use similar strategies by selecting a few issues at a time in preference to diluting their limited resources over the whole spectrum. In the fight against poverty, Oxfam, first on the scene, has recognised the political dimension, and has now been joined by many others with varying degrees of political involvement. In Britain the peace movement is dominated by the Campaign for Nuclear Disarmament (CND) which has combined large demonstrations with persistent behind-the-scenes lobbying.

Consumer power is a force which has already shown its muscle in achieving better and safer product design. Yet its potential is far greater. By boycotting goods from countries that violate human rights and from companies with bad pollution records, consumer groups have persuaded multinational and other large companies to change policies. As Earth awareness spreads, more and more consumers will stop buying goods that have been produced in ways that harm people, wildlife or forests. In this way, farmers, for example, will be encouraged to treat their land, crops and animals with more respect: our food will better for us and, by putting Earth first, they will be striking a blow for the future. Boycotting is potentially one of the most powerful weapons available to citizens otherwise impotent. Consumers could influence producers by 'voting' not to buy their wares until they have mended their ways. In this way companies felling rainforests, for example, might go home when they discover that vehicles made by their associated companies no longer sell. With consumer power, companies can be hit where it hurts them most: in the balance sheet.

Voters in more fortunate countries can already influence politicians more than they suspect. With re-election ever uppermost in their minds, politicians are extra sensitive to critical letters from constituents and face-to-face meetings at their 'surgeries'. Newspaper editors too, with one eye always on circulation figures, take heed of reader's letters — as indeed do politicians and other readers. All these approaches are grossly under-used. In view of the obstacles described in Chapter 12, change may more readily be achieved through the side door than by frontal assault.

Highly organised grass root organisations have the ability to empower people. The work of the American activist Saul Alinski, has inspired the growth of broad-based local organisations in the poorest areas of his native land. Collectively, these have now acquired the power to bring about significant changes on issues affecting people's ability to enjoy self-respect, justice and freedom. The most successful of these initiatives is the Industrial Areas Foundation, which now supports over 20 broad-based, multi-issue community organisations throughout the nation. Each is autonomous, financed by its members and totally accountable to them. With an active membership numbered in thousands, they wield real power.

The IAF identifies organised money and organised people as the prerequisites of power as understood by the Mafia and multinationals alike. Its role with the citizen's organisations is to train networks of local leaders in the realities of politics, where self-interest is the prime motivating force. Basing their work on the ideals of Judaeo-Christian traditions, organisations operate with professional acumen in the world, not as it could or should be, but *as it is*. In the public arena, they are gradually regaining an effective voice for the hitherto disadvantaged Blacks, Hispanics and Whites.

To overcome the apathy of these minorities over voting, the IAF initiated the Sign Up and Take Charge Campaign. This encourages those in inner cities and rural wastelands to register and then, without party political endorsement, advises them where each candidate stands on vital but generally neglected local issues such as pollution, education standards, roads, housing, and the provision of water to homes. The Campaign's realistic aim for the 1988 Presidential election was seven million votes. With such backing, the IAF had within reach — for the first time — the necessary political muscle to negotiate with candidates on all issues affecting the poor.

The IAF is only one of a number of US initiatives, burgeoning as local groups discover their potential to bring about change. The relevance of this phenomenom to the world crisis is apparent. It capitalises on our archetypal drive to form groups, and by relating self-interest and local needs to the greater whole, it takes our inherent tendency to be swayed and uses it to achieve escape from apathy and conditioning.

Its significance to the global problem of debilitating poverty and hunger can also be seen. Once the world's poor can be just as professionally helped to identify that the principal causes of their misery are jointly their own rulers and the total domination of international commodity and money markets by the Rich North, they too can be expected to discover their potential strength. When they do, they will accurately recognise themselves as the chief victims of the Poor South's crippling debt to the Rich North. Once awakened, they will exercise a legitimate concern over the ensuing annual interest payments which bleed their meagre resources to help maintain the North's enviable living standards.

Critical mass

According to one version of a story in oriental wisdom, an elephant had been brought into a house for exhibition in darkness where each visitor could feel it only with the palm of his hand. When one of them encountered its trunk he exclaimed, 'This creature is like a water-pipe'; when another touched its ear it seemed like a fan; and as another felt its leg he said, 'Truly this elephant is like a throne'. As each visitor heard a description of the elephant, he understood the whole only from the part he had touched. With a candle in each visitor's hand however the difference would have vanished.

So it is with the world crisis. Groping in the half light of our conditioning we cannot see the whole, but only that which is close and immediate, no more than what directly affects us. If indeed we can accept that there is any more to it, our limitations allow us no more than a blind guess: an underestimation, certain to be wide of the truth. To protect ourselves, we summon the anaesthesia of the Unthinkable. We not only mistake the part for the whole, we fail to see that the whole can be greater than the sum of its parts.

This need not be the formidable impediment to change that at first it seems. What counts is our inherent ability to feel and express concern about some specific issue, probably local, with which we can identify. That is the starting point. As with all else on Earth most issues worthy of our concern are connected to each other. So too, however informally, are the various groups. Their very interconnectedness likens them to a mosaic.

The analogy of a mosaic is useful. It implies an image or picture of the whole world crisis that cannot be appreciated by being too close. Each marble chip of the mosaic represents an issue in the crisis, while the distinctive shape and colour of each one signifies the nature of NGOs concerned with the issue. Until the craftsman sets to work to create the mosaic, each chip lacks significance to the intended picture. As he builds it however, clusters of chips grow and identifiable portions of the overall picture successively reveal themselves. Once this occurs each chip acquires not only meaning in its own right but also a relevance to the whole.

At a certain moment, well before the mosaic is complete, all the chips connect and the craftsman's work acquires a kind of *critical mass*. In a flash of recognition, anyone standing far enough away can see the picture as a meaningful whole. Those still obsessed with examining the parts, however, would miss this revelation — they may even choose not to for fear of what they might see. When the picture is complete, all who want to take an overview will see it. In such a way ideas can create a ripple effect capable of unstoppable momentum. At a certain point they generate a total energy infinitely more powerful than the mere arithmetical sum of each individual's capacity. Once enough people have become involved in specific issues dealing with aspects of the world crisis, they will connect and generate a synergy powerful enough to bring about change.

Synergy has been described as 'peak experience'. We experience the phenomenon as individuals when, for example, extreme danger requires us to take flight. Boosted by adrenalin, each organ in the body reaches a peak of performance that enables the whole to think more quickly, run faster and jump higher or further than is normally possible. The phenomenon is not always easily explained by normal rationality. We sense it in the presence of genius, that 'gift' which enables its possessor to live in a higher state of evolvement, specifically or sometimes generally, than any amount of hard work upon the Self would normally produce. It can be witnessed in Nature when seemingly stupid creatures such as fierce wasps or aimless termites acquire the magic number necessary for them get together and build vast and beautifully engineered living quarters. Something akin to it occurs in physics when vibrations acquire the property of instant resonance: the critical high musical note that can shatter a glass; or when a marching regiment, failing to break step when crossing a bridge, can cause its sudden collapse. It is evident in the critical mass reached when water boils, or when light of a specific frequency or colour is stimulated to cross the laser threshhold and acquire an immense increase in power. Synergy is never more dramatically apparent than when hydrogen molecules are induced to reach the critical mass of nuclear fission. As a species we experienced the phenomenon long ago when, after a million years of torpor, our collective consciousness crossed the Rubicon and, within the 'cosmic tick' of a few thousand years, we invented technologies that transformed the face of Earth. Our hopes for the future gain strength when we observe through history that once life-affirming ideas catch on they can prove unstoppable.

As earlier pages have indicated, we inherently give ourselves wholeheartedly to causes greater than ourselves. Since we no longer live in survival groups this imperative now constitutes a flaw in our behaviour, for we tend to commit ourselves to causes without due regard to their aims. It is a flaw that has helped to lead us into crisis. Yet we can put the flaw to good use. There is no need for every one of us to appreciate the complexities of the whole problem: much of this overviewing can be undertaken by people who have concentrated on the preparatory work for years. Indeed many have devoted their whole lives to grasping the full implications. Their efforts have not been in vain. In universities, libraries and NGO offices, innumerable shelves, filing cabinets and computers are packed with diligently acquired research findings waiting for keen minds to apply them.

That they lie idle is now easier to understand: they are too powerful. In conventional scientific methods of reductionism, the whole is dissected and examined. In the phenomenon of critical mass the parts come together to create a whole — even Earth awareness.

Yet change need not be painful: society can be eased through the transition from breakdown to breakthrough. And we do not have to wait frustratedly on the sidelines: we can each join in.

Starting point

By now it should be apparent that to rescue the future there must be a state of balance between what humankind takes from the Earth and what we give back. Less clear may be the vital connection between this principle and the way we live our daily lives. Yet until the connection is appreciated, little of consequence will change. We all find it far easier to debate the whole issue as a national and international problem than to do anything practical about it. Whenever any solution to a problem threatens our own material standard of living, we tend to relegate it to the unthinkable.

The concept of 'voluntary simplicity', frugality or living simply — it answers to several names — is not new. The Simple Life is a frequent television topic, occasionally a catalyst for change, always good for a snigger. Yet there is only one way to discover whether it is to be taken seriously, hurts in practice, or can indeed be a happy liberation from never being satisfied with what we already have, and that is to try it. There need be no compulsion to sell or give away everything, wear rags, sleep on the floor and live on bread and potatoes as from tomorrow: no rush to quit work, find a small farm and keep goats. It can be done by staying put. The idea is not so much ascetism, more an attitude of mind than any defiant gesture or hasty attempt to shed guilt. It implies a deep concern to take less from the Earth and others and to give back more instead. And importantly a measure of it is perhaps the only practical way we can exercise the restraint that is central to the new values of the future.

Voluntary simplicity has many facets. It may bring home the sense in getting rid of unnecessaries, giving up a few dubious habits, perhaps letting someone with no home occupy a spare room in the house. It could in time entail a move to a smaller house or to more ethically acceptable work. Or it might not. Would-be practitioners may be helped by some well-tried basic principles. In brief, these invite us to avoid buying anything unless essential, and even then preferably secondhand; to mend or recycle; to share if possible, to grow as much of our own food as makes sense; to make whatever we can ourselves, with recycled materials if possible; and finally to avoid waste at all times.'

More to the point than rules, however, are the motives and aims in making the change at all. Many who have done so speak of the release from stress it can bring, the meaning it can impart to life, and the better relationships with people it can generate. They tell of feeling genuine concern and desire for action over poverty and injustice; a fresh awareness of aesthetics and natural beauty. And they say how it enables them to find more time for family — children especially; as well as time and desire for involvement in community affairs, in political action, 'good works', adult education, and active sport. They speak too of fewer work worries, less guilt and better health. E. F. Schumacher has written about the benefits of getting necessity and 'creative leisure' into balance, of spending time on 'invisibles' and not just on 'visibles'. In 1972, Horace Dammers, while the Dean of Bristol, founded the Life Style Movement. Originally for those who sought contact with others of like mind, this has now become a national organisation, as it says, 'for people who, as a sign of their commitment to global justice, try to live a more thoughtful, sharing, responsible and ecologically sustaining lifestyle'. To avoid undue introspection, members are encouraged to take part in political or other appropriate, outwardly directed action.

In whatever way we may choose to reject conspicuous consumption, its value is undeniable. Throughout a million-year period, we were archetypally designed for a life style with few possessions. It should come as no surprise then to find that, far from granting us the elusive well-being we seek, too many possessions add to our ongoing stress. By reducing the clutter of consumer durables in our lives, we move closer to our original nature. When we examine our own life styles, we are prompted to discover that life can have a more rewarding focus than 'getting and spending'. We may begin to see our work as beneficial, neutral or harmful to others, and to act accordingly. We may begin to question why in the Top Twenty we should assume that we have an automatic right to a bigger share of Earth's good things than the majority of humankind. And, above all, in the crisis which jeopardises the future, we may end up taking a positive step towards moving from being part of the problem to part of the solution.

Social inventions

To reclaim the future, we have to invent techniques and social devices that will re-create as closely as possible the conditions for which we were designed. Much of what we take for granted must be challenged. One of the first institutions to face scrutiny must be the nuclear family. Society, perhaps, should not regard couples struggling on their own as the only way, or even the best way, to raise its children.

In general, living, working and governing patterns have become over-rigid, heedless of our true and basic needs as individuals. And, since men, rather than women, are chiefly responsible for the world crisis, it is for them that techniques and devices are most required. Society will be a better place when it can turn to its advantage their inherent drive to plot and plan together in groups away from home. The magnitude of the tasks ahead should keep men happy for decades.

Opportunities abound: waging war on poverty; fighting injustice; plotting peace; devising means to manage better with less rather than more technology; using fewer material resources rather than more; as well as making towns and cities places fit for people — organising, planning, diverting roads, creating squares, precincts and walkways, landscaping parks and gardens, and planting trees. And if after all this they still have unburned calories left over or problems of residual adrenalin, there is always participatory sport to supplant the giant business interests of spectator sport. Spare resources spent on playing fields and swimming pools could divert energies in ways that could well save Earth from the depletion of even more resources.

As the ozone layer thins and sunbathing loses appeal, people may be persuaded to travel less for hedonism, more as a way to gain understanding of how others live. Any steps to transform remote people from statistics to human beings just like ourselves would lessen the propensity to kill them in war. For those willing to open themselves to fresh experiences, travel in order to witness poverty could have its own rewards.

A crucial focus must be a new work ethic to replace the old. Not till then will Earth be safe and humankind liberated to find a valid meaning for life. The formal economies of most industrial societies depend on the concept of a lifetime of paid, full time employment for all who can be spared from 'home duties'. In practice the right to work can only be fulfilled by some; millions of others are denied work. Formal though such economies may be, they plainly malfunction.

In one industrial country after another, alongside the dominant formal economy an 'informal' alternative is growing fast. People in cities and country districts alike are seeing the merits of working locally primarily to meet local needs. It is purposeful and important activity, paid and unpaid, pursued by people both individually and in groups. Going by the name, 'ownwork', it embraces community enterprises, DIY and any self-reliant activity that people consider fulfils a genuine need. Aided by the Guaranteed Basic Income (GBI), the pattern is seen as part of the new future for work: a flexible mixture of part-time employment, family work at home and voluntary work, mixed in with spells of full-time employment for as long as the formal economy is able to provide it. As crisis deepens and the formal economy breaks down, so will ownwork supersede it.

This concept of working and living within a definable community goes a long way to satisfying our inherent image of life in small survival groups. Within it, children grow up surrounded by the familiar faces of other children and adults with whom they may expect close, continuous contact as practised in Steiner schools for years — even for life. Because the concept furthers the process of decentralisation, it enables people to regain more control over their lives. It stimulates the creation of 'villages within suburbs', each with its centre for meeting and socialising. It challenges the supremacy of the Wealth Machine. The chief limit to its growth is our acceptance of a lifetime of paid work.

The sense of community we once enjoyed can be restored. The limited success of latter day attempts to start intentional communities may be due to the difficulty in escaping from conditioning and the suddenness of the change. Ancient groups had their origins further back than memory. We must look to other means.

In the management and design of cities, past criteria no longer apply. Now typically 'ecological disaster areas', cities neither sustain human health nor nurture natural resources. To avoid repeating past errors, Professor Tjeerd Deelstra, environmental planning and design chief at Delft University in The Netherlands, has advocated that a city should be treated as a closed economy and run like any natural system. Among other measures to reduce inputs, energy-intensive, polluting traffic should be minimal; waste should be reduced and recycled.

With economics redefined — in the words of E. F. Schumacher 'as if people mattered' — cities would have more 'islands of Nature' in built-up areas with 'green corridors' linking them with the countryside. This would be a small step towards reducing the isolation of cities from the needs of the 'real world' outside that engenders myopic city attitudes. Cities remodelled on a scale to suit the needs of people rather than traffic, would have a variety of meeting places and play areas for children. Parks, gardens and boulevards would be balanced by informal people-only streets and squares where intimacy and bustle could add excitement and opportunities for fantasy to what otherwise could be manicured, sterile and inhuman. Any steps to reduce ongoing stress, whether from loneliness and boredom or noise, pollution and overcrowding, all help to reduce the crisis.

The pressing need today is not for the patentable products of technological inventions but for new social services and imaginative solutions to social problems. Anticipating the future, the Institute for Social Inventions began work in London during 1985 to meet this need 'by tackling social problems before they become crises, through public participation in continuous problem solving, and by promoting small-scale innovative experiments'. To these ends the Institute has run competitions, conducted 'workshop' courses in schools, and built up a network of over 400 'social inventors'.

Innovation is also needed to replace the supportive groups of kith and kin, now largely dispersed in the socially and geographically mobile societies created chiefly by the car. Since neither bureaucracy nor professionalism can fill the gap, new societies will have the task of re-creating caring groups. Every street, district or village deserves at least a meeting place, whether or not the neighbourhood boasts a giant leisure centre.

Pursuing grass root initiatives, people in rich and poor districts alike are forming neighbourhood associations. In varying degrees most of these embrace three overall aims: caring for each other, improving amenities and acting as a pressure group. In these ways they are able to augment or replace an ailing bureaucracy to improve the lot of children, the sick, elderly and disadvantaged; they can protect and improve their environment with trees, playgrounds and gardens; reduce traffic hazards and noise, and fight intrusions from unwanted developers and insensitive planners.

Some associations fare better than others. In poor districts problems can be acute. They are another world. Before an association can be started, leaders must be found and people helped to grow out of passive consumerism. Most people are relucant to do anything at all: anyone prepared to stand out from others takes unaccustomed risks by attracting ridicule, envy, suspicion. Guilt too holds many back. People join an association for a time, then drop out. Women tend to be the more ready to escape from the telly and come forward — if their husbands will let them out. Most men's interests go no further than the pub. In typical deprived areas remote issues have no meaning; Earth awareness doesn't stand a chance. The overriding aim of most is simply to survive another week — or even another day.

Something to sing about

All over the world people are dancing, singing and playing musical instruments, painting and drawing, decorating artifacts, recounting myths and telling stories. Art is all of this and more. It is as old as consciousness and as universal. Fired by joy and suffering, extinguished by affluence, this uniquely human instinctive drive wells up, even where we least expect it.

To those who would persuade us that the myth of progress and growth is real, art is irrelevant, even dangerous. Outside of gallery, theatre and classroom, our misguided culture has little place or time for it. Whether as music, dance, clowning, painting, sculpture, photography, drama, poetry or written word, art can reveal the ecstacy and intensity of existence. It can remind us too vividly of what we seek but cannot buy: for art dares to proclaim that everything significant above sheer survival lies beyond the capacity of 'getting and spending' to deliver. Fearful of its power, the persuaders seek to capture and tame it. In their hands, it degenerates to acquisitior Great Names, status, Box Office, money and a hedge against inflation.

Suggestible as ever, we too easily succumb. Abusing art no less than other human qualities, we demean it to a print on the wall to match the decor, the jingle in the cornflakes commercial, the architectural carbuncle, showbiz 'soap', PR, Page Three, and the aural sewage of electronically engineered pop. Once perverted, art becomes non-art.

Since art, whether as music, words or movement, cannot be divorced from the use for which it is commissioned, artists forever encounter the temptation of misdirected purpose. They hover on the brink of banality, for art too easily sinks to the sludge of persuasion and propaganda. Art however is the twin of the drive that sends us questing for a cause, and, since underneath we are not reasonable animals, to the upholders of conventional wisdom it is threatening. Reason may pierce the intellect, but art can touch the heart. Moreover, since emotion is more powerful than logic, language illuminated by art's magic can be powerful stuff, whether literature, drama, rhetoric or sales talk. Those who seek to bring about change of any kind, be it acceptance of an alien ideology, conversion to a new religion, or simply a switch from one leading brand name to another, know that non-art in the deft hands of their professionals is an instrument almost impossible to resist.

If we were not so submerged by the outer world and distracted from the inner world, more of us would be stimulated to express our feelings, fears and aspirations in art. As Edward Hyams has aptly put it: 'The poet is not an athlete among men of ordinary muscular development and control, but a fit man among the crippled and disabled.'

Although artists need have no compulsion to convey a message or serve a cause, throughout history excesses of suffering, indignation and rage have inspired poetry, music, drama and painting of such potency that, willingly or not, they become instruments of change. Today, when words and images can encompass the world in an instant, true artists, motivated by concern, find themselves at the threshold of either unprecedented opportunity or spiritual annihilation.

Already, artists, composers, script writers and actors, hired chiefly by press and television, daily employ non-art posing as art to persuade millions, not only to 'consume, consume', but increasingly and more subtly, to take up causes. So far, the messages of this newer dimension have been predominantly political: propaganda from both East and West for the conflicting ideologies of communism and capitalism. However, now that technology has brought about a new and dazzling globe-spanning platform for mass persuasion, political ideologies are being joined by the powerful new forces of evangelism.

Throughout the world, ordinary people are still reeling under the future shock of computers. Before long they will have to come to terms with a dramatic new medium in the shape of satellite television. Demolishing distances, frontiers and language barriers, this numinous force promises to impart a new meaning to the benign concept of global village. Once the new technology becomes an accomplished fact, competition for the hearts and minds of five billion highly suggestible 'villagers' will escalate to become a global struggle. Most of us, easily led, vulnerable and searching for meaning, are already no match for the hypnotic influence of television and its professional operators. Confronted by this new weapon, we shall be devoid of defence.

Doubtless many of the aims promulgated on global TV will be worthy, many of the people involved sincere. Yet our track record demonstrates that the scene will not be filled with the righting of wrongs, the fight against oppression and injustice or the threats to our future — the kind of issues that have traditionally inspired artists — but overwhelmingly by self-interest: the persistence of the status quo, protection of property and wealth, the perpetuation of injustices and the inventing of enemies. The new medium promises to be a stage reserved strictly for the super-rich. Any cause not backed by vast funds will be excluded. By comparison, lesser media competing locally for hearts and minds will have little chance of competing.

Neither will art. And neither at first will planet Earth. At some point however, when connections with the deepening crisis can no longer be ignored, when the existing system begins to break down, when the voices of protest from the grass roots have coalesced into effective groups, art will find a laudable role. All that is implicit in Earth awareness, its urgency, universality, the richness of its meaning and mysticism will be ripe for the potent magic of poets, artists, photographers, writers, dramatists, composers, choreographers, dancers, singers and other musicians, whether pop, folk or classical. Where reason has failed, art will have the capacity to touch hearts and spread hope.

With Earth awareness we shall know what it is to be whole, in touch with the stuff we are made of. As we live now however, we are all victims of our conditioning, constrained by the values of our misguided culture. In this climate, artists understandably find themselves, as Edward Hyams has put it, 'working against the grain of life'. The outcome is predictable. 'Poetry which runs against this grain . . . may still be profoundly impressive,' he admits, 'but so may any clever, bitter act of perversity and destruction.' Earth awareness promises to release artists from the influence of a poisoned environment that can only generate more poison. In exchange it may open up vistas of creative freedom.

A scenario of the future can be tentatively depicted. As the old order encounters critical collapse, the propaganda it emanates, especially through the new technology of satellite television, will become less and less credible. At the right moment, a vacuum of truth will be formed ready to be filled by the hope that comes with Earth awareness. Non-art will give way to art, for a cause so crucial as rescuing the future will be no fit milieu for hacks. Artists of all kinds, whose work has been hitherto overshadowed by the power of the new technology, will find they are needed and heeded. Their creations will not languish 'underground'. More and more will join them to create a critical mass of visionary ideas.

Those who elect to fill the vacuum in the global platform will be accompanied by aware, frustrated programme directors and producers hungry for long-denied opportunities. Together they will be able to speak for people everywhere who are eager to make amends for the betrayal and heal past damage. In ways such as this, technology itself may be transmuted and so enable humankind to attain the stature appropriate to our power. Future events may not accord with this scenario: instead our species may disappear. Yet if such a resurgence seems right for us, there is no reason why, with the special magic of every kind of artist, we should not make it happen.

We may conjecture that at some point, when crisis has deepened further, one or more charismatic, individuals might emerge to reach out and articulate all of humankind's deep and archetypal longings. To reach minds they would have instantaneous translation; to reach hearts the magic of music and art; through today's technologies, moreover, the means to reach a worldwide audience all at once. In a host of ways, the magnitude of the crisis is capable of being matched by the means to meet it.

In essence the vision of Earth awareness is natural excellence regained. We need not be daunted if it remains elusive. There is inspiration to be had in the words of Theodore Taylor, a physicist who turned from designing the Bomb to working on renewable energy: 'It is better to strive with all our hearts to achieve a future that may seem too good to be true than continue to drift towards one that is too dreadful to contemplate.'

All that is needed is the will.

The final chapter goes deeper into the implications of Earth awareness, makes clear the connections between all its aspects and presents it as a meaningful whole.

15: Earth Awareness: the Vision

My mind feels as if it aches to behold and know something great and indivisible Coleridge

Earth awareness has qualities which distinguish it from other radical alternatives. The counter-culture of the Sixties is a case in point. This well-meaning but short-lived Western phenomenon failed, not only because society absorbed the threat it posed by commercialising it, but because the movement was founded not so much on positive aims as on reactive rebellion and escapism. A believable alternative to our present society must deliver more than a dreamlike Utopia.

Earth awareness does not imply that people should take second place: that a person should be sacrificed to save a mouse, that anyone should starve for the privilege of admiring virgin forest, nor that millions be rendered idle through curbs on industrial exploitation, whatever nonsense its critics may concoct. Once we can appreciate that as a species, despite all our technology and all our efforts to quit the web of life, we are still part of it, then we shall see that each one of us can — and should — enjoy the same rights to satisfy our basic needs as the rest of life. That is part of natural principles. To *earn* that right, rather than wrest it from Nature, we have only to make adjustments to our attitudes and behaviour.

With Earth awareness we see through conventional economics. We spot the crucial difference between wealth produced from renewable resources and from finite ones. We also see the contrast between wealth resulting from extraction compared with the kind that comes from rearranging materials already around us. At present our inability to appreciate connections hides the uncomfortable truth that little or no wealth is in fact created when the true, full costs of production are taken into account. They cancel it out. Pollution, health and accident risks, exploitation and other hidden costs are too often borne by others excluded from benefiting from the wealth produced. One man's wealth then creates another's poverty. Similarly, the net amount of wealth created is either diminished or cancelled out when the production of it interrupts Earth's critical cyclic flows. The cost may then fall on our children. Replenishment is paramount.

Few have summed up the situation more aptly than Gandhi with his assurance that there is enough for everyone's need but not for everyone's greed.

Freedom from the slavery of the work ethic is implicit in the new awareness, yet this does not mean a wasteland of idleness. An immense task lies ahead: repairing the damage done, restoring to Earth what has been robbed or borrowed, and coping with the twin problems of material and spiritual poverty.

Earth awareness begs the awkward question: 'By what right does any person — or nation — deserve a larger share of Earth's limited resources than any other, if everyone else's share is reduced by the exercise of this claimed right?' In an ideal world the short answer would be: 'None whatever'. Critics of it might counter that we do not live in an ideal world and assert that, since the right is enshrined by tradition, just reward, military superiority, political clout or economic strength, its possessors would never give it up. This being so, until we are closer to an ideal world, a more sensible answer might be: 'We have no right, but let us move at a sensible pace towards a more equable distribution while we still have time.' Such a move would meet human needs no less than those of Earth. It has been said prophetically that: 'The good we secure for ourselves is precarious and uncertain until it is secured for all of us and incorporated into our common life.'

Equitable distribution of wealth requires a massive transfer of resources away from exploitation into restoration. It calls for an imaginative redirection of the intellectual muscle, materials, energy and aggressiveness currently focused on weaponry and other life-destroying activities. It will be on a scale never before undertaken. Barry Commoner made the issue clear when he wrote: 'Human beings have broken out of the circle of life, driven not by biological need but by the social organisation which they have devised to "conquer" nature. . . The end result is. . . a crisis of survival. Once more, to survive, we must close the circle. We must learn how to restore to nature the wealth that we borrow from it.' Our spur will once again be survival.

The one resource more precious than gold, iron or oil is soil. Synonymous with life itself, it is irreplaceable. Having resigned from the soil community, we have to seek re-admission, quitting our role as soil destroyers in favour of soil makers: a rediscovery of a true ecological niche and a readmission to the web of life.

Earth awareness renews our connection with the material of which we are made. It is an experience which Edward Hyams has described as '. . . a kind of wholeness, a feeling for the pattern of the whole organism which is life.' He sees the concept manifested as a kind of tact, felt and employed sensitively by all whose work requires them to manipulate the parts of the whole in their quest to understand the pattern. As he explains, 'These powers enable them to work *with the grain of life rather than across it.* And this is true even of those activities which involve not only the manipulation of matter, but of ideas and feelings.'

Once we are mature enough to treat Earth with tact, and ensure that our actions do not inadvertently worsen what we have already done, we may be entrusted to rebuild the soil. It means a worldwide programme without precedent. For once, science and technology will be required to pay more attention to what is under our feet than over our heads. Politicians and economists will have to see the sense in switching from unessential resource-depleting activities to constructive alternatives. These will involve halting erosion and desert encroachment, rebuilding topsoil from subsoil, terracing, replanting land with soil-holding plants and wind-breaking trees, fertilizing and irrigating, resettling people and helping farmers adjust to their new role. Land degraded by rubbish tips and pollution can be reclaimed. Good land will no longer be lost either through dumping or to building. Economics and accountancy will have to adjust to the new situation with fresh values. In assessing the standing of a country and its economy the Soil Standard should take precedence over the Gold Standard or any other purely financial criterion. Priceless lessons have already been learned. Degraded land that once took years to reclaim can now make a quick recovery by planting with pastures of brown bent and clover, with gorse and with alder and silver birch trees. In a host of fields, experience gained through piecemeal restoration could be incorporated into plans for afflicted regions worldwide.

Because agriculture in excess is incompatible with Earth's needs, it has been a major culprit all along. Human population keeps doubling, farming methods become ever more violent. As a result wilderness disappears, soil everywhere grows fewer plant species and the rest of life suffers. Of all the issues we shall debate and agonise over in the coming years, none will rival those concerned with food and soil fertility. Yet if farmers could be encouraged to change to 'low input', organic methods, with more biological controls and fewer chemicals, damage to our life support system would fall dramatically. Already such methods are beginning to make economic sense.

Soil gives life to most of the species on which we depend. Since our bodies consist entirely of secondhand plant life, it is imperative to halt the genetic loss of species now under way. In areas of rainforest, felling has to give way to replanting.

Good land unfit for crops can become 'managed' forest to supply timber. By establishing national parks and nature reserves worldwide, we can safeguard wilderness for future generations. As we become aware of the importance of diversity and interrelationships, we shall conserve and restock wilderness with the wildlife we now render extinct.

Redistribution of resources will not be confined to rebuilding soil. In getting away from dependence on throughput and investing in renewal, alternative energy technologies deserve to be taken seriously. In Britain, by comparison with the research budget for nuclear power, the allocation of resources for alternative technologies has been derisory. Tidal, wind and solar power all have a role to play. In the Poor South especially, investment in intermediate technology to harness the Sun's energy would pay handsome returns in well-being for people and planet.

All of these measures are in our own self-interest as a species. Yet on their own they amount to little more than the planet management we need for breathing space. For our survival into a remoter future, eventually we shall have to embrace something more fundamental. Entirely compatible with the longer term aims of Earth awareness is the perspective of 'deep ecology', originally proposed in 1972 by the Norwegian philosopher, Arne Naess. 'Shallow ecology' focuses on single issues that protect, 'the health and affluence of people in developed countries,' as he put it. Deep ecology, in contrast, emphasizes the oneness of all things. It detaches humankind from the centre stage and lays stress on the interdependence of *all* aspects of Nature, whether alive or not.

It proposes that no living organism has greater intrinsic value than any other. Firmly rejecting the accepted idea that the non-human world possesses nothing more than 'use value', it asserts that no nation or person has any right to own land. While any individual of any species has the right to occupy the minimum territory for its needs, it cannot do so in perpetuity, nor to the total exclusion of other species. Earth belongs equally to all life, just as all life belongs to Earth.

Seeing humankind as no more than a single strand in the complex web of life, deep ecology is a revolutionary and disturbing concept that is also essentially spiritual. By shifting the emphasis in our culture from material growth to spiritual development, it challenges many of society's present beliefs and values. Although it belongs to the future, the concept is already stirring. If we ever embrace it, we shall do so only when enough of us have reached the degree of Earth awareness at which, as Theodore Roszak has said, '. . . we are ready to embrace nature as if indeed it were a beloved person in whom, as in ourselves, something sacred dwells.'

Few writers have captured the spirit of Earth awareness and deep ecology better than the American author Henry Beston, who in 1949 advocated a wiser, more mystical concept of animals. '. . . the animal shall not be measured by man.' he wrote. 'In a world older and more complex than ours they move finished and complete, gifted with extensions of the senses we have lost or never attained, living by voices we shall never hear. They are not our brethren; they are not underlings; they are other nations, caught with ourselves in the net of life and time, fellow prisoners of the splendour and travail of the Earth.'

Prospects of hope

If we are to avoid the trap of 'thinking ourselves into demise' we need to cultivate an air of informed optimism: 'informed' implying not only an understanding of crucial connections, but a healthy knowledge of the obstacles, coupled with the will to surmount them. Uninformed optimism, in contrast, merely encourages us to believe erroneously that change will come about simply because it should. By tempting us to do too little to achieve our objective, such unjustified optimism plays into the hands of those who stand to gain by keeping things as they are. While informed pessimism can be constructive for the balance it can introduce to any debate, uninformed pessimism, on the other hand, usually offers little except escape into defeatism.

We need optimism just as desperately as we need idealism, but it has to be grounded in reality. If we deny our own capacity for evil we are virtually certain to project or displace it onto others, whether perceived as individuals, social classes, other nations, or social or political systems. Our world view is then distorted, our judgement impaired, and any ensuing actions unlikely to be fruitful.

It is useful to distinguish between what can be changed and what cannot. Spurious human nature can be changed. The laws of physics cannot. At a price, natural principles can be ignored, but they cannot be changed. We can repress our original nature, but deep within us it remains unchanged, for us to find and revive if we wish. We can change the direction of our cultural evolution: at a time when industrial society faces breakdown, and nervousness has become a permanent feature of the international power struggle. If so, we can change the social environment that engenders our ongoing stress — possibly more easily than ever before. And we can change our all-out war against the rest of life so that it again becomes muted competition.

If we neglect to make such changes, it will be because we have failed to understand that nothing can change the natural principle that when Earth is no longer able to support us, we shall disappear. The prophecy of the French author, Roger Garaudy, will come true: 'If we live the next thirty years as we did the last we shall be killing our grandchildren.'

Yet a disastrous future is not inevitable, deep though the global crisis has become. Despite all the best endeavours of world leaders and the Wealth Machine, ordinary people still have free will. The human spirit, flickering though it may be, still lives. Close as we are to the point of no return, we may not yet have arrived there. Short of a miraculous intervention, on which we would be unwise to bank, all that can save us from imminent extinction are the gifts which we have so far largely abused and the wealth we have borrowed from the living Earth. The stirring among us that is Earth awareness asks that we use our gifts and the common wealth to heal the living world that supports us. It is a cry from Earth herself. We have to recognise that we are still part of Nature, governed by the same natural principles. It is only by taking them into account that we can ever hope to make the man-made world work properly. Once we begin to do so, the all-powerful Life Force will begin to work for us instead of against us. Life-enhancing ideas will gain critical mass and enable us to reach heights of co-operation and achievement we never dreamed possible. With Earth awareness the impossible can become commonplace.

As a starting point, we have to confront our 'shadows', both personal and collective. We shall not get very far if we continue to consign anything that disturbs us to the realm of the unthinkable. Whether it is the threat of war, the spectre of mass poverty and hunger, our plague-like overpopulation or the demise of our industrial, throughput societies, the Unthinkable has to be faced.

This time of crisis must be seen for what it is: the opportunity to build on our strengths and overcome our weaknesses. Inept we may be at observing the crucial connections so important in wider issues, but we are uniquely brilliant at specifics. We have to be far cleverer in the way we select the specifics that consume our energies and Earth's resources alike. We shall have to defeat the Sumer syndrome that impels us to abuse the surplus we create and instead divert it to the supreme cause of renewal. In our industrial societies, there is unceasing conflict between natural principles, the inherent drives of our original nature and our limitations. We have to reconcile all three and restrain our readiness to promote ourselves to the level of our incompetence.

The most creative act imaginable is that of restoring to Earth the natural excellence of which we were once a part. Since the abuse of Earth is the abuse of Self, we need to put Earth's needs first — the very essence of Earth awareness. This is what renders it the equivalent of the next stage in consciousness since we attained self-awareness.

The greatest force that we can tap is the tremendous potential of the ancient, inherent drive that impels us to give ourselves to causes greater than ourselves. It is a force that has no adequate means of expression in the spiritually deadening materialism of today's industrial societies. 'Getting and spending' are simply not enough. They ignore the fundamental spiritual dimension of our true, original nature. Denied expression, this dimension intensifies our ongoing stress and lowers the quality of everyday life. As Ronald Higgins has written: 'Many who feel uncomfortable with the vocabulary of the churches are being persuaded that our most haunting concerns are essentially religious. We may begin with anxiety as to how Planet Earth's fragile envelope of life is to be preserved, only to end up with the conclusion that this will finally depend, not on technology or economics, but on how we can restore our reverence for life and our joy in creation for its own sake.'

Sceptics will point to the fact that none of the seven seers who originally crystallised the ancient spiritual drive into the major orthodox faiths of the world has yet succeeded in changing the world. This is undeniable: if they had, we would not be in our present predicament. Yet never before has the collective lunacy of a single species threatened the whole of creation. Never before has a species enjoyed the gift of consciousness and thus been potentially aware of the full consequences of its actions. Neither has humankind ever had the means to convey instantly to almost every member of the species just what these consequences are and what an effective response should involve. The challenge is unprecedented and so the extent of the response is unknowable. Yet, as previous chapters have chillingly spelled out, what *can* be predicted with chilling certainty are the stark consequences of failing to respond.

Whatever the response, it must come from the grassroots. Its new values must infiltrate the power structure. All the brains, creativity and energy that are currently misdirected to the abuse of surplus will be needed to spread the healing message of Earth awareness worldwide. Every non-violent means to implement it must be used: education, reason, argument, debate, persuasion, proselytisation, lobbying, demonstration, boycotting, politics and communication — from face-to-face encounter to global television.

Since women and children have the most to gain, they need no longer be pawns in the power games men play. Only women have the means to convince men of the urgent need to grow up and willingly to re-impose the constraints on the excesses of humankind that once existed naturally. If men and women together cannot learn to behave like responsible adults, they stand accused of not loving their children enough. They are guilty of allocating to their children's future a lower priority than the games, power struggles and collective lunacy that threaten it. It is a serious charge that requires each of us to examine closely the way we live.

There is within each of us the sense of that which is greater than ourselves, even greater than all of humankind put together. We catch a glimpse of it in the presence of genius and other gifts that come to us from outside us. It is the source of all aesthetic appreciation, the embodiment of all that surpasses reason and touches the heart. It is the sheer, down-to-earth goodwill expressed by people everywhere when neither threatened nor under stress. Above all it is love, the word we defile for fear of what love may do to us. We ignore what it may do *for* us. Yet we need love now, just as desperately as Earth needs it, for what it will do for us both while there is still time. Nothing stands in the way of putting things right except ourselves.

Complete Earth awareness is the goal of a future that should be, yet will never be unless we make it so. The pages of this book have shown how each of us may help to make it a reality. That it may never be complete should not deter us. A Chinese proverb reminds us that a journey of a thousand miles begins with a single step. The more of the tenets of Earth awareness that we can realise, the more certain and agreeable will the future for our children be. The less we do so, the more difficult will it be to look them in the eyes.

Earth awareness is rock hard in the firmness of its convictions, founded on both the continuum of the past and the urgency of the present. The evidence of Earth's need for it is impeccable. Yet it is also fragile, born of idealism and so a target for the slings and arrows of cynics. All who think they stand to gain by keeping things as they will interpret it as either menacing or ridiculous. Their attacks and ridicule will be formidable. Yet for others, children most of all, Earth awareness means hope. Even more than hope: a matter of life or death.

Previous pages have progressively hinted at, spelled out and explained what it means; now the time has come to draw its parts together and and make clear the connections between them. In this way the vision may be made whole.

The vision

Reunion with Earth

These are the changes we have to make if children are to inherit a world worth living in. They embrace the principle of reunion with the natural world that we have left behind. This reunion is a return after a long absence; a wish to make peace after protracted conflict. Yet it is more a leap forward than a step back; more an issue of self-interest than morality. The changes mean that wherever we can we restore to Earth the wealth we have borrowed and heal the injuries we have inflicted.

In a profound sense, it is a rediscovery of the niche we left millennia ago. To the extent that a niche is an *occupation*, the work of healing Earth qualifies our species for a return to the web of life.

We can expect a sustainable future only if we rearrange our lives and societies in ways that will enable us to live in harmony with natural principles. Totally dependent upon Earth for life as we are, our future lies in conquering neither space nor Earth, but simply in reconciling our needs with hers. Such a conscious shaping of our destiny promises to be the most momentous undertaking humankind has ever known.

As the crisis deepens, more of us will put the needs of Earth first. This perspective means recognising and understanding the connections between humankind and Earth, and the consequences of ignoring them. It means establishing the wider implications of significant actions and, where there is doubt, withholding action rather than incurring needless risks to life, now and in the future. Those who choose otherwise will become the new outsiders.

When dangers increase and the old order starts to break down, so will the challenge elicit appropriate responses and crisis become opportunity instead.

With Earth awareness, as if looking down from a circling satellite, we see ourselves as just another species, temporarily dominant but with neither more nor less rights than others, no matter how much power we may wield. From this vantage point, we reconsider our impact on the lonely planet below and examine the nature of our relationships, not only to each other, but to other species, past and present. We then see that we can expect a future only by abdicating from the presumed god-given, science-driven right, embedded in our culture's beliefs and values, totally to control and dominate Nature.

Earth awareness does not pretend to be the One Big Explanation that will magically put everything right. It is the sum of many parts — conservation, environmentalism and planet management. Though rooted in the green imperative, it embraces more than ecology and it is more down-to-earth than Pantheism.

The sooner we embrace it, the longer we put off our demise; the more we neglect it, the bleaker our children's prospects become. With radical change we could live in muted competition with the rest of Nature and in harmony with each other for as long as the sun shines. With some change, we may expect a future measured in decades, even centuries. With none at all, even tomorrow is shrouded in doubt.

Deepening crisis and individual action

Since we cannot leave the task of rescuing the future to those who imperilled it, we have to undertake it ourselves: from the grassroots, seeking out others of like mind. We begin by changing the inner world of the Self, the better to change the outer world. We stop blaming Them and admit that the problem is Us. We confront our 'shadows' and extricate the prospect of extinction from the realm of the Unthinkable.

It is no mean feat to imagine a world without humans. Yet since we are each able to live every day with the certainty of our own death, we should be able to accept that one day our own species too could die. Then, just as we take measures to delay our own death, so shall we see the point of taking measures to delay the demise of our species.

We can all join in. If conceivably one person or one group by their efforts were to postpone demise by a few minutes, the efforts would be worthwhile. Muliplied by millions, similar efforts would reclaim the future. Too many do nothing simply because they can only do a little.

Others have already begun. Throughout the world, pioneers have changed their lives and shown their deepening concern in a growing number of life-affirming groups. Through their endeavours, seeds of hope have taken root and fresh green shoots are already breaking through the barren soil of intransigence.

In the end it all amounts to a question of love. With enough love, almost all problems can be alleviated, if not solved. Without love, reason can be lethal. Without love, life is a kind of lingering death. Yet we cannot expect to love all life, planet Earth or indeed anyone beyond family and friends if we are unable to love ourselves. Damaged as we are, guilty though we may feel about our species' collective madness, nevertheless it is within ourselves that the quest has to begin.

Its meaning to each of us

For our forebears, Earth awareness was enshrined in the images and instinctive drives they enacted every moment of their lives. When, as their successors, we had begun to make war on Nature we sentenced this awareness to the prison of our collective 'shadow'. In today's crisis we can no longer profess ignorance of such warlike behaviour. Since the war is manifestly unwinnable, the time has come to make peace. This we can do by releasing the prisoner and re-enacting its languishing images and drives.

Earth awareness is humankind's next evolutionary leap. It involves exercising a degree of responsibility appropriate to the power we wield as a species. With concentrated but rewarding work on the psyche, well within most people's ability, many of us may achieve this level of consciousness within the span of a single lifetime. Since evolution is now largely cultural, to do so is to advance the evolutionary clock in one quantum leap.

We live our lives, conscious of our limitations as a species and as far as possible in ways that will enact the inherent images and drives of our original nature. Acquired when we were part of Nature, these imperatives pose no threat to her, neither do they require us to ignore natural principles.

Because they are universal, by enacting them we bring closer the global unity so vital for rescuing the future. Representing, not the differences that divide us, but all that we have in common, they can help to reverse the misunderstandings and distrust that fuel the crisis.

Earth awareness will satisfy the drive inherent in each of us to embrace a cause greater than ourselves. Concerned as it is with survival, it is the one cause capable of uniting all humankind. This inherent drive, repressed by poverty and affluence alike, will liberate the human spirit and guide it along alternative paths to the one down which it has been led.

Its effect on society

The emerging culture will be founded on a new body of knowledge, beliefs, values and rules, in harmony with our original nature. Its social inventions will re-create as far as possible the environment for which we were designed. In small, lasting groups, each one united in a common aim, we may rediscover a long lost source of energy and intelligence. The ensuing society will be one in which we feel at home. Free from stress, our behaviour will reflect our original nature rather than our acquired substitute. Responsible and mature, it will no longer exacerbate the crisis.

Our new awareness will affect the way we eat, work and play; how we bring up and educate children; how we build, travel and grow our food; how we perceive and treat each other, especially the opposite sex; and how we behave towards other forms of life.

Humankind's resources — intellectual, technological, monetary and spiritual — will undergo a massive switch from exploitation to restoration. Surplus will be appropriated as it should be. Wealth will be defined differently, putting quality before quantity. The lunacy of heedless material throughput will give way to the cyclic, caring ethos of conservation. Giantism and runaway growth will be constrained. The future will no longer be sacrificed on the altar of present expediency.

Since injustice is an abuse of surplus, it is central to the focus of our concern. Rescuing the future therefore involves the relief of present widespread and unnecessary suffering. It has a direct bearing on our reunion with Nature and her excellence of natural design.

The essence of the vision is society without oppression, production without exploitation, politics without violence, religion without intolerance, and plenty without greed. Although it is unlikely to be realised in our time, it is a legacy we owe our children to atone for our ruinous mistakes.

Appendices

Appendix A
Ways of becoming involved

Non-governmental organisations (NGOs) vary: some have local branches, some offer annual membership, some are fund-raisers, some are pressure groups, some publish literature and/or regular journals, some invite voluntary, practical work, some run education programmes. All of them welcome a large SAE from inquirers for information. The few listed below have been selected from the huge total. Brief descriptions are given in parenthesis where titles are enigmatic.

Environment, ecology, conservation

British Trust for Conservation Volunteers (tree planting etc., cleaning up the environment) 36 St Mary's Street, Wallingford, Oxford OX10 OEU.
CARE Britain (worldwide tree planting) 35 Southampton Street, London WC2E 7HE.
The Conservation Trust (information on environmental matters on request) George Palmer Site, Northumberland Avenue, Reading RG2 7PW.
Council for the Protection of Rural England (CPRE) 4 Hobart Place, London SW1W OHY.
Friends of the Earth 377 City Road, London EC1V INA.
Greenpeace 36 Graham Street, London EC1V INA.
National Trust 36 Queen Anne's Gate, London SW1H 9AS.
Ramblers' Association (campaigns for access to natural landscape) 1–5 Wandsworth Road, London SW8 2LJ.
Tree Council (fosters rural and urban tree planting) 35 Belgrave Square, London SW1X 8QN.
Woodland Trust (owns, protects and manages woodland) Autumn Park, Dysart Road, Lincolnshire NG31 6LL.

Wildlife and animal protection

Compassion in World Farming (campaigns against factory farming) 20 Lavant Street, Petersfield, Hants GU32 3EW.
National Anti-Vivisection Society 51 Harley Street, London W1N 1DD.

Royal Society for the Prevention of Cruelty to Animals (RSPCA) The Causeway, Horsham, Sussex RH12 1HG.
Royal Society for the Protection of Birds (RSPB) The Lodge, Sandy, Bedfordshire SG19 2DL.
Urban Wildlife Group (sets up urban nature reserves) 11 Albert Street, Birmingham B4 7UA.
World Society for the Protection of Animals (WSPA) (farm, domestic, marine, wild, experimental) 106 Jermyn Street, London SW1Y 6EE.
The Wildfowl Trust Slimbridge, Gloucestershire GL2 7BT.
Worldwide Fund for Nature (WWF) Panda House, 11–13 Ockford Road, Godalming, Surrey GU7 1QU.

Peace

Campaign against Arms Trade (CAAT) 5 Caledonian Road, London N1 9DX.
Campaign for Nuclear Disarmament (CND) 22–24 Underwood Street, London N1 7JQ.
Christian CND as above.
European Nuclear Disarmament (END) 11 Goodwin Street, London N14.
Foundation for International Security The Rookery, Adderbury, Banbury OX17 3NA.
Freeze (campaigns for international nuclear freeze) 82 Colston Street, Bristol BS1 5BB.
National Peace Council (information on peace NGOs) 29 Great James's Street, London WC1 3ES.
Pax Christi (Roman Catholic peace NGO) St Francis of Assissi Centre, Pottery Lane, London W11.
Peace Through NATO 46 Chancery Lane, London WC2A 1JB.
Peace Tax Campaign (proportion of income tax *re* defence expenditure withheld) 1a Hollybush Place, Bethnal Green, London E2 9QX.
Quaker Peace and Service Friends House, Euston Road, London NW1 2BJ.
Women for a Nuclear Free and Independent Pacific (no nuclear tests) 62 Purser House, London SW2 2JA and 7 Furnace Cottages, Crow Edge, Sheffield.

Women's groups

A Woman's Place (drop-in and information centre) Hungerford House, Victoria Embankment, London WC2N 6PA.

Gingerbread (for one parent families): 52 Wellington Street, London WC2E 7BN.
National Council for One Parent Families: 255 Kentish Town Road, London NW5 2LX.
Rights of Women (legal resource, research, advice and information centre) 52–54 Featherstone Street, London EC1Y 8RT.
Wiser Links (international women's resource centre) 173 Archway Road, London N6
Women in Collective Action (WICA) (aims to improve the position of women in the community) c/o Student Unit, Oxford House Settlement, Derbyshire Street, London E2.
Women's Information and Enquiry Service (WIRES) (information service *re* women's liberation groups) PO Box 20, Oxford.
The Working Mothers Association 23 Webbs Road, London SW11 6RU.

World development and poverty relief

Age Concern Bernard Sunley House, 60 Pitcairn Road, Mitcham, Surrey CR4 3LL
Child Poverty Action Group 1 Bath Street, London EC1.
Christian Aid PO Box 1, London SW9 8BH.
Help the Aged St James's Walk, London EC1R OBE.
Intermediate Technology (researches, funds and installs technology for Poor South) 9 King Street, London WC2E 8HW.
Oxfam 274 Banbury Road, Oxford OX2 7DZ.
Population Concern 231 Tottenham Court Road, London W1P OXH.
Quaker Peace and Service Friends House, Euston Road, London NW1 2BJ.
Save the Children Mary Datchelor House, 17 Grove Lane, London SE5 8RD.
Servas (international hospitality network) 6 Addison Road, Hove East, Sussex BN13 1TN.
Shelter (campaigns for the homeless) 157 Waterloo Road, London S.E.1.
Voluntary Service Overseas (VSO) 9 Belgrave Square, London SW1X 8PW.
War on Want Three Castles House, 1 London Bridge Street, London SE1 9SG.

Farming and food

Henry Doubleday Research Association (organic growing and seed sales) Rylton-on-Dunsmore, Coventry CV8 3LG.

The Soil Association 86 Colston Street, Bristol BS1 5BB.
Working Weekends on Organic Farms (WWOOF) 19 Bradford Road, Lewes, Sussex BN7 1RB.

Politics and economics

Amnesty International (campaigns for political prisoners and refugees) British Section 5 Roberts Place, London EC1; International Secretariat 1 Gaston Street, London WC1.
Campaign for Press and Broadcasting Freedom (CPBF) 9 Poland Street, London W1V 3DG.
Ethical Investment Research and Information Service (EIRIS) (portfolio advice) 9 Poland Street, London W1V 3DG.
The Green Party 10 Station Parade, Balham High Road, London SW12 9AZ.
Liberal Ecology Group 77 Dresden Road, London N19 3BG.
The New Economics Foundation (organises 'The Other Economic Summit', TOES) 27 Thames House, South Bank Business Centre, 140 Battersea Road, London SW11 4NB.
Socialist Environment and Resources Association (SERA) 9 Poland Street, W1V 3DG.

Unclassified

The Fourth World (for small nations, small communities and the human spirit) 24 Abercorn Place, London NW8 9XP.
The Future in Our Hands (FIOH) (advocates non-exploitative life styles) UK Information Centre, 120 York Road, Swindon, Wilts. SN1 2JP.
The Institute for Social Inventions 24 Abercorn Place, London NW8 9XP.
Life Style (advocates non-exploitative life styles) Manor Farm, Little Gidding, Huntingdon, Cambridgeshire PE17 5RJ.
The Samaritans (befriends the suicidal and despairing) 17 Uxbridge Road, Slough SL1 1SN.
The Schumacher Society (for discussion, development and use of 'Small is beautiful' ideas) Ford House, Hartland, Bideford, Devon.

NB: More environmental and associated NGOs are listed in the *Directory for the Environment*, Routledge & Kegan Paul, London.

Appendix B
Bibliography

ATTENBOROUGH, D. (1979). *Life on Earth*, Collins/British Broadcasting Corporation, London.

BELLINI, J. (1986). *High Tech Holocaust*, David & Charles, Newton Abbott.

BESTON, H. (1949). *The Outermost House: a Year of Life on the Great Beach of Cape Cod*, Holt, Reinhart & Winston, New York.

BRONOWSKI, J.(1973). *The Ascent of Man*, British Broadcasting Corporation, London.

CAPRA, F. (1982/3). *The Turning Point*, Simon & Schuster, New York; Wildwood House, London; Flamingo/Fontana, London.

COLINVAUGH, P. (1980). *Why Big, Fierce Animals Are Rare*, Allen & Unwin, London.

COMMONER, B. (1971). *The Closing Circle*, Knopf, New York.

COTGROVE, S. (1982). *Catastrophe or Cornucopia*, John Wiley, London.

CROSBY, A. W. (1986). *Ecological Imperialism*, Cambridge University Press, Cambridge.

DAMMERS, A. H. (1982). *Life Style: a Parable of Sharing*, Turnstone, Wellingborough.

DARWIN, C. (1972/5). *The Origin of Species*, Dent & Sons, London; Rowman & Littlefield, New Jersey.

DIXON, W. M. (1937/58). *The Human Situation*, Edward Arnold, London; Pelican Books, London.

EDBERG, R. (1979). *The Dream of Kilimanjaro*, Heinemann, London.

GARAUDY, R. *Appel aux Vivants*, Paris.

HIGGINS, R. (1978). *The Seventh Enemy*, Hodder & Stoughton, London.

HYAMS, E. (1952/76) *Soil and Civilization*, Thames & Hudson, London; John Murray, London.

HUXLEY, A. (1984). *Green Inheritance*, Collins, London.

ILLICH, I. (1973). *Tools for Conviviality*, Harper & Row, New York.

JONES, A. (1983). *Beyond Industrial Society*, The Ecologist, Vol. 13, p. 141, No. 4.

JONES, A. (1987/8). *From Fragmentation to Wholeness*, The Ecologist, Vol. 17, No. 6, p. 236 (1987) and Vol. 18, No. 1, 1988.

JUNG, C. G. (1953/78). *Collected Works*, Routledge & Kegan Paul, London; Pantheon Books, New York.

JUNG, C. G. (1958). *The Undiscovered Self*, Routledge & Kegan Paul, London.

KOESTLER, A. (1967). *The Ghost in the Machine*, Hutchinson, London.
KOHR, L. (1957). *The Breakdown of Nations*, Routledge & Kegan Paul, London.
KULL, S. *War as a Species Disorder*, Peace and Common Security, Berkeley, USA.
LEAKEY, R. & LEWIN, R. (1977). *Origins*, Macdonald & Jane's, London.
LOVELOCK, J. (1979). *Gaia, A New Look at Life on Earth*, Oxford University Press, Oxford.
MACK, J. E. (1984). *Resistances to Knowing in the Nuclear Age*, Harvard Educational Review
MCNEILL, W. H. (1963). *The Rise of The West*, University of Chicago Press, Chicago.
MOSS, T. (1976/9). *The Probability of the Impossible*, Routledge & Kegan Paul, London; Paladin, London.
PETER, L. J. & HULL, R. (1969). *The Peter Principle*, Morrow, New York.
PONTING, C. (1987). *Politics and the World Crisis.*
REICH, C. A. (1980). *The Greening of America*, Random House, New York.
RIFKIN, J. R. (1987). *Biotechnology and the Environment*, The Green Alliance, London.
ROBERTSON, J. (1987). *The Sane Alternative*, J. Robertson, London.
ROSZAK, T. (1978/9). *Person/Planet*, Doubleday/Anchor; Victor Gollancz, London.
RUSSELL, P. (1982). *The Awakening Earth*, Routledge & Kegan Paul, London.
SAHLINS, M. (1974). *Stone Age Economics*, Tavistock, London.
SCHUMACHER, E. F. (1973). *Small is Beautiful*, Blond & Briggs, London.
SEYMOUR, J. & GIRARDET, H. (1986/8). *Far from Paradise*, British Broadcasting Corporation, London; Green Print, Basingstoke.
SHELDRAKE, R. (1981/3). *A New Science of Life*, Blond & Briggs, London; Paladin, London.
STEVENS, A. (1982). *Archetype, a Natural History of the Self*, Routledge & Kegan Paul, London.
TOYNBEE, A. (1976/8). *Mankind & Mother Earth*, Oxford University Press, Oxford; Paladin, London.
TURNBULL, C. M. (1961/74). *The Forest People*, Chatto & Windus, London; Jonathan Cape, London.
VELIKOVSKY, I. (1982). *Mankind in Amnesia*, Doubleday, New York; Sidgwick & Jackson, London.

The Gaia Atlas of Planet Management, (1985). Pan Books, London.
The Global 2000 Report to the President, (1982). Penguin/Allen Lane, London.

The Human Story, (1985). The Commonwealth Institute, London.
The Limits to Growth, (1972). Pan Books, London.
The Living Economy, (1986). Routledge & Kegan Paul, London.
Man the Hunter, (1968). Aldine Atherton, Chicago.
Man's Place in Evolution, (1980). British Museum (Natural History), London and Cambridge University Press.
World Resources 1986, (1986). The World Resources Institute and The International Institute for Environment and Development, Basic Books, Inc., New York.

Index